Welcome Home, Jellybean

Welcome Home, Jellybean

Marlene Fanta Shyer

GRANADA
London Toronto Sydney New York

Granada Publishing Limited
Frogmore, St Albans, Herts AL2 2NF
and
3 Upper James Street, London W1R 4BP
866 United Nations Plaza, New York, NY 10017, USA
117 York Street, Sydney, NSW 2000, Australia
100 Skyway Avenue, Rexdale, Ontario M9W 3A6, Canada
PO Box 84165, Greenside, 2034 Johannesburg, South Africa
61 Beach Road, Auckland, New Zealand

Published by Granada Publishing 1981
First published in USA by Charles Scribner's Sons 1978

Copyright © Marlene Fanta Shyer 1978

ISBN 0 246 11558 0

Printed in Great Britain by
Richard Clay (The Chaucer Press) Ltd,
Bungay, Suffolk
Phototypesetting by Georgia Origination, Liverpool
Set in Plantin

Granada ®
Granada Publishing ®

*With thanks to
Joseph Colombatto, Director
of Woodhaven Centre,
Temple University, who
thinks he knows all the
answers, and did.*

One

When my sister turned thirteen the school where she lived got her toilet-trained and my mother decided she ought to come home to live, once and for all.

My father and I weren't so sure, but he agreed that we would all give it a try, and he and I got the suitcase out of the storage room and loaded up the trunk of the car and drove to the gas station to have the tank filled while my mother was still up in the apartment writing with the whipped-cream squirter on a cake she had baked: WELCOME HOME.

Which my sister of course cannot read.

My mother's idea was that my sister would be able to taste WELCOME HOME and also appreciate a little bunch of flowers she put on the window sill in her room, which used to be the dining room until the superintendent, Mr Parrish, had a wall with a door in it put up and turned it into a bedroom.

I'm not sure what my father thought because he has just grown a new moustache, and his mouth disappears under it and it's hard to tell what his expression is. Usually when he drives he hums along with the car radio or complains about traffic, but it was my mother who seemed to be doing most of the talking today.

A few times she asked my father to slow down and then, when we passed a bunch of cows in a meadow, she said that my sister had probably never seen a cow in her life, or a horse.

Then she talked about a farm she'd visited one summer and she went on and on talking about how she had loved the chickens and pigs and used to shuck corn, which had nothing to do with anything. My father asked my mother why she was so nervous, and my mother said she wasn't nervous a bit, and she told my father to please slow down. To me she said, 'Neil, please close the window,' and a few miles later, when we'd stopped to eat our sandwiches, she turned right around and looked at me and said. 'Why did you close your window, Neil?'

It seemed a longer drive than usual, but finally I could see the school in a valley below us, a whole bunch of green roofs a little darker than the houses in a Monopoly set, short roads between them and a few benches set here and there under trees. Not bad. My sister seemed to like the school most of the time and only once in a while cried when we left after a visit.

Inside it looked okay too, although the whole place smelled like the stuff our cleaning lady, Mrs Shrub, uses to clean the bathroom, and once when I just wanted to get some fresh air and tried to open a window, the window let out alarm screams like the phantom of the opera and people came running from every direction like I'd set the place on fire.

Most of the rooms were big, with beds in rows and a bunch of lockers at one end, and a TV set and a chair in the corner for the guard. The guard sat there all night to make sure everybody slept. My mother said not to call the guard a guard. The guard was an attendant, she said.

Anyway, the attendant told us my sister was in the dining room having lunch and we would have to wait, and my father asked if it would be all right if we went into the dining room to see if she was finished. The attendant said it was against regulations, and when he said that, he sounded like a guard, not like an attendant.

So we sat on my sister's bed and waited and waited, and my father kept looking at his watch and finally he said it was getting late and he didn't want to get into heavy traffic and why didn't we just walk in the direction of the dining room and peek in and wave at my sister to hurry up?

My mother knew the way. We went through a lot of empty corridors and one that wasn't empty. An attendant was wheeling a sleeping person in a wheelchair and talking to him at the same time. I couldn't figure out why he was talking to someone asleep until we came up close, and then I saw that the man in the chair wasn't sleeping at all. His neck was just bent down like that, his head resting on his shirt as if he were trying to push his chin into his pocket. And he was wide awake and looking at us, especially at me. When we passed the chair, the man never moved, but his eyes just followed us as we went by. He had very fierce, dark eyebrows over staring eyes, but I pretended not to notice, because my mother had warned me about a hundred times to expect to see people behave in ways that might seem peculiar but not to embarrass anybody by bugging out my eyes and staring or asking, 'What's wrong with *him*?'

My mother said that even if the people here had been doled out a little less smartness, it didn't mean they had any less feelings.

The dining room was in the next building, so we had to go outside. We passed a fenced-in area where a group of girls were sitting in a circle on the ground and doing what looked like exercises with a leader. One of the girls was lying outside the circle flat down with her face smack in

9

the grass, and another girl was racing along the fence, grabbing it here and there and waving to us. I remembered what my mother had said about people's feelings, and I waved back.

The dining room door had two portholes. They were too high for me to see into, but not too high for my father. We were about to go in and just wave at my sister to hurry up, when my dad suddenly said, 'I don't think we should,' and he stopped dead and turned his back to the door. I guess he'd just taken a peek and changed his mind. I thought that was funny since it had been his idea in the first place, and I guess my mother thought it was strange too, because she just looked at him without saying much and then suggested she take just one step inside alone and see if she could find my sister.

'I want to go too,' I said. I guess I was curious to see if it was anything like our school cafeteria, but the minute we stepped inside, I knew it was a lot different.

Almost immediately a lady jumped out from nowhere and blocked our way. Her hair was the same ghost white as her uniform. 'I'm sorry, no guests are allowed in the dining room,' she said. She sounded like my old fourth-grade teacher, Miss Drummond, who'd had a voice like the loud notes on an electric organ.

'We're just here to –' my mother started to say, but the lady had each of us by one elbow and was trying to turn us right around so we wouldn't see what was going on.

I only had a glimpse and I'm not sure my mother saw what I saw, but right away I figured this dining hall was one reason my mother wanted my sister to come home to live.

All the kids were wearing the same big white bibs marked 'Green Valley Regional Training Centre', and they were all eating off plastic plates. They didn't have knives or forks though, just little spoons. And everybody was eating the same thing – no kidding – baby food. On every plate was a little orange pile of baby food and a little grey pile of what looked like the same stuff. There were older people here too, some who looked older than my father, and they were wearing bibs and eating baby food too. Some were being forced to eat it. Attendants were holding their jaws open and spooning it into their mouths. I saw my mother turn her head away and I didn't much want to look either, so we allowed ourselves to be ushered right out again the way we'd come, but not before I'd seen that a lot of the people there, seated at the long tables, were tied into their chairs with heavy leather straps.

To save time, we decided to open my sister's locker and pack her things into the suitcase before she returned. The attendant came and opened her locker and we took out her stuff: a little bunch of clothes, four crayons, papers with her drawings, a flashlight without a battery, part of a tea set my mother had given her on her birthday, and a Christmas card I'd sent her two years ago.

My mother called the attendant after she'd put everything in the suitcase. 'Where are the rest of my daughter's things?' she asked.

'Is anything missing?' the attendant asked. He was yawning, maybe from having to stay up all night watching everybody else sleep.

'But this can't be all! I sent my daughter a little radio just two weeks ago! And what happened to her drawing pad and the big box of pastels? Where are the picture books and the lacing cards? Where are the rest of her *clothes*?'

11

The attendant shrugged. 'Things get stolen here all the time,' he said.

My mother's face turned very red. She looked at my father. My father took her arm. 'Forget it,' he said. 'It's all over.' He looked into the large suitcase we'd expected to fill and then at my sister's things, which were bunched up in one small pile, and he didn't say another word. My mother shook her head and looked down at the floor while he closed the bag and set it at the foot of the bed.

The girl who sleeps in the bed next to my sister got back from lunch first, and I didn't know whether I was supposed to say hello and pretend I hadn't noticed the contraption on her head or just look down at the floor and act as if I hadn't seen her at all. I was really scared for a minute; if they had to keep her head in a cage like that, was she maybe dangerous?

But she just laughed and said hello like any other person would and we all said, 'How are you?' and the attendant came over and unstrapped her cage so she could lie down and take a rest. The cage actually looked like the white skeleton of a football helmet with a chin strap. The girl lay down on her bed and I noticed the bed had sides, like a crib; there were also rubber pads all around on the floor, in case she fell out anyway. Later, my mother whispered to me that the girl often had seizures and the helmet protected her if she fell suddenly to the floor. She explained that seizures are blackouts that happen very suddenly and without warning.

Other kids started coming in from lunch and pretty soon the dormitory was almost full, except for my sister.

My mother and father kept staring at the door, wishing my sister would hurry, anxious to leave, but I knew why she was going to be the last one in, for sure. She is not

12

that fast at walking and has a funny step, as if she never quite got the hang of putting one foot in front of the other. Her toes point in towards each other and it's almost as if she's learning a new dance routine and wants to get it really right. Step/step, step/step.

In she came at last and sure enough, she was the next-to-last kid back from lunch. She stepped in and I took one look and my mouth flew open. Of course, I hadn't seen her for quite a while, not since last Christmas, but good, grey grief! What had they done to her, anyway?

Two

My sister's name is Geraldine, after my grandfather, Gerald Oxley, who was famous. Well, not exactly famous, but he did play with the American Piano Quartet on the radio in 1944, and had his picture in the newspapers quite a lot when he entertained troops during the Second World War. He was my father's father and he died before I was born, but my father liked him a lot and still keeps his picture in a frame right up on the piano, next to mine.

My father takes after my grandfather too. He has perfect pitch and plays really well, although he is not a professional musician; he is a stockbroker, but he can do fantastic things with the keyboard, and he writes songs. He wrote 'You Put the Oh in Love' and a rock group almost made a record of it for RCA last year, but the deal fell through.

My father wants me to play too, and I try, but my fingers seem to slip a lot and hit the wrong keys, although Mrs Reinhardt, my piano teacher, says where there's life, there's a possibility of a Mozart.

Geraldine was born a year before I was, and at first they thought she was okay. Pretty soon, though, my mother noticed that Gerri couldn't suck her breast enough to get milk and when she cried, she sounded more like a toy you wind up with a key than a baby. She wasn't getting any bigger, either. When it was time to take Geraldine home from the hospital, she'd gotten smaller instead of larger.

The doctors agreed she was impaired but couldn't agree on why. My mother told me that Gerri's condition was no easier to explain than it was to explain a birthmark. So Gerri, who was born damaged, stayed on at the hospital and my mother came home.

Geraldine didn't grow for a long time. After she did begin to grow, she could never learn to hold up her own head. My mother said if she didn't hold it up for her, it would flop right over like a flower in a downpour. Later, when other babies were sitting up, Geraldine just lay in her crib. She couldn't turn over and she couldn't seem to learn to hold things in her hands, or to laugh. My mother wanted to bring her home, but she got pregnant with me then and people started giving her advice. My mother says she's had so much advice she's gotten allergic to it; she says it makes her itch. Everybody told my mother to put Geraldine into a home where she'd be better off, and my father said, 'Do whatever you think is best,' and so Geraldine was put into the Roxbury School, which was closed down after two years for health violations, and then she was sent to the Woodstream Academy, which was very good but went bankrupt, and then the Lower River School, which was too overcrowded, and finally my parents had to send her here, to the Green Valley Regional Training Centre, which is so far away we rarely got to see her. My mother said the Woodstream Academy had been better. One thing is sure: in all the years we'd been coming on holidays and long weekends, we'd never seen Geraldine looking like this!

I heard my mother gasp. My father turned white around his moustache. He said to the attendant, 'What's happened to Gerri? Why does she look like that?'

The side of my sister's head was blue-black and there

15

was a bump over her ear. What was even worse was that where the bump was sticking out, hair was missing, as if it had been pulled out by the handful or shaved clean off her head, leaving just a few wisps that couldn't cover the bulge.

The attendant and my parents moved off into the attendant's corner and got into a huddle; whatever it was that had torn the hair out of my sister's head was going to be super hush-hush, judging by the way they were whispering, looking her way and nodding. It was like they wanted to keep the secret right in that corner, like a wrecked piece of furniture.

As awful as her head looked, it didn't seem to bother Gerri. All this time she was holding on to my sleeve, or running over to pick up the suitcase and set it down again, or coming back and hugging me and wrapping her arms around my arm. You would think with all the moves she'd made, she'd be used to it. Or did she understand she was coming home? Geraldine has this funny laugh that sounds like it's climbing a ladder, up and up, higher and higher, like *ho, ha, hee,* and then *YEE!* She was talking too, but when Gerri talks, no one understands what she is saying because – no kidding – the words all come out sounding like she's reciting the names of Santa Claus's reindeer: Dasha, Dansa, Donda, Blitzen – like that.

Sometimes, between words, Gerri forgets to close her mouth and just leaves it open. That's when she looks all wrong and funny; otherwise, when her hair is combed right, she looks pretty much like every other kid and a lot prettier than some of the girls in my class. Her top teeth are crooked, but mine were too, until I got braces, and although my father doesn't think it's necessary to put Gerri through all that trouble, my mother says she hopes we'll be able to get Gerri a toothpaste smile exactly like mine.

16

I couldn't help noticing that the girl in the next bed wasn't sleeping at all. She was watching us through the metal protecting bars, just lying there, not moving, not speaking.

When it was time to go, my father lifted the suitcase and held out his hand. 'Come on, Gerri,' he said. 'Time to leave.'

Gerri opened her mouth and stared, not moving.

'Come on, let's go,' Dad said. He took a step in her direction and Gerri backed up and moved away from him.

'Hey, what's wrong?' Dad said.

Gerri made a sound in her throat. It sounded like 'Donner' or 'Donde' or 'Dahnda'. You could see her tongue moving in her mouth, like it was trying to find the right place to land. 'Dahanda, dahan.'

My mother rushed over to put her arm around Gerri. She pulled her very close. 'What's wrong? Don't you want to come with us?'

'Dhanda.' Gerri's mouth stayed open. It was wet in one corner. She'd backed right up against a locker.

My mother turned to me. 'Neil, can you understand her? What is she saying?'

I didn't know. She could have been talking Czechoslovakian for all I was getting.

The girl in the next bed all of a sudden pulled herself up on the steel protecting bars and pointed to my father. 'His moustache,' she said. 'She's scared of it.'

'Of course!' my mother cried, sounding very relieved, and we all had a laugh. When Gerri saw everybody laughing, she joined in, and little by little Dad got closer and closer to her until she finally let him take her hand and move it up under his nose to feel the brushy new

17

hair. Gerri's laugh went higher and higher and then she said, 'Tash.' I heard it and Mum heard it and Mum said, 'Hey, I think Gerri said "moustache",' but when we asked her to say 'moustache' again, she said, 'Blixen.'

More weird words came out of her when she saw that we were going to get into the car. She'd been for a few automobile rides, but she didn't get to go very often. I guess she felt about our old blue 'ord' (the F has been missing off the back for about five years) the way I feel about roller coasters: that's how her voice sounded as she climbed in, like oh-boy-here-it-comes! Then for the first half-hour she never shut up; it was like having a tape recorder sitting right there next to me on the back seat. I even saw my father look over at my mother and smile a couple of times, and when we passed the cows we'd passed coming up, out came the old *ha-hee-hi-YEE*, with Gerri pointing out the window and bouncing in her seat like she was sitting on a spring.

Then, O gross, no warning, she just got quiet for a couple of minutes, put her head down, and threw up. Just like that.

Dad pulled off the highway and drove a few minutes until we found a gas station, and while my mother walked Gerri in the fresh air to clear her head, Dad and I went to the men's room to get some paper towels and to fill our thermos with water for the cleanup, and Dad all of a sudden turned to me and said, 'Neil, it's not going to be easy,' and I thought he was talking about cleaning up the back of the car and I said, 'I know.' But later, when we finally got home and had that awful scene in the elevator, I realized Dad wasn't only talking about the mess in our car.

Dad was trying to warn me about what it was going to be like living with Gerri.

18

Three

I'm going to be honest and come right out and say it: I
don't like school. It's not that the place itself is bad; to
look at it you'd say it was pretty nice, modern and bright,
with red carpets and green blackboards. What's bum
about the school, aside from some of the lunches they
serve in the cafeteria, is the kids. It's not even that the
kids aren't nice either, it's that they come in bunches, like
grapes. There's the jock bunch, and they all hang out
together near the gym, and then there's the East End
bunch, who all live in the same housing development and
cluster upstairs in the corridor, and there are the brains
and they flock together near the maths office. There's
also the music and drama set, who all clump together
near the auditorium. When they aren't huddled in these
places, they sit together in the cafeteria or outside on the
steps. Where do I fit in? That's the problem. I am not a
jock, not an East Ender, not a brain, and not a
music/drama person. I like to take pictures and paste
them in albums or fool around at the piano or just fool
around; what's more, I'm sort of new. All the kids at
Franklin Pierce Junior High came either from Remington
Elementary or Lady of Mercy Parochial School.

I came from private school, and that, to the kids, is like
I'm from the North Star. I didn't know any of the kids
everyone else knew and I didn't know any of the teachers
and I had a different way of doing maths and I had read
all the wrong books; like I said, practically like coming

19

from a secondary planet. Half the time I wished I were back in private school where my friends are, but when my mother decided to have Geraldine come home to live, she had to give up her job and we couldn't afford the tuition.

I shouldn't say I have *no* friends in school. I have one friend, Joe Newbolt, who is in the music/drama group and wants to have his name changed to Jason Newley. He thinks a name like Joe Newbolt is not good for his image and now wants everyone to call him Jason. Half the time I forget and Joe/Jason gets mad, so we have our ups and downs, but he's someone I talk to.

When I told him Geraldine was coming home to live, he gasped. He practices gasping for theatre a lot, and does it really well. 'Watch out,' he gasped, 'just watch out.' Then a minute later he said he really dug the name Geraldine – it had a tragic ring. Finally, he said, 'Well, it should be a real trip, Neil-boy,' and I couldn't help remembering those very words when we first took Gerri up in the elevator.

We live on the sixth floor, so with or without her suitcase it was never a question of walking up, although we should have been smart enough to realize that a first ride in the elevator for Gerri might seem like a parachute jump for anyone else. The funny thing was that she was gung ho to get on and followed Dad right in without hesitation. What happened, unfortunately, was that in addition to Dad, Mum, me, and Gerri, there were two other people on board: Mr Rasmussen from the fifth floor with his Scottie dog, and Miss Gropper from the fourth. Just as the elevator door began to close, another person, the delivery boy from the nursery, carrying a tree in a tub, squeezed in. The doors closed and the delivery boy pushed the button for the seventh floor. Dad had pushed

20

six, of course, and Mr Rasmussen had pushed five. Miss Gropper had pushed four.

I guess Gerri, watching everyone press a floor button, figured that it was a requirement of all elevator riders to push a button; before anyone knew enough to stop her, she reached over and pressed the most colourful, eye-catching, brightest of all the buttons – the one clearly marked EMERGENCY.

Immediately an alarm went off that sounded as if it were signalling the end of all life on earth, a scream of an alarm that must have been heard by the dead and the deaf, a shriek that felt like it could put a hole right through the side of the building. The button had jammed. Geraldine went wild. I guess she realized she'd made a mistake, and went to correct it. She leaped forward to push another button to try to make up for the goof and – no kidding – it turned off the lights and stopped the elevator dead with a jerk somewhere between two floors.

Gerri began to jump and scream, scream and jump, and was immediately joined by Mr Rasmussen's Scottie, who started to yelp. Mr Rasmussen is nervous (as I later found out) and tried to outscream Gerri, the alarm, and his dog. He was not just screaming screams, he was screaming words, but I didn't quite catch them. I think one of them was *Help*.

Miss Gropper is a heavy-type lady, with the sort of body that seems to fill up clothes and the sort of arms that use up whole sleeves. She began slapping the walls and making sounds like you might hear coming out of an orchestra pit when the violinists are tuning up. My father kept saying, 'Calm! Stay calm!' but his voice sounded like someone was trying to push him off a cliff, and just hearing his voice come out so high took all the breath out of me. My mother sounded like she was practicing

21

reciting the vowels. She was saying 'Aah, oh, eee, ooo.' I could hardly breathe I was so scared. Was the elevator hanging there by a thread? Were we all going to plunge into the sub-basement and end up as a pile of broken bodies and bones in the cellar or just explode into bits in mid-air?

Finally my father (or someone) turned the lights back on. First thing I saw was the delivery boy holding his neck with both his hands, crouching in the corner behind his tree, looking as if he were waiting for death. Mr Rasmussen, who had picked up his dog and was holding him under one arm, was hanging on to Miss Gropper with the other. Miss Gropper was hanging on to Geraldine, who was looking straight up and still screaming her head off.

Suddenly, the siren stopped. My mother had punched it with her fist and it turned itself off. The elevator wobbled and started up, shaking only slightly on its way to the fourth floor.

Miss Gropper, wiping her left eye with a tissue, was helped off. On her way out I heard her say, 'Those kinds of children should not be allowed on elevators!' but I don't think my mother or father heard. Mr Rasmussen, with my father's help, his head and body shaking like he was treading water, got off with his dog on the fifth floor. He said a bad word just as the doors closed behind him.

Gerri had calmed down, but my mother and father had to help her out of the elevator. She was breathing very hard, taking big, loud gasps, the very opposite of me, who was still hardly getting any air in my lungs at all. I kept thinking that if this was a sample of what life with my sister was going to be like, we were probably making a monster mistake.

22

Four

My mother was looking worried too, and I saw her holding Gerri's hand tight while my father opened the door to the apartment. Actually, I don't think she needed to, because the minute the door opened, Gerri calmed right down as if she were about to step into a museum or a church or someplace where you had to be really quiet. My mother took her right through the living room and I followed them; I was really anxious to see what Gerri would do when she saw her own room.

My mother had put my old stuffed rag doll, Woodie, on the bed (Woodie has the vest with the buttons and buttonholes and laces that taught me how to tie a bow), and Geraldine made a beeline for it and laughed and said 'Blixen,' or something like that, and then she just lay down on the bed and hugged and hugged the doll and held it like somebody was going to try to take it away from her. My mother looked at me with this funny look like she was going to laugh with one side of her mouth and cry with the other side, but then she just smiled and put her hand on my shoulder. I guess she'd decided right there and then that elevator disasters or no, having Gerri home was going to be worth it.

My father was standing in the new doorway and smiling too.

'She seems to like it here, doesn't she?' he said.

Gerri had noticed the flowers on the window sill and was already on her way to examine them. 'Smell them,

Gerri,' my mother said, and Gerri put her face right smack into the vase and practically knocked it over trying to breathe in the perfume. 'Dasha,' Gerri said and she inhaled again. I'd never seen anybody in my life who appreciated flowers that much, or for that matter, everything. My mother showed her the chest of drawers full of her new clothes and the wicker chest she'd filled with some of my old picture books and a xylophone with a little hammer and a top that never really worked right. Everything – bedroom slippers, comb and brush, wooden bank shaped like a train – went over very, very big, like we were giving her the lost treasure of the Incas or something.

She liked the Welcome Home cake too, although – believe it or not – she didn't seem to know what it was for. The minute my mother took it out of the refrigerator Gerri looked like she was going to make a dive for it with both hands. It looked beautiful and I could see which way she was heading right off, but luckily my father saw the look in her eyes too, and got to the cake just in time. He pulled it out of her reach and said, 'No, no, Gerri, we *eat* this!' and he cut her a nice big piece with a cake cutter and put it on a plate for her and set it down on the table. My mother gave Gerri a fork and tried to show her how to use it, and Gerri sat down at the table and oh, good, grey grief, she couldn't eat the cake.

I mean, she couldn't get a piece speared on the fork. And when my mother had helped get the cake and fork together, Gerri couldn't seem to aim it towards her mouth. My mother said, 'They've never really taught her to feed herself properly, Ted,' and my father nodded. Then, with my mother's help, once she got it into her mouth, she didn't really get the hang of how to chew it.

'I'll unpack her things, Margery,' my father said, and I

24

said I'd go help him put her suitcase away. I guess neither of us wanted to watch Gerri learn how to eat.

In fact, when we got back from putting Gerri's suitcase in the basement storage room, my mother was still wiping up the mess in the kitchen; there was whipped cream everyplace you wanted to look. There was even a little whipped cream on my mother's forehead, but my mother was smiling. 'Gerri loved the cake,' she said.

'But wait until you try to give her carrots,' my father said, smiling, and he disappeared into the living room, while my mother was still sponging the floor. She'd given Gerri a sponge too, and Gerri was helping, if you can call waxing the floor with whipped cream helping.

Every evening when he comes home from work, my father plays the piano. He usually practices scales, then he runs through some of the pieces he's written. He hums along with the music with his head to one side (as though he can concentrate better if his head is tilted) and sometimes he sort of half closes his eyes like he's trying to remember which note comes next, or maybe he's thinking of something altogether different, like who won the Spanish-American War or what we're going to have for dinner. He says he has to play to relax and when he plays I'm not allowed to disturb him unless it's a real emergency, like the bathtub overflowing or a stove fire.

Tonight, the minute the sound of the very first note came plinking into the kitchen, Geraldine went absolutely zonkers. She dropped the sponge and sat smack on the wet floor and threw her head back and said, 'Eee! Donneh, donneh.'

Then she was dead quiet for a long time listening. My mother winked at me. 'Looks like your sister likes music, Neil.'

25

It did look that way. She shuffle-shuffled into the living room and pulled a chair next to the piano and climbed aboard, like it was the back of a pickup truck and she was going on a hayride. She just plumped herself up there and crossed her legs and tilted her head to one side like my father's and just sat up there smiling her head off.

My father had stopped playing, of course, and just sat there staring as if he couldn't believe his eyes. 'What's going on?' he said.

'Gerri seems to like your playing a lot,' my mother said, coming out of the kitchen smiling, the whipped cream still on her head.

'Listen, she can't sit on the piano,' my father said. He wasn't smiling a bit.

'Geraldine, get off the piano,' my mother said.

Even though his moustache was hiding his mouth, I could tell my father was annoyed. My dad loves his piano. It's a big Bechstein, and no kidding, it's the size and colour of a hippopotamus when it comes out of the water at the zoo. It was my grandfather's and is a hundred years old, but it plays great. It takes up a big corner of our living room and my mother said that when we moved in, they couldn't get it into the elevators and had to pull it through the windows on pulleys and ropes, in pieces. To my father, his piano is like something behind glass at a museum, like priceless. He never even opens it, because he doesn't want the dust to float into it and mess up the strings, and he won't let my mother put wax on it, either. He doesn't trust wax any more than he trusts dust.

Geraldine got the message right off; she could tell she'd goofed by my Dad's tone and climbed right off the piano, but not before she'd knocked the picture of my grandfather to the floor on her way down. The glass luckily

26

didn't break or anything, but my dad jumped up and rushed to pick it up and examine it for cracks.

'She didn't mean it, Ted,' my mother said, helping Gerri down. 'Tell Daddy you're sorry, Gerri,' my mother said, and Gerri said, 'Vixen, vixxxen.'

My dad was now looking over the piano, trying to find scratches. Gerri said, 'Vixen, blixen,' but my father didn't pay any attention. He was too busy running his finger back and forth along a little mark he'd found along the edge.

'I think she apologized, Ted,' my mother said, and my dad finally looked up.

'I know she didn't mean it, Margery,' he said and then he said, 'You have whipped cream on your forehead, did you know it?' but he still looked serious.

My mother wiped the cream off her forehead with the back of her wrist and said, 'I think I'll give Gerri something warm to drink and put her to bed. She's exhausted,' and she took Gerri by the hand and led her back to the kitchen, which is where we were now eating since we had given Gerri the dining room.

My father sat back on the piano bench and looked at me.

'I'm tired too, Neil,' he said. 'Really tired. Aren't you?'

'I guess so,' I said.

'It's been quite a day,' he said, and he struck up a minor key chord and closed his eyes. 'Quite a day,' he said, sort of to himself. I just sat on the sofa and listened to him play, but I should have gone right to bed. I didn't know that within a few hours I'd find out what had made the bumpy bald mess out of my sister's head.

It had been quite a day. It was going to be quite a night too.

27

Five

I went to bed before ten with the idea of reading one chapter of the book I'm supposed to do a report on for English, but I hardly got through one page. I didn't know if it's that I'm just not that interested in spear-fishing in Canada or if the long trip to Geraldine's school wore me out, but I could hardly stay awake long enough to reach over and switch off the light next to my bed.

When you're sleeping, time gets all mixed up, so I couldn't say whether I'd been lying there for hours or whether I'd just fallen off to sleep, but I do know that one minute I was sleeping and the next minute I was as wide awake as morning, as if my alarm had gone off. Only it hadn't gone off at all, and the digital dial, when I could get my eyes into the right focus, was glowing 1.08.

The funny thing is that I woke up scared, as if something was going to happen, or had already happened. It was dark as a cave in my room, probably because my mother had forgotten to leave on the bathroom light, and the digital numbers 1.09, 1.10, 1.11 threw just enough of a gold-green glow to remind me of the Night of the Living Dead.

Then! A sudden, hard thump – the sort of sound a fist would make striking a . . . well, a coffin – and again, the same, hard, scary knock, coming from very nearby.

I waited, not daring to move or to scream. The knock came again, then again, in a repeating hollow drum rhythm: *BLAM BLAM BLAM BLAM.* Was someone

28

trying to break into the apartment, smash in the special dead-bolt locks my father had put on the front door after the neighbours were robbed last year?

Then I remembered Gerri. The room my parents had enclosed for her was next to mine. Was Gerri making these cemetery noises in the dead of night? What in the name of the avenging spirit was going on at 1.12, 1.13, 1.14 a.m. in her room?

I didn't bother with slippers. With my heart going in my chest like somebody had cranked it up, I tiptoed through the black hall to the kitchen. Now I discovered why my mother hadn't left a light in the bathroom: she'd left the small one over the stove on in the kitchen instead. It shone directly into Gerri's room, and was probably supposed to keep her from getting scared if she woke up in the middle of the night. I guess they didn't figure *I* might wake up and die of fright, but it now seemed like a good possibility.

I peered into Gerri's room until my eyes got used to the dim-dark, trying to get my bearings and preparing myself for who-knows-what waiting in there for me.

Who-knows-what turned out to be my sister, all right. Gerri was kneeling on her bed, slamming her head into the wall – *BLAM BRAM BLAM BRAM* – like it was a normal, everyday thing everybody did in the middle of the night.

'Geraldine! Stop it!' I said. I admit I was really shook. What was she trying to do? Knock herself unconscious? Put holes in the plaster? No wonder the hair was worn thin on her head. No wonder she had that big, fat welty bump on her head.

'Stop it!' I said again. 'Will you please cut it out!'

But it would have been easier reasoning with a ghost in

29

a sheet. She just kept right on, *BRAM BRAM BRAM*, like she had a quota of crashes to fill and didn't want to be interrupted.

Was she determined to wake everybody in the world, let alone this building? Just when I was trying to decide whether this fell into the category of the same sort of emergency as overflowing bathtubs that justified waking my mother, she came running in.

'Gerri!' she said, 'Oh, Gerri!'

She ran over to my sister and sat on the bed and threw her arms around her and held her head against her shoulder and started rocking her, rock-abye-baby style, and saying 'Gerri, Gerri,' and humming off key. It was something to see, my mother holding someone Gerri's size practically on her lap, but it seemed to calm Gerri right down. Gerri started to hum too, but I guess it was a different tune from my mother's, because it sounded awful.

I think it was Gerri's humming that finally woke my father.

He came shuffling in, his eyelids looking pasted together, the belt from his robe trailing behind him on the floor. 'Hey, what's going on here?' he said, but his voice sounded as if it were coming from another floor.

'Everything's all right now, Ted,' my mother said, still rocking, interrupting her humming for a minute. 'Problem's solved.'

'What'd she do?' my father said, coming a little more awake, but not much.

'You know, the head-banging thing,' my mother sort of whispered.

Why she was whispering I couldn't figure out since it was certainly no secret that my sister had practically put a hole in the pink wall and would have put her head right through the bricks if we hadn't come running in to save her and the apartment.

My father nodded as if it were the most natural thing for someone to wake up at one in the morning and work out against the plaster.

'Why does she do that?' I asked. I heard myself whispering too.

My mother gave me sort of a high sign over Gerri's head, like we wouldn't discuss it in her presence but she'd tell me later. Dad put his arm around my shoulder and walked back to my room with me. He put me under the covers, which he hasn't done since I had my tonsils and adenoids out, and sat on the edge of my blanket. A minute later my mother came in and sat next to him, and my dad said, 'I hope your sister didn't upset you, doing that?' and my mother said that it was a little scary but not to be worried. I wasn't frightened, was I? And I said I wasn't, but why did she want to do that, *hurt* herself like that?

My mother sighed and looked at my father, and he was just playing with the cord of his pyjamas and looking at nothing, and my mother said that it was just a way that Gerri had of trying to beat the frustrations out – like some people might kick a ball real hard or jog until they fell down exhausted.

'Gerri can't do what most children her age can do,' my mother said. 'It upsets her. And when she speaks and we don't understand her, it frustrates her terribly. And when she can't walk right or catch a ball or eat a piece of cake, and when people laugh at her – *especially* when people laugh at her, or run away from her – it's like there's a hard knot of unhappiness she can't untie – and believe it

31

or not, banging her head, even when she feels the hurt, makes her feel better.'

I understood, but I didn't really want to understand. Long after my parents left me alone in my room, long after everything was peaceful and still, I turned it over in my mind. I tried not to think about how it would be to be Geraldine, how it would feel to be spending your first night with your own family instead of being one person in a room filled with rows of beds and a guard, how it must have been to call for your mother at night at the top of your voice, even scream for her when everything was black and still, and know all the time she'd never come and that only the guard, who didn't care at all, would hear you.

I just lay there in bed and every now and then I looked at the glowy numbers of my digital clock: 2.46, 2.47, 2.48. No kidding, I just couldn't get to sleep. For the longest time, I couldn't seem to get my own knots untied.

Finally, though, I did fall asleep and I had the weirdest dream. I dreamed I found a diamond the size of a light bulb under my desk during old lady Bowring's English class. Wow, it weighed a ton and it had a shine like Christmas and in my dream it made me like the rajah of the school. Everybody wanted to be my friend.

What a letdown when I woke up. I was back to being just me, diamondless, no rajah, and pretty much alone as usual. But there was a surprise waiting for me, and believe it or not, it did happen in old lady Bowring's English class, fourth period.

Six

It is said around school that Mrs Bowring was born around the turn of the century but that nobody can figure out which century. I guess she must have been a good teacher once when her systems were all in working order, but lately she can't see or hear beyond the third row. If you're lucky and manage to get a seat in the fourth or, better still, the fifth or sixth row, it's like having a free period. Some of the best fights at school are fought over the back seats in Bowring's class, and nobody is ever late for English, because aside from a couple of the brains, everyone whizzes into her room way ahead of time to be sure to get the farthest seats from her desk.

Which is where Joe/Jason and I have most of our conversations.

Today, while Bowring plodded through Canadian spear-fishing, Joe/Jason and I played a couple of games of Dots and Tic-Tac-Toe, and I decorated my notebook with the flags of the world, which I have pretty well memorized.

All of a sudden, Joe/Jason whispered, 'Say, you know how to play the piano, don't you, Neil?'

I never know how to answer a question like that because I can play 'Country Gardens' and two Chopin études pretty well and I can play 'Happy Birthday to You' like a virtuoso, but if you want to hear anything else, better call my father or look in the Yellow

33

Pages under Piano Players because even if it's easy, I'll sure as anything botch it.

'Not too good,' I said, and I put the finishing touches on a real good Greek flag in the corner of my book.

'Listen, we need a piano player for the Franklin Pierce Follies,' Joe/Jason said.

'Count me out, Joe,' I said, and he gave me a killer-look. 'Count me out, *Jason*, I mean,' I said.

'Listen, Neil, don't be a dummy,' Joe/Jason said. 'It just means learning a couple of easy pieces and playing with the band. It's like this: The band does most of the work, and every once in a while, like for emphasis, the band stops and you go *Plink Plink Plink*. It's not Tchaikovsky, sweetheart.'

'Forget it,' I said. 'Blot it right out of your head. Anyhow, what's the Franklin Pierce Follies?'

'A big show the drama group is putting on. Come on, Neil, if you hit a couple of wrong keys, is the world gonna stop turning? Who'll know the difference if you get a plink or two wrong?'

He had me and he knew he had me; if I got involved in the Franklin Pierce Follies, maybe I'd work my way into the drama bunch, which wouldn't exactly turn me into a rajah but might get me out of this singles act. Also, the drama kids are not a bad bunch, actually.

Old lady Bowring was looking in our direction, or at least her glasses seemed to be aimed at us. 'Keep a low profile,' Joe/Jason whispered, 'and think it over. You can start working on the Battle Hymn of the Republic and I'll get the rest of the music to you as soon as I can.'

'You call the Battle Hymn of the Republic *Plink Plink Plink*?' I said.

'Shhh. You can do it!' Joe/Jason whispered.

I admit I flew home right after school and started exercising my fingers, doing scales and chords and tearing the place apart looking through every old song-book for the Battle Hymn of the Republic. I found it in a book mixed in with Christmas carols and the Brahms Lullaby: it had lots of sharps and flats and might impress whoever was supposed to be in charge of tryouts if I could get it right, no easy job.

My mother and Gerri were out at the park, according to Mrs Shrub our cleaning lady, so this should have been a nice quiet time to play, but no luck. Mrs Shrub brought the upright vacuum cleaner into the living room and planted it smack next to the coffee table, not so she could vacuum, but so she could lean on it and complain about her back, which hurts her a lot down on the right side. So instead of practising, I sat on the piano bench and listened to Mrs Shrub's health problems and also answered a lot of questions about Geraldine that Mrs Shrub probably didn't like asking my mother. And every time I answered a question about my sister, Mrs Shrub said, 'Poor thing,' and shook her head and then quick thought up another question. Finally, when Mrs Shrub heard my mother's key in the lock she remembered she hadn't cleaned the bedroom and disappeared, dragging the vacuum behind her.

My mother was too tired to be surprised to see me practising the piano of my own free will and just flopped down on the couch and took her shoes off. Gerri, hearing the vacuum going in the bedroom, shuffled off; my mother said Gerri had been trying to help Mrs Shrub clean all morning, and she added, 'Poor thing.' She meant Mrs Shrub.

Then my mother told me that she was exhausted after

35

her outing with Gerri because Gerri was now afraid of the elevator and my mother had to walk down six flights on the way out and walk up six flights on the way back. She also said Gerri has a habit of going up to perfect strangers and just throwing her arms around them and hugging them. Before my mother could stop her she had hugged two old ladies, an ice-cream vendor, and a sleeping bum, and we were going to have to start teaching Gerri to shake hands before we all got into a lot of trouble . . .

CRASHO. My mother and I looked at each other; the sound and Mrs Shrub's voice could be heard travelling through the apartment air like a Chinese gong. *'Geraldine!'*

My mother and I jumped up, prepared for the worst, and there it was in the bedroom. Gerri had pulled down my mother's big, fancy draperies, complete with rods, tassels, and rings. They were lying there on the floor in a big messy heap under the bare window, making the whole room look like we'd fought a war in it.

My mother said, 'Oh, Gerri!' and I could see Gerri was scared; she had her mouth open and was backing into the corner where my father keeps his clothing valet; was she afraid my mother was going to *hit* her?

My mother reached over to try to stop the valet from going over and Gerri got so scared, probably thinking my mother was going to grab her, that she let out a couple of shrieks that sounded like dawn in the jungle. Just then my father stepped into the bedroom. With all the commotion, nobody'd even heard him come home.

His face looked like it didn't believe what it was seeing. 'What's happening here?' he said, and he had to say it a couple of times before anybody really heard him, because

36

of the noises Gerri was making.

'The little girl pulled down the curtains,' Mrs Shrub said, meaning Gerri, who is taller than she is. She was shaking her head and looking very sad, as if someone had died.

'Why did she do *that*?' my father asked.

My mother still had her hand on the wobbling valet. 'I think maybe she was watching Mrs Shrub pull the sheets off the bed and got mixed up. She's never seen a room with curtains before, Ted. There were no curtains at the home. She might think they don't belong on the windows.'

My father shook his head. 'I think I'll go have a drink,' he said and then he stopped, turned to me, and said, 'Want to come to the kitchen with me, Neil, keep me company?'

'I thought I'd go in, practise the piano for a while,' I said. My father's mouth flew open under his moustache, and no kidding, just then he looked a lot like Gerri. I never noticed until that minute that they had practically the same nose and the same shape head, only his bald spot is on top. 'You're going in to *practise the piano*? Without anybody putting even the slightest squeeze on you? Or is this April Fool, Neil?'

I had to tell him then about the Franklin Pierce Follies tryouts and you should have seen how excited he got. He forgot all about the draperies and the drink and flew right over to the piano and sat on the bench and patted the place next to him and said, 'Come on, Neil, we'll work on this every night until we get it right,' and then we had to get up so he could shuffle through the music we keep in the piano bench to find a simpler version of the Battle Hymn of the Republic, which he finally found in a book

37

of patriotic songs. He put it on the music stand and turned on the metronome and began to play it very slowly so I could follow what he was doing with his left hand, and sure enough, he hadn't played two bars before Gerri appeared and one, two, three, she had dragged over a chair and was climbing up on the piano again. My father had to stop and say, 'Geraldine, get off!' and rescue the photo of Grandpa that was wobbling and ready to fall.

Which is when the doorbell rang.

I was in no mood to have anybody come into our apartment and see my father trying to get my sister off the piano and to hear the commotion from the bedroom where my mother and Mrs Shrub were trying to rehang the draperies, but the doorbell rang again and I had to answer it.

If I'd known who was coming to see me, I wouldn't have opened the door at all. I would have pretended we were all out or asleep or didn't want to be disturbed, but of course, I had no idea who was waiting out in the hall.

'I'm coming!' I called, and I looked through the peephole that lets us check out visitors to make sure they're not crooks, and no kidding, I had to look twice to make sure I was seeing right. Oh, good, grey grief, what was *he* doing here, anyway?

Seven

My mother had heard the doorbell too, and was almost behind me when I opened the door. 'What are *you* doing here, Joe?' I said.

'*Jason, Jason, Jason,* for crying out loud!' said Joe/Jason. 'I brought you the sheet music, for the tryouts. What are friends for, baby?'

I had the door open just a crack so Joe/Jason couldn't look into the apartment. 'Thanks,' I said, and I took the music and tried to close the door.

Although Dad had gotten Geraldine away from the piano, I wasn't sure what she was going to do next. 'Well, I'll see you around,' I said, but my mother heard me. 'Aren't you going to invite your friend in, Neil?' she asked, and then it was impossible not to.

Joe/Jason was dying to come in and look around anyway; I could tell by the way he accepted the invitation right off and the way his eyes were jumping all around the place like they were electric. I kind of don't know Joe/Jason well enough to figure out if he's really my friend or was just curious to see if Gerri was some kind of freak who would take off her clothes and dance around the carpet in her underwear or do something just as wild that the kids at school would love to hear all about. I just crossed my fingers and prayed that Gerri wouldn't do anything too weird.

'Would you and your friend like a snack?' my mother asked.

At the moment, Gerri was sitting on the floor near the couch and pushing her fingers into the rug. I thought if we just went straight to my room Joe/Jason might not even notice her.

'No thanks, Mum. We'll just go hang around.'

But I was dead wrong. We hadn't taken one step when Geraldine spotted us, and one look at Joe/Jason and she let out one of her *ha-hee-hi-heeees*, which rooted Joe/Jason right to the floor. It was sort of a welcoming laugh and in a minute she had scrambled up and was coming right towards him – shuffle/shuffle, shuffle/shuffle. She was learning to put speed on it.

I could see Joe didn't know what to do and so just stood there frozen, not moving, the way people do when a two-thousand-dollar vase is about to topple off a table.

Which gave Geraldine a great opportunity to come over and throw her arms around Joe/Jason and give him a hug like he was her best friend and she hadn't seen him in five years.

Poor Joe/Jason. He let a sort of little laugh come out of his throat and his face turned the colour of sunsets and his eyes rolled up in his head.

'That's enough, Geraldine,' I said, and she let go. She said, 'Dasher-dancer,' and let her mouth stay open like she was going to say something else.

'What did she say?' Joe/Jason wanted to know.

'Let's forget it. Let's go to my room,' I said.

'Vixen-blix', Gerri said, and Joe/Jason said, 'What did she say? Is that how she talks? Can you understand her? How do you know what she's saying? Why is her head banged up?' And then we passed my parents' bedroom and he saw the mess in there and he said, 'Hey, you're not moving, are you?'

40

'Listen,' I said, trying not to get annoyed. 'Did you come in here to visit or to ask questions?'

'Take it easy,' Joe/Jason said. 'Don't be sensitive. She's not that bad. Really.'

I was glad Joe/Jason wasn't there that night, at dinner. My mother made meatballs and spaghetti because she thought those foods would be soft enough for Gerri to chew, but I guess Gerri didn't like the look of what was on her plate, or maybe it reminded her of something she didn't want to be reminded of. I remembered what Dad had said about trying to get her to eat carrots. She wouldn't touch the spaghetti. My mother begged her and I showed her how to wrap it around a fork and my father said, 'Come on, Gerri, dig in,' but Gerri just sat at the table staring at the food and looking as if she was going to burst into tears.

My mother's face was very red, partly from cooking and partly from worry. She said Gerri hadn't eaten anything except oatmeal for breakfast and an ice-cream cone at the park and might get undernourished if she didn't learn to eat solid food.

She put the fork in Gerri's hand and tried to guide it into her mouth, but the spaghetti fell off the fork and some of it fell on the table and some slid into Gerri's lap. I said, 'Yuk.' My father got up and said he really wasn't that hungry and would just grab a sandwich before he went to bed. A minute later we heard him at the piano and my mother and I had to practically sit on Gerri to keep her from running into the living room after him.

Then I got a really great idea. 'I think she's just used to mushy food,' I said, and I ran to the cupboard and looked for something soft she might like. I found a jar of applesauce and put it into a dish. Right away Gerri's eyes lit

41

up. I set the dish on the table where she could see it and I said, 'Spaghetti first, then applesauce.' I pointed to each thing to make it clear that she had to eat some of what she thought was the bad stuff to get the good stuff, and you know, it worked! I'm not saying she didn't make a mess of the spaghetti; the kitchen looked like we'd had a tomato-sauce explosion – but a plate of spaghetti and one meatball went down Gerri's hatch! My mother told me she didn't know what she'd do without me – and now would I please take out the garbage? Some reward!

'Why do I always have to take the garbage out?' I said because that's what I say every night when my mother or father reminds me to do it, and all of a sudden Gerri said, 'Bobbidge', very clearly. 'Bobbidge.' It didn't sound like any of the reindeer; she was trying to say 'Garbage'! 'Did you hear that, Mum?' I asked, and I could see my mother had heard it all right; she was standing at the sink with the dish rag in her hand smiling from ear to ear.

'She wants to take out the garbage!' I said. 'And I'm sure as anything going to teach her!'

At first my mother looked uncertain, but then she said, 'I suppose it's safe enough,' and she handed me the bag of trash out of the container and said, 'Please, be very careful and stay with her every minute, Neil.'

So Geraldine and I went down the hall to the incinerator, which is a sort of closet in which there's a little door in the wall that opens like an oven, and you simply throw the bag of garbage through the door and it travels down a chute to the basement. Easy. Geraldine looked really interested. She watched me do it, then I took her back to the apartment and gave her a paper bag and filled it with some junk I pulled out of a wastebasket and I said, 'Now you do it, Gerri.'

Gerri and I went back to the incinerator together and sure enough, she pushed her own bag of garbage down the incinerator very efficiently, just like she'd been doing it all her life. 'Great!' I said. 'Good job!' and she looked really thrilled. She said, 'Bobbidge, bobbidge!'

I felt great. She loved doing it! From now on, it would be *her* job. I'd never have to take out the bobbidge again!

Eight

It was another bad night. I woke up at the inky hour of 2.24 to the sounds of Gerri's head blamming against my wall. Going back to sleep was out, so I lay awake counting blams, hoping they'd stop of their own accord, and trying to work out ways we could keep a pillow tied around Gerri's head so we could all get a good night's sleep.

Pretty soon I heard my mother's bed creak and then her footsteps heading for Gerri's room.

Then I heard the telephone.

It rang and rang, and finally I heard my father pick up the receiver. I couldn't hear everything he said, but I did hear a lot of 'sorrys' and 'We're doing our bests.'

I heard him tell my mother that it was Mr Rasmussen from downstairs and that he'd said he'd lived in this building for twenty-two years and in all that time he'd never heard this kind of commotion and if we were going to practise for the Olympics up there, would we do it while he was at work?

Finally I heard my mother rocking Gerri and humming, and pretty soon the place quieted down and I went to sleep thinking how funny it would be if we had to tie a pillow around Mr Rasmussen's head too.

Being up half the night meant I had to make up for lost sleep sometime; unfortunately, I fell asleep during Miss Lynch's third-period history and was late for old lady

Bowring's class, which meant my seat next to Joe/Jason was taken up by Beef Adams, who is called Beef because his arms look like something you'd see hanging in the window of a butcher's shop and he has the brains of a hamburger. I sure was not going to displace Beef, so I had to move into the last available seat, so close to old lady Bowring's desk I could be asphyxiated by her perfume, which smells like an explosion at the florist's.

'Neil, in last night's reading, you learned that the hero of the story "October Saturday" by Lionel Wycks made a very important catch. Can you tell the class what that catch was?'

Old lady Bowring was probably zeroing in on me because she hadn't seen my face up this close since the beginning of the year. I thought fast, remembering the spear-fishing in Canada assignment I hadn't read, and I crossed my fingers. 'Blue mackerel?' I said. I did not say it loud because I wasn't sure it was right, but I said it loud enough for her to hear.

She screwed up her mouth and opened her eyes wide like I'd told her I'd just tied the principal to the flagpole. 'Neil Oxley, did you say "blue mackerel"?' she said in a voice that sounded like it was coming out over the public address system. *Blue mackerel?*'

The class went wild. It turned out that 'October Saturday' was not a story about Canadian spear-fishing, it was a football story and the catch in question was a forward pass, not a fish. Everybody laughed for about ten minutes while I felt the blood rushing up to my head and turning me the colour of October leaves, and finally old lady Bowring held up her hand to shut everybody up and ordered me to do not one but two reports, one on last week's spear-fishing story and one on this week's football

45

story and to have them in by tomorrow, *or else.*

As if that wasn't enough, as soon as English period was over, every kid in the class went out of his way to call me blue mackerel at least twice and to stop me in the hall later to ask me what kind of bait to use for a touchdown and did I keep worms in my helmet. Even Joe/Jason, supposed to be my friend, came over to ask me to tell him 'about the quarterback that got away.'

'Not funny,' I said. I was really down now, because it might take me all afternoon and half the night to do those reports, which would hardly leave me time for sleeping, let alone practising the Franklin Pierce Follies music. I had looked the music over, and what Joe/Jason had called *Plink Plink Plink* was six pieces, long enough to give even Beethoven piano-player's cramp.

Now Joe/Jason broke another piece of bad news. Wendy Wellington had decided to try out for the piano solos too. Wendy Wellington is no older than I am and she hasn't been playing any longer either, but when Wendy Wellington sits down at the piano it sounds like she has twenty-five fingers and an extra ten keys.

'Oh no!' I groaned, when Joe/Jason broke the news.

'Tough break,' Joe/Jason said.

It was a bad day for the blue mackerel.

The moment I walked through the door at home, Gerri came from out of nowhere and threw her arms around me and gave me one of her specialty hugs. I took a minute to show her how to shake hands instead of hug and she said, 'Blixen blix.' It was anybody's guess if she understood what I was trying to tell her.

I didn't stop for a snack or anything, just said hello to my mother and went straight to my bedroom. I had to get

46

going on my reports if I didn't want to be up all night, but right away Gerri was in the doorway, wanting to keep me company and talk reindeer talk to me. 'Buzz off,' I said. 'I'm busy. Go. Can't you see I'm *doing* something?'

'I have to go out for a short while to get some groceries, Neil,' my mother called from the kitchen. 'Will you keep an eye on Gerri for a half-hour or so?'

What could I say? Mum can't take Gerri to the market without climbing up and down six flights of stairs, and there's no telling what kind of a commotion Gerri would cause hugging the fruit-and-vegetable man, the checkout ladies, and who knows how many customers, so I pulled up a chair and gave Gerri some of my photo albums to look at while I read. She sat in the chair and turned the pages and was very careful not to rip the pictures like I told her, but she kept making sounds and talking – 'Dasha, dansa' and so on – making it very hard for me to concentrate on anything, let alone striped bass and halibut, which are not exactly the world's most interesting subjects anyway.

I don't think I'd read more than three pages when my father came home. He was early, and before he'd even taken off his jacket, he was in the doorway of my room asking me why I wasn't practising for the tryouts. I told him I had this important English assignment to finish first, and he looked just like Gerri had looked when we tried to make her eat spaghetti – like he was being punished. He said he'd come home early to help me work on it since we only had three more days to get it perfect. 'Neil, do you think you could work on your English assignment after dinner?' he said.

I couldn't let him down if he'd come home especially to help me. I put aside the reports, and he and I went into

47

the living room and sat down together at the piano and he began to play the first piece through so I'd get an idea of how it should sound. Of course, Gerri came shuffling in right behind us.

My father stopped playing. 'Gerri, please go play in your room for a while, honey,' he said.

Gerri looked at me; she looked at Dad.

She was working her lips as if she was going to say something, but it was as if her mouth was temporarily out of order; nothing but a little squeak came out. I wouldn't have minded her sitting on the floor listening, but I guess Dad was afraid she was going to try to climb the piano again.

'Go on, Geraldine, go to your room,' he said.

Geraldine gave me a sort of sad, good-bye look and turned and went step/stepping to her room. After being put away so long I guess Gerri now wanted to be in on everything. Dad said, 'I think it'll be easier to concentrate now, don't you, Neil?' and he began to go through the first piece again, pointing out the tricky part right near the end where I'd be playing six complicated chords in a row.

Not a minute later, *FROOM!* A noise that sounded like a mid-air jet collision came from my sister's room and, no kidding, I almost jumped a foot off the piano bench. Dad and I went running, bumping into my mother in the hall. She had just come in and was still holding her bag of groceries and trying to catch her breath.

My sister had done it again – torn down the curtains and curtain rods, like she wanted a better view or – and I couldn't help thinking this – more attention.

Now my father looked really annoyed and he turned to my mother and said, 'I think she needs a bit of discipline,

48

don't you?' and my mother nodded her head yes, but didn't answer.

'If you don't get firm, it's going to get out of hand, Margery,' my father said.

Gerri was sitting on the edge of her bed with Woodie in her lap. Her mouth was open and the corners were wet. Her eyes looked watery too. With Gerri it was always hard to tell what she was thinking, but I was beginning to be able to tell by the way she held her head and the way her eyebrows moved over her eyes how she was feeling. Now I thought she was feeling scared.

My mother set down the groceries and went over and sat next to her and put her arm around Geraldine's shoulders. 'Gerri, please don't do it again,' she said, very quietly. Gerri's head turned very slowly on her neck, like there was a battery in it and it was wearing down. She just looked right straight at my mother and her tongue moved in her mouth like she was trying hard to say something but it wouldn't come out.

Then my father made a sound that was half cough and half snort and he said, 'Margery, do you call that discipline?' and he turned, put his hand on my shoulder and headed me back in the direction of the piano.

It was really not easy to concentrate. Although I kept my eye on the music, I kept making mistakes, hitting the wrong key or hitting two keys with one finger, and I had to start the same piece about four times before I could get three bars played without a mistake.

'Ted! Is she in here with you? Where is Gerri? I can't find her!' My mother came running into the living room. She had a wild look in her eyes. 'I just went into the bathroom for two minutes and when I came out, she'd disappeared.'

49

'She must be in the apartment,' my father said, jumping up from the piano bench. My father had put special locks on the windows so we knew she could never get out that way. Still, my parents looked worried, so I checked out all the closets and looked under the beds. There was no sign of Gerri anywhere in the apartment.

Dad found her out in the hall a few minutes later. It was funny, but not really funny.

She'd gone to empty the 'bobbidge' all by herself, just the way I'd shown her. Only instead of the trash, she'd thrown my mother's unpacked bag of groceries down the chute.

How would I explain to old lady Bowring tomorrow that now I had to run down to the supermarket to buy the stuff that Gerri had thrown away while my mother started dinner and my father worked on trying to put back the rods in Gerri's room? How would I tell her that after dinner I'd have to help my mother clean up the mess Gerri would make with the pot roast and mashed potatoes and that I'd then fall asleep right in the middle of 'October Saturday' before I'd written one word of the report? How would I explain that although I'd set my alarm to wake me an hour early in the morning, the midnight head-blamming kept me up for so long that I not only slept through the alarm but almost missed the school bus?

I couldn't tell her. Which is why fourth-period Wednesday turned into Black Sunday, and sent me to the principal's office for the first time in my life.

Nine

I practically had to pinch myself to stay awake during third period. Miss Lynch was discussing the Continental Congress, and if she hadn't shown some gory slides of the battle scenes of the Revolutionary War, I would have been off to dreamland. Which is the last thing I wanted, since I absolutely had to be in Bowring's class early if I wanted even a fighting chance to get a back seat.

I figured if I got a back seat today, Mrs Bowring was sure to forget the assignment she'd given me and I'd have another day to get it down before the hatchet fell. On the other hand, if I had to sit anywhere in her three-row radar range, she'd remember the two reports and it would mean the frying pan for the blue mackerel.

I really flew from Miss Lynch's class on the second floor to old lady Bowring's on the first. My feet hardly touched the ground. Sure enough – and what a relief! – I was one of the first kids in class and there were lots of seats left in the last few rows. I slid into my usual seat next to Joe/Jason, who was already in his, studying the script for his part in the Franklin Pierce Follies. The actors had tried out last week and as usual, Joe/Jason got one of the leads: he was going to play Franklin Pierce and already had the home-economics bunch sewing him a custom-made sheet for the scene where he appears as Pierce's ghost. Everyone liked Joe/Jason, especially Joe/Jason. 'How does this sound?' he said to me and read the first line: 'I've come back from the dead. What's new in town?'

'Great,' I said. 'Sounds great.'

'Should I put more emphasis on "new" or "town"?' he said, re-reading his script. I was more interested in keeping an eye on the door to see if maybe I was going to get a real shot of luck; could Bowring please be absent just for this once in my lifetime?

Not a chance. She probably hadn't been absent since Franklin Pierce was President and they built, not this school, but the school that used to be here before this one. Sure enough, with books under each arm, in she came, glasses, white hair, flowered dress and all, and plumped all her stuff on her desk, ready for action.

At which time, Beef Adams, hair flying, shirt flying, face the colour of a slice of bologna, came into class just as the bell was about to ring. He made his way to the back of the classroom, although it was clear as glass to me that the only seats left were the ones in the front, and believe it or not, he was heading right in my direction. Actually, he wasn't only heading right in my direction, he was heading for my seat, although it was obvious that someone was in it. Me.

He planted his big beefy self smack in front of me and had the nerve to say. 'This is my seat, so swim off, blue mackerel.'

Old lady Bowring was checking through the attendance book and couldn't see back this far anyway, so she wasn't aware of what Beef was doing.

'What do you mean, *your* seat?'

'My seat,' Beef said, and he pointed at the desk. There, carved fresh into the wood, were his initials – B.A.

While I'd been wasting my time drawing flags of the

world in my notebook, he'd been monogramming school desks.

'Get up, Fish,' he said again.

Now Joe/Jason leaned over and said to Beef, 'Leave Neil alone, willya? You can see he was here before you.'

Now here's what I mean about Franklin Pierce Junior High School. Beef Adams was dead wrong, anybody could see that, and I was dead right, as any fair jury would admit. But Beef is an East-Ender and old lady Bowring's class was full of other East-Enders. Right away, they overruled Joe/Jason and turned against me.

'Come on, Mackerel, Beef hasn't done his homework, give him a break,' one of them whispered.

Another one said, 'Go swim upstream, willya, Mack?'

And another one said, 'Let's get a net and pull him out of his chair!'

While Beef had his group pulling for him, all I had was Joe/Jason, and it was no contest. With everybody cheering for Beef, he got a big surge of self-confidence and he leaned over and tried to lift me out of the chair with his big steaks-and-chops arms. I wouldn't budge. He pulled, I resisted. While Joe/Jason said, 'Come on, Beef, lay off,' in one trying-hard but single voice, four other guys and one girl were in there for Beef.

'WHAT...IS...GOING...ON...BACK...THERE?'

Good, grey grief! Had old lady Bowring had her eye-glass prescription changed? How come she'd noticed us back here anyway? Her voice ricocheted around the room like they'd emptied a cage of parakeets in here. Now she was headed this way!

Even with Bowring coming at us through the aisle a mile a minute, Beef didn't stop. He had me by the shirt and was trying to pull me up. I was holding on to the desk

53

with both hands. He had his cheering section and I had my Joe/Jason and it made quite a commotion: a lot of furniture seemed to be shaking, and under my feet, the floor didn't seem all that steady, either.

'WHAT...IS...HAPPENING...HERE?'

Beef let go. I let go. Everybody shut up, one-two-three.

Bowring grabbed my shoulder and Beef's arm. Was she trying to perfume us to death? She squinted at us through her glasses.

'Come to the desk, both of you,' she ordered. I expected fire to come out of her nose and mouth, or at least smoke. That's how mad she sounded.

I followed Beef up to her desk. He followed her. She asked what was going on back there. I mumbled, 'Nothing,' and Beef mumbled, 'Nothing.' She did not look happy with two nothings. She asked for Beef's assignment. Beef hadn't done it. She asked for my assignment. I hadn't done it. She turned blue. Well, not exactly, but she looked like she might.

She told us to get our books and to go sit in Mr Guttag's office. She said she would have no fighting in her classroom. She said no one would accuse her of being permissive and encouraging wanton behaviour. Nobody knew what 'wanton' meant but we knew it wasn't good. She said she knew times were changing but they weren't going to change in *her* classroom. I wished like anything times would change and that it would be July or August when schools were closed. Instead, here were Beef and I, making our way to Mr Guttag's office.

'Sit down, boys,' said Mr Guttag's secretary, who hardly looked up from her typewriter. 'Mr Guttag is in his private office now. He'll see you in a few minutes.'

While we waited I tried to listen for screams to see if

54

somebody else was really getting it in there, but the typewriter was making so much noise there was no telling. Besides, my stomach felt like high tide and I had to concentrate on keeping it under control. Beef just sat next to me relaxed as anything, humming (humming!) like he was sitting here waiting for the light to change, like he did this every day.

But Mr Guttag did not seem to recognize Beef. He just stepped out of his office and strode over to us in three or four big steps and stood looking down at us as if he were trying to decide whether to throw us into a reptile pit or simply tie us to these chairs and beat us with chains for a couple of hours.

'Boys,' he said. He made the word 'boys' sound like the Gettysburg Address spoken by Lincoln to a million people. Even the secretary stopped typing to listen.

'Boys, Mrs Bowring just called me on the intercom to tell me that you caused a disturbance in class.'

Mr Guttag made 'disturbance' sound like 'holocaust'. Then he paused. 'She said that there was a . . . scuffle. Is that correct?' He made 'scuffle' sound like 'earthquake'.

I nodded. Beef had stopped humming. He nodded.

'Boys. I want you to understand that we are not going to tolerate this sort of behaviour in our school. I am putting this to you in the form of a warning, since this is a first offence. Let me make it clear by putting it to you this way: I expect you to behave at all times like gentlemen. Is that understood?'

I nodded. Beef nodded.

'In short,' said Mr Guttag, 'I do not want to see you in this office again.'

Right. I was for that, one hundred percent. I didn't want to be in Mr Guttag's office ever again, either. Beef nodded. I nodded. Mr Guttag shook my hand, then he shook Beef's hand. I was so relieved, I felt like doing a dance right outside the office in the corridor. No snakes! No chains! We were free!

'Don't worry,' I wanted to say, 'you'll never see me in this office again, Mr Guttag!' But I was wrong.

I didn't know it then, but I was going to be back very soon – and the next time was going to be a lot worse.

Ten

There was no fooling around this time. I came home, went right to my room, closed the door, and got to work on my English reports. With the house this quiet, I could practically zip through the work, so by the time my mother and Gerri got home, from wherever they'd gone, I'd finished one report and gotten halfway through the other. My mother was in a very good mood. She said she'd found a school that would take Gerri for a few hours every day and teach her letters and numbers. My mother was sure Gerri could be taught to read first-grade words.

Gerri did seem to love turning the pages of books. She couldn't seem to get enough of my photograph albums. I had pictures of all my friends at the old school pasted in there, and some very good shots I'd taken at Lake Alfred, where we always rent a summer cottage. I took a picture of a deer that could have won a contest (except part of his tail was cut off by the camera) and a picture of my mother and father sitting in a rowboat before my father grew his moustache.

Gerri was full of 'donder and blitzens'; she was talking a mile a minute as she was turning the pages of my albums; I thought I ought to tell my mother to buy Gerri a scrapbook and some scissors and get her started with a hobby that would take her mind off pulling down curtains. Gerri was being so quiet in my room I actually got to finish my second report and no kidding, it turned out better than my first. I stuck it into my ring-binder notebook and felt pretty pleased with myself. I might even go sit in the first row of old lady Bowring's class tomorrow to give her a break and knock all the kids off their chairs with surprise.

I was in a great mood. My reports were done, I could smell chicken frying, and I'd even have time to work on my Follies piano piece after dinner. I looked over at Gerri sitting in my rocker and it was like Joe/Jason had said: she wasn't that bad. Once she stopped banging her head and the black-and-blue bumps went down, she would look fine. In the meantime, she was calming down and I didn't mind her hugging me all the time. She wasn't a spoiled brat like other sisters I knew either; you could give her any little thing, like a blue cake of soap or something, and she'd just act like it was Christmas. And no kidding, even if she laughed in the wrong places sometimes, I think she understood a lot of what was going on. Like teasing. She was terrific to tease. If I threw Woodie up in the air she screamed like she was being attacked by the vampire bats, but then – here's the best part – she'd never even try to tell on me. I was tattleproof.

When Dad got home, I could tell right away he was in a good mood too. He said on the way home he'd gotten an inspiration for a new song he was going to call 'You Put a Firecracker in My Heart' and right after he helped me with my Follies piece, he was going to get to work on it.

Dinner went well too: we had the applesauce routine down pat – Gerri knew she'd get some in a dish if she ate some food she had to chew, and tonight she almost looked as if she liked the drumstick my mother gave her. She smiled and laughed a lot of *ha hi hees* and my father looked really pleased.

After dinner, my mother said she had to put up her aching feet for a few minutes, and she went into the bedroom to lie down and watch TV. Dad and I cleared the table and loaded the dishwasher and Gerri took out the garbage (I watched very carefully to make sure that only garbage went), and I also tried to teach her to sweep, which she loved. Unfortunately, she took forever to get the crumbs into the dustpan, and as soon as she'd gotten them all swept up she'd pour them out on the floor again so she could start all over.

As soon as Dad and I had the kitchen spic-and-span, we sent Gerri in to watch TV with my mother and headed right for the piano.

Dad thought I should warm up by playing some scales first, so I played the C and G scales and some chords, and Dad gave me some pointers about how to hold my wrists down. Then I tried to run through the second Follies piece and it was harder than the first – written in the key of B flat and very tricky in the chorus. 'It needs a little work, but don't worry, you'll do fine,' Dad said, but I was worried. Tryouts were the day after tomorrow, I was up against Wendy Wellington, and I hadn't even had the time to go through all the pieces once.

Dad saw my face and gave me a little lecture on trying hard, perseverance, staying power, and never quitting. He told me how his father had forced him to play for two hours every day and how he'd hated Grandpa for it at the time but was now very grateful and wished he could write a letter to Grandpa in heaven to tell him. I pointed out that I only had two days to practise and it looked pretty hopeless, and Dad said that there was no such word as hopeless in his vocabulary. He said we had the whole evening before us and now, the apartment being peaceful and quiet, there was no excuse for not diving right into the piece and working it through until I had it down pat and perfect, and to please note that it said '*Vivace*', which meant brisk and lively.

I began to play briskly and lively, and couldn't have played more than six bars when we heard my mother scream. It wasn't a regular 'Dracula's attacking!' scream, it was more the sort of 'Oh, no' cry, like in an opera when the soprano discovers that her boyfriend has been stabbed through the heart by a clown. It had come from the kitchen.

My father jumped up. I jumped up. I saw my father's teeth for a second under his moustache and I heard him say, 'Damn,' which I think he didn't want me to hear him say. He also said, 'Margery, what's happened now?'

I couldn't believe the kitchen scene. Every can of food and soup was out of the cupboard, lined up all over the place. My mother was standing at the stove, both hands clapped over her mouth. Gerri was backed up against the refrigerator. She'd taken about three-quarters of the labels off the cans, and left what looked like a million plain tin cans standing in unidentifiable, identical bunches on the table, chairs, and floor.

'I was watching television and must have fallen asleep,' my mother said. My mother was talking through her hands, which still were covering her mouth and made it hard to understand her.

My father's eyebrows moved towards each other. 'Geraldine! What the hell did you do that for?' he cried.

Geraldine burst into tears. She cries funny, in very loud, crazy gasps. She started crying and gasping and all of a sudden turned her head toward the refrigerator. Oh, no! She wasn't going to do the head bit now? Sure enough, she began thwacking her head against the Westinghouse and the racket was terrible. My mother rushed over and put her arms around her. 'Gerri, Gerri, please, please! It's all right, darling, it's all right!'

The telephone began to ring.

My father shook his head. 'Oh, Margery,' he groaned, and he kept rubbing his moustache and shaking his head. Then he said, 'I'm sorry,' but I don't think my mother heard him. The thwacking noise was awful.

My father pretended the telephone wasn't ringing; he just ignored it. He put his arm around me and he said, 'Come on, Neil, let's go out for a walk,' and he and I left my mother and my sister and we walked out of the apartment.

I was really worried about leaving my mother alone there with Gerri; I knew the telephone call was coming from Mr Rasmussen or someone else who was really mad. What would he do if no one answered? Would he call the police or come upstairs himself and try to push his way into the apartment? My father told me not to worry. He said the door was locked, my mother was safe, and he wanted to get me out of the house for a walk and a private little talk.

On Sundays we sometimes go to a little park near our building, but at night the park isn't safe, so my father and I walked eight blocks to a new ice-cream place on Albermarle Avenue, even though it was drizzling and we hadn't taken an umbrella.

All the time we were walking, he didn't say much. When we got to the ice-cream place he looked up at the sign listing the twenty-five flavours and he said, 'I can't make up my mind. What would you like, Neil?' and I said I wanted pistachio mint, a double dip, so my father ordered that for me and he ordered a single cone of butter pecan for himself, but when it came, he just took one lick and said he really wasn't in the mood for ice cream and he threw the whole cone away!

I guess he wasn't in the mood for talking much either, because all he said was that he thought I wasn't practising enough piano, and that he wasn't practising much either. Then he just stood there looking around and waiting for me to finish my cone, like he was more in the mood for thinking than talking.

On the way home, he hardly spoke at all until we were on the corner of Albermarle and Third, waiting for the light to change. Then he suddenly asked me if I'd be happier if we sent Gerri back to the Training Centre.

The question really surprised me. Had Dad really thought of doing that, no kidding? I couldn't imagine Dad packing Gerri into the ord and taking her back to the school, dumping her off back there with her suitcase, and leaving her there for good.

I didn't want to tell him that sometimes she reminded me of me, and that a lot of times I thought that what happened to her could have happened to me if I'd been born first.

'What do you say, Neil?' my father said. He was looking up at the sky like someone up there was going to throw down an envelope with the answer in it.

'I don't think so. She doesn't bother me that much,' I said, and I know he heard me, but he didn't answer, and all the rest of the way home, he didn't say a word.

When we got back to the apartment, everything had quieted down. Gerri was in her room (I could hear her talking to Woodie) and my mother was putting away the last of the unlabelled cans.

'We brought home some ice cream,' my father said, and my mother put it into the freezer.

'We're going to be glad to have good desserts, because something tells me with all these unmarked cans we're going to be eating some really funny meals,' my mother said. She tried to smile, but only the right side of her mouth seemed to want to go up.

'Why do you suppose Gerri wanted to take all those labels off the cans?' I asked her.

'I don't know, but I bet she had a perfectly logical reason,' my mother said.

I didn't really believe my mother then, but I found out Gerri's logical reason the very next day, and I think it took about ten years off my life.

Eleven

It had been another bad night. Head-banging, the telephone, and something new: another neighbour pounded on our living room wall with what sounded like lead boxing gloves – probably Mr and Mrs Rawlings, who had a new baby and lived next door in 6-D.

Pretty soon we would have to either get pillows for everyone on the floor to tie around their heads or furnish Gerri's room with sandbags. While I was lying there, trying to get myself back to sleep, listening to my mother rocking Gerri, I heard my father's voice in the bedroom. He said a bad word. I heard it. Then I heard *CRACK*, and I wasn't sure what had made that sound until later, when I heard it again. It was my father's fist, hitting the wall.

When my alarm rang, I didn't hear it. I slept right through, as if it were Saturday. When I did wake up, it was so late I had no time for breakfast and hardly enough time to brush my teeth or comb my hair.

Then! I couldn't find my ring-binder notebook. I flew around the apartment like my shoes were on fire; my English reports were in there, both of them! I couldn't show up in Bowring's class without the reports today!

My mother is the best looker-for-lost-things – she always finds whatever is missing. This time, though, it was Dad who found it. It was hidden in the piano bench, of all places, and of course, we all knew who'd put it in there. Late as I was, I took a minute to run into Gerri's room to scream my head off at her. She just pulled the covers over her head and pretended she didn't hear me.

In the elevator, I met Mr Rasmussen, who had his Scottie on a blue leash. 'What's going on in your apartment?' he said to me. 'What are you people doing in there?' He looked angry. He also looked tired.

I didn't know what to say. It's very hard for me to tell people about Gerri. I just looked down at the dog and I didn't answer.

'You people are making such a racket the whole building's up in arms about it,' Mr Rasmussen said. 'Something's going to have to be done,' he said.

'Yes sir,' I said, and I was really relieved when the elevator stopped in the lobby and I ran out.

I was in plenty of time for Bowring's class, in a seat that wasn't in the back but wasn't really up front either. I still had about two minutes before the period started and Bowring arrived, and although Joe/Jason was calling me to come in back and tell him how the practising was coming and sit next to him and listen to how he'd memorized some more lines, I decided to look over my report one more time before handing it in.

I opened my notebook, looked at my report, and good, grey grief, I think all the blood ran out of my head. No kidding, I expected to see a red puddle right at my feet on the floor. My report – all that careful work about Canadian spear-fishing and Saturday football that took me forever to put together, which I copied in my best handwriting, which I'd put in the gorgeous blue folder and lettered ENGLISH REPORT in the most careful, indelible-ink letters, measured with a ruler – was covered with the labels from our canned goods!

Gerri! While Dad and I were out having ice cream last

65

night, she must have been busy making a scrapbook by sticking in paper labels that read Tuna, Ravioli, Beets, and Mandarin Orange Sections!

I guess she'd gotten the idea from seeing me paste stuff in my photo album, borrowed my glue and wrecked my report!

In a minute, Bowring would be in here, asking for it, opening the blue cover, seeing the Campbell Split Pea Soup label, the Kernel Corn label, the Green Pea label with the Jolly Green Giant on it. If she looked up and said to me in front of the class, 'What is the meaning of this, Neil? Why did you paste green-pea labels in your report?' and if she then held it up for the class to see, turned the pages, squinted at them through her glasses while the class rolled on the floor laughing, it would feel like Gerri had torn *me* up into little bits.

I couldn't face it. I had only one minute to run, and I jumped up, grabbed the book, and no kidding, I ran. I flew out of Bowring's class like someone had flung me out the door like a frisbee. I whooshed through the halls and, not knowing where to go, ducked into the boys' room just as the bell rang. She hadn't seen me. I was safe.

A few East-Enders were in there passing around a cigarette. One of them was from English class, Dick Franzella, who, it was said, only attended classes on Franklin Pierce's birthday. 'You cutting Bowring too?' he asked me, and offered me a drag. I didn't like the smell of the cigarette so I shook my head.

'Yeah, I'm cutting Bowring too,' I said.

'Join the club,' he said.

To tell the truth, this was the first time I'd ever cut a class, and I felt like I felt the first time I'd been out on my uncle's sailboat on Lake Alfred – like I was going to tip

66

over, maybe drown. Any minute I expected the door of the boys' room to open and a teacher to burst in and line us up against the tile wall and ask each one his name and why he wasn't in class. A few times the door slid open, but it was only some kid or other wanting to go to the bathroom, but each time it was like my heart left my body and just hung in the air waiting to get back in my chest and start beating again. The other guys were just sitting around smoking and rapping and telling dirty jokes; they were used to this and looked like they were having fun.

I just stood around waiting for the period to end; half the time I just sat in one of the cubicles so that if a teacher did come in I wouldn't be caught.

Finally, after what seemed like a longer time than an all-night hike, the period ended. When the bell rang I walked out in the hall and pretended to act normal, although any minute I expected old lady Bowring to pop out in front of me, grab me by the T-shirt, and drag me off to Mr Guttag's office.

Which never happened at all. I stayed pretty much out of sight, steered clear of the cafeteria, the library, and the central corridor, and it turned out not to be a bad day at all – until last period. I was at my locker getting my jacket when Beef Adams came up.

He made a fist and punched me in the shoulder, which is his idea of a friendly greeting. 'Whaddya say, Neil,' he said, very friendly.

'Hi,' I said. I was kind of surprised, since I never get any attention from Beef unless it's a putdown or an argument. I was alert.

'You cut Bowring, huh?' he said. It was like a compliment. His eyes were shining with new respect.

'Yeah,' I said, trying to sound casual. Even the word

67

'cut' makes me think of swords and knives and gives me the jitters. Had anyone heard?

'How come?' Beef asked. No one else was around, but I didn't want to talk about my cutting at all, least of all to Beef.

'She knows you cut, y'know,' Beef said. He said it really casual, like he was telling me what size shoes he wears or that it's going to rain.

'She knows?' My own voice went right up, like I was trying out for the seventh-grade choir. 'How does she know?'

'When she took attendance, some helpful kid, I think it was Sally Brown-noser Gibbons, yelled out, "He's here; I just saw him," and somebody else chimed in "yeah, he's here all right," like that. Only you weren't.'

My heart moved right out of my body again. I just stared at Beef. Of course, I knew I'd be caught. Everybody who cuts gets caught sooner or later (even the bunch in the bathroom, who love being suspended). Still, I thought that maybe I'd get away with it this once.

'Listen, it ain't that bad for a first offender,' Beef offered. 'Guttag just hangs you by your thumbs for a couple of days, first time around, haha.' Beef was practically doubling over at his own joke.

'Problem is, it's not exactly first time around,' I said in my own crazy new voice, having to remind him we'd just done a little time in Guttag's office yesterday.

Beef looked thoughtful. 'Oh yeah,' he said. Then his face brightened. 'Don't worry, Neil. I can fix it for you,' he said.

'You can?' I said. 'How?'

'I've done it a hundred times. I got a friend, works in the guidance counsellor's office during his free period.

When the cut slips come in, he makes yours disappear, that's all. That way they never get to Guttag's office, and they never get sent home, either.'

'No kidding.' In spite of myself, I was feeling as if someone had given me a little bouquet of hope.

'Only thing is, I got to give my friend two dollars.'

Leave it to Beef to try to make a little money on other people's misfortunes. He was probably going to keep one dollar himself. Maybe both.

I then remembered I didn't have two dollars. 'I only have one dollar,' I said. If I'd gone to the cafeteria and eaten lunch today, I wouldn't even have had that.

'Okay, just this once, as a special favour to me, maybe he'll do it for only one dollar,' Beef said, and he snapped the money right out of my hand the minute I took it out of my pocket.

'Are you sure you can take care of it?' I asked.

'Good as done, Neil, rest your mind and keep cool,' he said, and he tucked the dollar into his wallet and pushed the wallet into his back pocket.

'Thanks, Beef,' I said, and the truth is, I felt much better. Dummy that I am, I actually trusted him.

Twelve

At home, after my mother stopped me from threatening my sister with one of my old galoshes to illustrate what I was going to do to her if she ever touched my school stuff again, I tried to peel the food labels off my report and maybe salvage some of it, but the pages tore, so I had to start working from scratch. This time nothing short of an invasion from Mars would stop me from finishing the report and handing it in to Mrs Bowring tomorrow.

If there was time I'd practise the piano tonight, and if there wasn't, I'd have to get up at five in the morning and practise then. If I didn't, I wouldn't have a chance of being in the Follies. I'd go through the rest of my school days alone – the weird kid without a group, wandering around the place like the man without a country.

My mother was in Gerri's room, trying to teach her how to tie shoelaces. When I calmed down I told her three times I couldn't be disturbed. Despite the galoshes, Gerri gave me a big smile and a shriek. Her head bumps looked bluer than ever and I noticed that the curtains were down again. My mother said she understood I needed privacy and quiet for studying, and speaking of studying, how was school today?

I started to tell her about cutting English, but at the last minute I changed my mind. My mother was getting those circles under the eyes that old people get and she was hardly smiling any more. I told her school was fine. She told me Gerri would not be starting her school until autumn, which seemed a long way off.

She suggested I go into the kitchen for milk and cookies. She'd wanted to surprise me by baking some with Gerri's help, but when she tried to teach Gerri to break an egg into the batter, Gerri threw the shell in too. In the end my mother had to throw out the batter and go to the store for the cookies. Never mind, I told her, they tasted fine.

I think I cheered her up; a few minutes later she came into the kitchen to show me some pictures she'd taken of Gerri in the park with a Polaroid camera, and she was smiling. One of the pictures, where Gerri's head was turned good side to the camera, came out pretty nice. My mother had bought a really neat frame for it that looked like real white leather, and she said she was going to put it on top of the piano next to the photos of me and Grandpa. Just as she was about to go into the living room with the picture, the telephone rang.

My mother took the receiver off the hook, and although all she said was 'Hello,' right away I could tell something was wrong. She was standing there with the telephone in one hand and the picture of Gerri in the other and no kidding, her face turned practically the same colour as the picture frame.

Usually, when my mother talks on the telephone, she talks. I mean she talks and talks and laughs and talks. This time, she just held the receiver up to her ear and nodded and said, 'Yes,' a couple of times, and finally, she put the receiver back in its cradle and she just stood there looking at me.

I stopped eating and said, 'What's the matter?' and she pretended that everything was fine and said, 'Oh, nothing. You want some more cookies?' and I said, 'Who

71

was that on the phone?' and then my mother just sank into the chair opposite my chair at the kitchen table and she shook her head and looked down at the place mat like she'd never seen it before.

'It was Mr Parrish.'

Mr Parrish is the superintendent-manager of the building we live in. He's in charge of everything that goes on – sort of like the big boss of everyone who lives here. He's also pretty tough; I once saw him hold two kids he thought were trying to open the coin boxes in the laundry room until the police came. You don't fool around with Mr Parrish.

'What did he want?'

'He wants to come up and talk to your father and me tonight,' my mother said. She was drawing on the place mat with her finger.

'What for?' I said, but I didn't have to ask. Mr Parrish was coming up to talk to my parents about Gerri. 'Are you letting him come up?' I asked, when my mother didn't answer.

'What else can I do?' she asked.

My father ran to the piano the minute he came home. He said he had an inspiration for the release of 'Firecracker' and wanted to get it on paper before it disappeared out of his head. He reached into the piano bench for blank sheet music and began to play chords with his left hand and write with his right. I was sitting on the couch listening and my mother was giving Gerri a bath. Dad suddenly stopped. 'Hey, what's this?' he said, spotting Gerri's picture on the piano.

'Mum took it at the park,' I said. 'It's pretty good, isn't it?'

'It certainly is,' Dad said, putting it back between my picture and the picture of Grandpa. 'Not bad at all.' He went back to playing chords and writing them down.

My mother had heard the music and suddenly appeared with Gerri. Gerri was in her nightgown and robe and, as usual had to be held back from trying to climb on the piano.

Dad was in a pretty good mood. 'Hi, Gerri! How's my photogenic girl?' he said. He hit a great big beautiful chord, and Gerri let out a squeal. Suddenly, she said, 'Gee! Gee! Gee!'

My father stopped playing to look at her.

'It's the key of G,' my father said. He played it one more time, never taking his eyes off her.

'Gee!' Gerri yelled.

My father looked really exicted. He turned to my mother and lifted his eyebrows.

'Try a different chord,' my mother said. She was holding Gerri's towel and squeezing it in her hands.

My father tried another chord.

Gerri squealed, 'Gee! Gee! Geee!' again.

My father's face fell. 'That wasn't a G chord. It was E sharp,' he said. 'For a minute there, I thought –'

He stopped talking and played an arpeggio, using both hands and what looked like his elbows and shoulders too. He didn't look at my mother, or at me, or at Gerri.

'You thought she might have perfect pitch too?' my mother asked, over the sound of the music. She was still in the doorway and still hanging like anything on to that wet towel.

'It was kind of a silly idea,' my father said. He kept playing, but his moustache looked like it was drooping.

'It's not a silly idea,' my mother said.

'In any case, she doesn't and it doesn't matter,' my father said.

Dinner that night was really crazy. With all those unlabelled cans, we were eating really weird combinations. My mother wanted to open a can of kernel corn and got breakfast figs instead. My father ate the breakfast figs with his lamb chop and asked my mother if he was going to have spaghetti and meatballs for breakfast tomorrow. The spinach turned out to be cranberry sauce. My mother made one more attempt at getting a vegetable on the table and let me pick a can. What we hoped was a can of asparagus stalks turned out to be chicken chow mein. For dessert, instead of pineapple, my mother opened a can of pea soup.

My father got up from the table. 'I'm not that hungry,' he said. 'I had a big lunch.'

'Let me give you coffee, at least,' my mother said, and was getting up when the doorbell rang.

'Who could that be?' asked my father.

My mother looked at me. She hadn't told my father about Mr Parrish. I suppose she didn't want to upset him and was waiting until after dinner to tell him, like she did the time my ten-speed bicycle was stolen and she wanted to break the news gently, on his full stomach.

'It's Mr Parrish,' she said, looking whiter than ever.

'Mr Parrish?' my father said and his face looked as if he'd opened the hall closet and the seven dwarfs had jumped out.

'Neil, would you keep Gerri in here while Dad and I go into the living room and talk to him?' My mother looked nervous, the way she looks when anyone runs a high temperature or goes out too far in the ocean at the beach.

74

I said I'd try. My father got up and said, 'What does he want?' but I could tell he already knew pretty well why Mr Parrish had come up here. He scraped his chair on the floor when he pushed it away from the table like he always tells me not to do, and he and my mother went into the living room.

I really wanted to hear what Mr Parrish had to say, so I stood at the door trying to listen, but Gerri kept up her steady stream of conversation, and what with all the prancers and dancers coming out of her mouth, I couldn't catch much of what was going on in the living room.

I kept saying, 'Shh, Gerri! Shh!' but she just went right on making enough racket to block out any other voices. Which gave me the idea of filling her mouth with food. If she was eating, she'd have to shut up, wouldn't she?

Where was the applesauce? There didn't seem to be any in the refrigerator. I looked into the cupboard, but aside from the rows of unmarked cans and some that still had labels that Gerri had missed, I didn't see anything that would appeal to her. Except, maybe those marshmallows on the top shelf? I thought I saw my mother give her one a couple of days ago. What were they doing all the way up there, anyway? Maybe Gerri liked them so much that Mum had had to put them out of reach?

'Want a marshmallow, Gerri?'

'Pranssssa, blix.'

I was beginning to understand her, no kidding. I dragged the step stool over to the cupboard and climbed up two steps and reached in the cupboard for the marshmallows, and while my back was turned and I was up on the ladder, would you believe it? Gerri just got up and started heading for the kitchen door.

'Hey, Gerri! Come back! I'm getting those marsh-

75

mallows down for you!' I called, but she didn't stop. She'd heard that strange voice in the living room and was heading his way, revving up her shuffle/shuffle to full-speed-ahead to make sure I didn't catch her.

I got off the ladder as fast as I could and ran right out of the kitchen after her, but she was already crossing the living room and heading straight for Mr Parrish, zeroing right in on him like she had a mission to push him out of the way of a falling building. His back was to Gerri so he didn't see her, but now I could hear what he was saying.

He was saying that he'd had to bring action against a man who had had all-night marijuana parties in his apartment and he'd had to bring action against a family that was raising rabbits in the master bedroom, but he hoped he wouldn't have to bring action against us. I knew that 'bring action' meant turning us out of our apartment, which is the apartment we've lived in ever since I was born.

My father's eyebrows moved together over his eyes, and he said that he wasn't having wild parties or raising rabbits and that Gerri needed time to adjust and why couldn't people be a little patient?

Mr Parrish was about to answer when he sensed or heard Gerri's footsteps coming his way and he turned around and just stared at her. She was heading directly at him and his expression was like – no kidding – he'd come face to face with twenty kids trying to vandalize the basement washing machines. His mouth went straight across like he was preparing to put a knife between his lips and his body seemed frozen to the corner of the rug, like he was not a person at all, but a wood carving decorating the room.

Gerri never hesitated for a moment. I guess she knew

76

all along why she was headed for Mr Parrish. She shuffled right up to him, said, 'Vixen, vix, blix,' and threw her arms around him in a great big bear hug.

For a second, Mr Parrish looked like he didn't know what hit him. When she let go of him, his mouth looked even straighter, his eyes rounder. There was a second or two of absolute what-next silence and then – no kidding – Mr Parrish grabbed Geraldine and hugged her right back!

I guess none of us expected that. In fact, all of a sudden, my mother turned her back on all of us; I guess she didn't want us to see her face when she wiped her eyes with the back of her hand. I guess that's the way my mother celebrates! It certainly seemed as if Mr Parrish really liked Gerri, and if Mr Parrish liked Gerri, he wouldn't bring action, would he? Even my father's moustache looked as if it was smiling.

I felt good too. I'd finished my reports and hidden my ring-binder out of sight. Beef would fix the cut slip, I still had hours to practise my Follies piece for tomorrow's tryouts, and now it seemed that we could stay right on in our apartment.

Things were looking up. I was sure everything would be smooth and sweet as those marshmallows in the kitchen cupboard and we'd all live happily ever after.

I should have remembered things always look brightest before the storm; no kidding, I'd never been so wrong about the future in my whole life!

Thirteen

My father and I decided if I got the first Follies piece absolutely perfect I'd have at least an even chance of getting the piano part, in spite of Wendy Wellington. There was always the possibility that Wendy wouldn't show up, or that she'd sprain a finger playing ball since she is also on the baseball team, or that just for once she'd hit all the wrong keys and I'd hit the right ones.

My father put aside his firecracker song to help me practise this one piece, which was called, 'Mrs Pierce, You Have a Lovely Baby Boy', when my mother came in to tell us that she hated to disturb the practising but that she couldn't get Gerri to sleep until I stopped playing; the music was keeping her wide awake and making her very excited. I said okay and closed the piano. I felt I had the piece down pretty good except for one really tough part with a lot of sharps and flats in the left hand, and I was getting pretty tired anyway. My father got up and walked around the room and said that it definitely needed more work.

I told him I'd planned to set the alarm to go off early tomorrow morning to get in some more practising before tryouts, and he agreed that that was a good idea. As for his own song, he told me he'd met a man who lives on Lafayette Avenue who said he'd let him use his piano now and then, and he was going over there now to work on the release so he wouldn't disturb anyone here.

He took his music out of the piano bench, went in to

kiss my mother good-bye, and told me to go easy on the right pedal. He wished me luck at the tryouts and he left.

In the middle of the night I heard Gerri's head whamming and blamming, although my mother had moved her bed way out in the middle of her room, hoping that getting her away from a wall would help. I guess Gerri just climbed out of bed and found a wall to use anyway, but I must have been getting used to it; it didn't keep me awake that long, just long enough to hear my father come home and take the phone off the hook when it started to ring.

When the alarm went off at quarter to five, I didn't much feel like getting out of bed, let alone practising piano. My body felt like somebody had tied a couple of weights to it, and I yawned about fifty times.

I guess I'm not at my best at that hour in the morning because when the piece was supposed to go *plink, plong, plang*, rest, *plinkity plong*, I kept hitting the wrong key and it came out sounding like *plink, plunk, flam*, rest, *plinkity, flam, flam*. I must have played it seventy times and every time it started right and ended wrong.

All of a sudden, mixed with the plinks and the plunks, I thought I heard a *bling-blang*, but I kept playing. I heard it again: *bling* and *blang*. The doorbell! The doorbell at five in the morning? Following the *blings* and *blangs* came a *whang* and a *bam-bam-bam*; no kidding, it sounded like a gorilla was out in the hall trying to knock our door down with his feet.

I was really scared, although the chain was still on and both locks were locked. I got up from the piano bench and went to the door. 'Who is it?' I asked. The banging and ringing stopped. A man's voice said 'Brszfrsk.' I said, 'Who is it?' again. The voice said, 'Mfmdnsk!' 'I can't hear you!' I called.

My mother appeared in her robe, which she'd buttoned wrong, her face looking like she wasn't really awake. 'What's going on, Neil!' she said in this voice that sounded like it was coming from down in a well. 'What's happening?'

'Someone's out there –' I pointed at the door.

'At this hour?' My mother started waking up. She went to the door. 'Who is it?' she said.

'Frtrskd!' said the voice.

'What do you want?' said my mother.

'FRTRSKD!'

My mother opened the door a crack, just the length of the chain, and we both peeked out.

Mr Rasmussen! He was standing there in a blue-and-white striped bathrobe and a pair of slippers. His Scottie dog was not with him.

'You took the telephone off the hook!' he said. He was red in the face.

'I'm sorry –' my mother started to say. 'I took a sleeping pill –'

'I'm up half the night listening to the drumming on the walls, the pounding, the crashing, and now –' his face got even redder, sort of like instant sunburn – 'you expect me to put up with the piano at five in the morning?'

'What happened was –' I started to say, but he cut me right off.

'I hardly slept twenty minutes since eleven o'clock last night!'

My mother tried to tell him again that she was sorry, but he wouldn't let her finish a sentence.

'I've had it up to here!' he said. He made a sign with his hands like he was going to cut his head off at the neck.

'Up to here!' he said, and without another word, he turned on his heel and marched off, his slippers slapping against the corridor floor.

My father had come into the living room, had heard the last few of Mr Rasmussen's remarks, and now flopped himself into a chair and stared at the floor.

My mother closed the door and turned to look at him. 'Poor man, I can hardly blame him,' she said.

'He's going to make trouble for us, Margery,' my father said.

'What can he do?' I asked.

'I don't know,' my mother said.

'Plenty,' my father said.

When I got to school I got the shock of my life. The minute I walked into home room, the teacher called me right to his desk. 'Don't go to your first-period class. You're to go directly to Mr Guttag's office. He's waiting for you.'

Waiting for me? Good, grey grief! Hadn't Beef fixed that cut slip? Waiting for me! Those words had an end-of-the-world ring that took the wind right out of me. The principal of the school, stopping everything to wait for *me!*

I made my way down to his office, but I practically had to hold on to the walls. My legs felt so weak, it was like I'd been sick with the flu for a week and was now allowed out of bed for the first time. I held on to the bannisters going downstairs and tried to take deep breaths for courage. I found out that taking deep breaths for courage doesn't work.

Mr Guttag's secretary hardly looked up from her typewriter when I came in. 'Sit down and Mr Guttag will be

81

with you in a minute,' she said.

I sat and imagined what was in store for me, a second offender. I imagined the screams that would come out of Mr Guttag's throat, the punishments he would invent for me. 'Go in now,' the secretary said, too soon. My stomach jumped right up into my throat. Another kid had just left Guttag's office and I wondered about him. He didn't look as if anything too awful had happened. On the other hand, he wasn't smiling either.

I went straight into the office and stood in front of Mr Guttag's desk. He put down the cut slip he'd been reading like it was his favourite book and stared at me for what seemed like ten years. 'Okay, Oxley, what's the matter?'

I didn't know what to answer, so I didn't answer.

'Did you hear me? What's wrong?'

'Nothing, Mr Guttag.'

'You were in here a couple of days ago for causing a disturbance in Mrs Bowring's class. *What is the matter with you, boy?* Is something wrong at home?'

How was I going to answer that one? I didn't answer. I looked at the little golf club paperweight holding down the papers on his desk and I swallowed a couple of times. I kept thinking how Beef had taken my dollar and flim-flammed me but good.

'This school has a strict cutting policy. Are you aware of it, Oxley?'

I said I was aware of it.

'Then why did you cut English class?'

'I didn't have my report.'

'And why didn't you have your report, may I ask?'

'It got messed up.'

'Messed up?'

I shut right up, I don't know why. It would have been impossible to tell him about Gerri. If I told him about Gerri, he'd call my mother and father and make a big thing. Then for all I know they'd send Gerri back to the Training Centre. Did I want that on my conscience?

'I'm not going to waste any more time. I'm going to suspend you from classes today. You'll sit right in that chair in the outer office until it's time to go home at three o'clock. You may leave only to go to the cafeteria during fifth period for half an hour, to eat your lunch.'

I got up and moved to the outer office thinking that there was absolutely no reason for me to go to the cafeteria for lunch since it was almost a sure thing I'd never be able to eat even one bite.

But I did go to the cafeteria during fifth period and it was one of the biggest mistakes I'd ever made in my life. It got me into even worse trouble than I was in already – and if Mr Guttag was tough with second offenders, he was practically frothing at the mouth the third time around!

Fourteen

I admit that by the time lunch period came around, I did want to eat, although I didn't do much in Mr Guttag's office to build up an appetite. Mostly I just watched Mr Guttag's secretary type and answer the telephone and saw who went into Mr Guttag's office, and what they looked like when he let them out. (Pale, mostly.)

About eleven o'clock another kid got suspended for calling his maths teacher a weirdo, and he and I played Tic-Tac-Toe for a while and it wasn't that bad. In fact, the kid said tomorrow he was going to call his home-room teacher a weirdo to make sure he'd get another day off. I told him I might cut again so we could continue our game, but I really didn't mean it. No kidding, I never wanted to be suspended again.

We were sent out to lunch at about twelve o'clock, and by that time my mouth was watering for the Friday special, cheese pizza. I got on the cafeteria line and was waiting my turn when I spotted Beef Adams having lunch at a table with a bunch of his East End buddies.

It was like somebody stuck an ice cube down the back of my T-shirt. Just seeing him sitting there laughing with his friends, probably telling them what a fast one he'd pulled on the big chumpo in his English class, gave me a chill. Seeing him eating his pizzas (no kidding, he had one in front of him on a plate and one in his hand) was ruining my appetite, especially when I figured I'd paid for one of them. I left the line and made a beeline over to his table.

'Okay, Beef,' I said, trying to sound like I was tougher and meaner than Mr Guttag and might even be carrying a knife or a hand grenade in my pocket. 'Give me back my dollar.'

Beef looked around at his friends and winked at one of them before he answered me. That made me even madder. 'What dollar?' said Beef. One of his finks laughed.

'The dollar I gave you yesterday, for fixing the cut slip you didn't fix, Adams.'

'I spent it. I bet it on the Yankees. Sorry, they lost.' All his friends went *ha ha ha* like they never heard anything so funny.

'Give me back the dollar, Adams.'

'I told you, the Yankees lost. Bug off if you don't want to be a loser too.' *Ha ha ha.*

'I want my dollar and I want it now.'

'Hey, didn't you hear me?' Beef said. 'Didn't you understand what I told you?' he said, and then he said something that made the red flag go up. 'What are you, retarded or something? Does it run in your family?'

It was like he stuck my finger into an electric wall socket. I went berserk. I picked the extra pizza off his plate, lifted it into the air, and mashed it right into his face. It caught the right side of his head, and no kidding, it actually made me feel good to see the tomato sauce and cheese running out of his ear.

Of course, he went wild. He threw the other pizza right back at me and caught my left shoulder and neck. Then he picked up his milk container and hurled it too, but I ducked and it hit a pole and sprayed a girl wearing glasses

85

who was sitting next to it. She just sat there with milk covering both lenses and running down her nose, looking ghostly and not knowing what hit her.

The entire cafeteria went wild.

The screaming was like in a football stadium. Beef's friends were pounding the table yelling 'GO! GO! GO!' like he was going to make a touchdown. Other kids were stomping their feet and leaping on the tables; an applauding, whistling crowd was gathering.

It didn't last long. Within a minute, I saw Mr Peck, the assistant principal, zigzagging towards us, his face looking like a death mask in the art museum. It was all over before you could say Reform School. 'Let's go, fellas, the party's over,' he said, and I didn't have to ask where we were going. I just wished that a hand would reach down from the sky – maybe Grandpa's, but I didn't really care whose – and grab me up out of the cafeteria, out of this school, and dump me somewhere else, preferably as far away from Mr Guttag as possible, like Venus or Saturn.

None of that happened. Mr Peck knew the way to Mr Guttag's office so well that we arrived there before I could finish even half of the Lord's Prayer. I was at 'give us this day our daily bread' when Mr Peck pushed us in our same old seats and told us not to move an inch. The secretary stopped typing and looked over her glasses at us.

Before I could even get to 'those who trespass against us', Mr Guttag's face, carried on his familiar body, made its way right towards us. I actually wished Gerri were here right now, to go over and throw her arms around him, change his expression from murderous to at least not-so-murderous, maybe soften his eyes from tombstone grey to just plain grey.

No luck. We were led to his office one by one, Beef first, then me, and I think stake-burning would have been easier. The inquisition lasted forever. What was wrong with me, he wanted to know. Did I realize that I was in danger of being expelled? 'Expelled' was a word I put in the same category as 'electric chair'. Things like that didn't happen to people in my family, or hadn't, until now.

At the very minute that thought fluttered through my head like a dark and terrible bat, Mr Guttag leaned back in his chair, stretched his lips above his teeth to make sure I could see he had none missing, and asked me what I thought my parents would say when they found out that I had caused a near-riot in the cafeteria. Would they be proud of a son who had assaulted another boy with a pizza without any provocation?

Since I didn't want to tell him about the provocation, I couldn't think of an answer for that question. What was more, I knew if I'd had another pizza and some more time, I'd have thrown one at Joe/Jason too, for blabbing it all over school about Gerri. At the same time, I didn't even want to think about what would happen when my mother and father found out. I even – believe it or not – thought it might be a relief to find a wall to bang my own head against to get some of the terrible it's-going-to-burst feeling out of it.

'What will they say when I tell them you've been sent to my office three times in the last three days? That you behaved in a violent and dangerous way?'

'I don't think they'll like it.' Here was the understatement of all understatements. I managed to say it, but not very loud.

'Well, let's find out,' said Mr Guttag.

To my absolute horror, it turned out that Mr Guttag was going to call my mother this very minute, while I was still sitting here, waiting for the hand from the sky to rescue me, and dying of fright a mile a minute.

Instead of a hand from the sky, Mr Guttag's secretary appeared with a card with who-knows-what written on it. Mr Guttag studied the card a few seconds and then he looked up at me. 'Your father's name is Theodore?'

'Yes,' I said. Nobody ever calls my father anything but Ted, although his mail is addressed to Theodore. Maybe Mr Guttag just intended to send a letter to my father instead of calling?

No. His hand was reaching for the telephone; I guess our telephone number was written on the card too.

Had they called Beef's house too? Beef had left Mr Guttag's office looking smug, giving me a big wink on his way past my chair as if he'd just gotten away with everything, had pinned it all on me, and was now getting the afternoon off to celebrate.

While Mr Guttag waited for my mother to answer the telephone, he looked at me with his I'll-get-you eyes and drummed on his desk blotter with his fingers.

'Hello,' he finally said, and my stomach did a complete somersault – I moved to the edge of the chair in case I had to run out of his office to the boys' room to throw up.

'Mrs Oxley?' he said, and there was a pause. 'I see. When will she be in?'

He'd gotten Mrs Shrub! I'd forgotten that Mrs Shrub had promised to stay with Gerri so my mother could go to the beauty parlour to have her hair cut, although today, Friday, was not Mrs Shrub's regular day.

'Will you have her call Mr Guttag at Franklin Pierce

Junior High School the minute she comes in, please? And please tell her I'm delaying Neil at school until I hear from her.'

'Delaying Neil' meant I was a prisoner in this office, until who knows when my mother would get home.

'I hope your mother calls early. I have an appointment in the city and have to leave school at five,' Mr Guttag said, looking at his watch.

Five! The tryouts were at three! I moved back in my chair, looked up at the clock over Mr Guttag's office door, and began to wait. It was 2:05. I crossed my fingers; how long could a haircut take?

What I never expected and what really surprised me was that my mother never called at all and that I not only lost my chance to try out for the Follies, but I lost something much more important as well.

Fifteen

It was my father who got the message from Mrs Shrub, and he didn't bother calling the school, he just came right over. It was almost five o'clock and I'd long since missed the tryouts and was sitting in Mr Guttag's office watching his secretary cover her typewriter when my father came in. He saw the tomato sauce from the pizza on my shirt first and must have thought it was blood; he looked really scared for a minute. 'What's happened to you, Neil?' he asked. 'Who did that to you?'

'Mr Oxley?' Mr Guttag came out of his office and he looked altogether different when he was talking to my father. He didn't look like he was going to throw punches or beat someone up with leather straps. He looked like somebody who might work at a bank or some other place ordinary people work who don't have to push kids around to make a living.

He almost looked as if he were going to smile, but instead he simply asked us both to come into his office and put us each in a chair, only this time it was more like we were going to have a tea party instead of a neck-wringing.

Even so, my father looked very uncomfortable, pulling at his shirt, his tie, and his belt, as if everything he had on was too tight. 'Is this very serious?' he asked Mr Guttag.

'I wouldn't have called your home if it weren't serious, Mr Oxley,' Mr Guttag said. He leaned back in his chair so far I was afraid he was going to tip over and bang his head on the plant on the window sill behind him. 'Mr Oxley, your son assaulted another boy today,' Mr Guttag said. I know it's nothing to be proud of, but he made it sound like a hatchet murder.

My father's eyebrows went up. 'It doesn't sound like Neil,' he said.

Mr Guttag looked at me. 'He caused a terrible commotion in the cafeteria. My assistant principal, Mr Peck, had a most difficult time restoring peace. Furthermore, this is the third time this week Neil has been sent to my office.'

Now my father's eyebrows really went up. 'I'm surprised,' he said. 'Really surprised. You never told us, Neil,' he said, turning to me.

I looked at the floor, then I looked at the little golf club on Mr Guttag's desk. Mr Guttag picked up the card that had my telephone number and, as it turned out, all my sins listed on it, and he began reading. 'He had a scuffle in Mrs Bowring's English class Wednesday. He cut that same class yesterday, and today, even though he was suspended, and apparently with very little provocation, he attacked another boy with a pizza.'

'Mr Guttag, I assure you, I couldn't be more surprised,' my father said. 'Neil has never been a problem in school or at home. If you check with his last school, you'll be convinced that he has a spotless record, without any discipline reports.'

Mr Guttag listened to my father sticking up for me, and he looked very thoughtful. A couple of times he nodded and glanced in my direction. Then he picked up his little golf club to fiddle with, and cleared his throat.

'Is there a special problem here at school, Neil? Is something bothering you?' He had taken the spikes out of his voice and sounded . . . well, almost friendly.

I said nothing was bothering me.

Then Mr Guttag turned to my father. 'Could there be a problem at home?' he said.

My father cleared his throat and he lifted his hand to his moustache and he rubbed his fingers back and forth across it a couple of times. A big silence fell into the office like rain.

'There is a problem,' my father finally said, kind of slowly. 'With Neil's sister.' His voice was funny, like it was going over bumps.

Mr Guttag seemed very alert now. He squinted down at the card with my telephone number on it, as if he were going to find a sister listed in with the sins, and then he turned back to my father. He said, 'We don't seem to have her listed here.' He picked up a ball-point pen and aimed it at the card. 'Older sister or younger sister?' he said.

'That's the problem,' my father said, and then he said it again. 'That's the problem.'

Mr Guttag looked at me, and he looked at my father, who wasn't saying much of anything else. 'Is it something we can discuss?' he finally asked.

My father said, 'I'd like to discuss it, yes. Neil, would you step out of the office for a minute, please?'

Why my father wanted to make a world-war spy secret out of Geraldine, I don't know. If everybody else would just keep cool and give her a chance to fit into the world better, she'd be fine. If she didn't think people were waiting to jump all over her for making mistakes, and would maybe try harder to listen to her reindeer talk and wouldn't point at her in the street and run away from her in the park, she'd stop crashing her head into walls and pulling curtains off windows.

I couldn't hear what my father was saying through the closed door, but I did hear his voice and Mr Guttag's voice, and here and there, I understood a word or a sentence. One part of a sentence I heard got my ears up. It was louder than the rest of the conversation and it came from my father. 'My wife refuses –' I heard him say, and I tried to figure out for myself what came next. 'Refuses to send her back to the school'? or maybe, 'Refuses to give her up'?

I guess I was glad I wasn't in there listening; I didn't want to hear any of it. I just sat there in my chair drawing flags of the world on my notebook, waiting for my father to come out and take me home. Maybe I'd ask him to take us out to Lake Alfred for the weekend – I could show Gerri how to fish if we could get an extra pole; she might like that. But just as I had the thought, the office door opened, my father stepped out, and I could tell in a second by his face that he was in no mood for fishing.

He shook hands with Mr Guttag, and Mr Guttag came over to me and, no kidding, put his arm around my shoulder! I was nearly knocked over by surprise. He said he knew I'd be making no more trouble at Franklin Pierce Junior High and could see I was under what he called 'stress' at home and said he understood perfectly. It all translated into his feeling sorry for me to have Gerri for a sister, but there was no setting him straight. He'd probably never even met anyone like her, so I don't think he could understand perfectly. I don't think he could really understand at all.

On the way home my father and I had a serious talk. Actually, it was my father who talked. I listened. He told

93

me that he understood how my sister was disrupting my life, because she was disrupting his life, too. He said he himself was very, very upset and didn't know what exactly could be done. He said that we were not going to continue living this way, that was for sure. I asked him what he meant and he didn't answer.

Suddenly, he remembered the tryouts. 'Did you play well? Did you make mistakes? How did you do?' he asked.

Of course, I had to tell him I'd been sitting in Mr Guttag's office the whole afternoon and had missed them.

'Well, they'll certainly let you try out Monday if you explain the circumstances, won't they?' my father wanted to know. I think he was more upset about my missing the chance to play in the Follies than he was about my throwing the pizza at Beef.

I said no, they were choosing the piano player today. In my heart I guess I knew I didn't have a chance against Wendy Wellington anyway.

Maybe I shouldn't have told him the bad news right then. I think it was too much for my father. A couple of weeks later, he moved out.

Sixteen

What happened was that for a long time my father couldn't get 'Firecracker in My Heart' written the way he wanted it. The refrain was great but the release never sounded right, and he said he could never concentrate enough to get good lyrics for the last eight bars with Gerri around. This time he wanted to make sure the song was recorded and the deal did not fall through, so very often after dinner he'd have to leave the apartment to go to his friend's house, where there was peace and quiet and no Geraldine.

One afternoon, when my mother was out and I was in my room, my father came home early. 'Anybody home?' he called the minute he opened the front door, and right away I could tell he was in a holiday mood. Gerri and I both came running immediately; that Fourth of July sound in his voice meant something good was up.

'Hiya, Neil! Hiya, Gerri!' he said, and he practically zipped across the living room to the piano, pulled his 'Firecracker' music out of the bench and set it on the music stand, then plopped himself on the bench and loosened his tie. 'I think I really have it, Neil!' he said. 'Right in the middle of a phone call from Cincinnati when I was quoting the market price for IBM, it just flew into my head from nowhere. I better put it down quick before it gets away!'

My father doesn't get excited often, but he was really excited now. He opened the piano, tilted his head, and began to play. He played about three chords, then he stopped. He looked down at the keys, touched a couple of them and tried another chord, 'What the devil is all over these keys?' he asked.

I went over and looked at the keys. I touched a couple of them. 'They're sticky,' I said.

'What from? What are they sticky from?' my father said. The Fourth of July went right out of his voice and the holiday expression disappeared from his face.

I figured applesauce, but it didn't matter; we both knew they were sticky from Gerri, that it was Gerri who had messed up the piano, that it was Gerri, again and again, who was fouling things up, snafuing everything.

My father got up from the bench and stalked into the kitchen. I followed him; I guess I wanted to help clean up the keys so he could hurry and get started before he lost all the stuff that had come into his head during his phone call from Cincinnati. I rushed around and found a sponge, and he held it under the warm-water tap until it was soft enough to use, and I found the Ivory soap he told me to look for and then followed him back into the living room, and oh, good, grey grief, Gerri was sitting on the piano bench and just lifting a crayon to the firecracker music, pretending to write notes all over it like my father does.

My father flew to the piano and got there just in time to grab the crayon out of Gerri's hand, before she'd messed up the whole page. Then he threw the sponge on the floor and he yelled at her.

Gerri started to scream and my father just stood there with his face turning redder and redder, holding on to the sheet music like it was a breathing baby and no kidding, his hand was shaking like there were no muscles or bones in it.

Finally, he pulled his eyebrows towards each other as if there was a stripe of horrible pain right behind them and he shook his head. 'I've lost it, Neil,' he said to me, and he made a fist with his hand and held it up to his mouth the way people do when they are trying to keep their hands warm. Then he slumped onto the piano bench and shook his head. 'It's gone,' he whispered.

Ten minutes later he was in the bedroom packing the suitcase he'd brought out of the storage room; it was the same suitcase we'd used to bring Gerri's stuff home from the training school.

Gerri was standing in the door of the bedroom, holding Woodie and watching. My father was opening drawers, pulling out socks and underwear and shirts, and stuffing them into the suitcase. His face was still red and his hands were still shaking.

'I've thought about this a long time, Neil,' he was saying. 'A long time. It's nothing sudden. The situation here – it's not good,' he said. I could see he was perspiring. His forehead was wet and a drop of wetness was moving down the side of his head in a straight line to his chin. 'As soon as I get another apartment set up, I want you to think about coming to live with me. I think it's important for a boy of your age to have a peaceful home life without the sort of... pressures we're living under here.'

'Dad, I don't mind,' I started to say, but even as I was saying it, Gerri had shuffled into the bedroom and begun opening dresser drawers and pulling out clothes and trying to stuff them into the open suitcase. I suppose I would have thought it was funny to see her pulling my mother's bras and pantyhose out of the drawers and think she was helping, but my father didn't think it was funny at all. I think he'd had enough. He just threw a ball of socks on the bed like he hoped the socks would put a hole right through the mattress and he yelled, 'GERALDINE, STOP IT!' in a dragon voice that could shatter eardrums and must have travelled through three floors.

Geraldine's eyes opened wide and her mouth opened wider. She looked as if she'd peeked into a jack-in-the-box and a fiend had jumped out. Then, oh, good, grey grief, she wet her pants. I looked down at the rug where she was standing and saw this awful dark spot that was getting bigger and darker and right away I could see that my father hadn't missed it either.

He just walked out of the room and I heard him open the piano bench and clean out the music. He came back to stuff it all into his suitcase. Then he snapped the case shut and picked it up.

'I'm going to leave it up to you, Neil, I know you'll make a wise decision,' he said, and he went into the living room, wrote a short note to my mother, pushed it into an envelope, pasted it shut, and gave it to me to give to her. 'I'll call you soon,' he said and he set down the suitcase and put both his arms around me. Then he just held me and held me and I thought maybe he was thinking it over and changing his mind and would go right back in the bedroom and unpack and just stay here with us like always. Instead, he just gave me one more squeeze and ran his hand over his eyes, and then he picked up his suitcase and walked out of the apartment for good.

Without my saying a word, my mother could see something was wrong the minute she came home. She put down her packages so she could read the note my

98

father had given me to give her, and she went over to the kitchen doorway and leaned against it when she opened the envelope.

Gerri had learned a new word, something that sounded like 'Womba,' which turned out to mean Mama. As soon as she saw Mum come in, she started saying, 'Womba, Womba,' because she was not only thrilled to see her mother come home but also seemed pleased with herself for improving her vocabulary. So while Mum read the note, Gerri kept yelling 'Womba, Womba, Womba' at the top of her lungs.

I said, 'Ssshh, Gerri, Shh,' really wishing I could stuff a couple of handkerchiefs in her mouth the way the crooks do on TV when they really want to shut somebody up, but I didn't want to upset my mother any more than she was already upset. So Gerri kept it up – *Womba, Womba* –sounding like a caveman about to throw a spear. I was watching my mother; her nose was getting red and she was pressing her lips together very tight. All of a sudden, she ran into the bathroom and shut the door; a minute later I heard water running. My heart felt like it was going *womba womba* too.

But she came out almost right away looking okay. She told me she wasn't really surprised that Dad had left. I told her exactly what had happened and she said she didn't blame my father, not one bit. Then she took Geraldine into the bathroom to clean her up and said that life was just going to have to go on and that we'd better start thinking about preparing dinner. She asked me to wash four baking potatoes and stick them in the oven. Then she quickly said, 'Not four baking potatoes, I mean *three* baking potatoes,' and she started to cry, and no kidding, it was awful.

I felt like running out of the apartment and going somewhere else like the laundry room or the garage or out on the street, maybe trying to find my father and make him come back, asking him to think it over, *please*. But instead I just went into the living room.

Almost immediately I could tell something was different. The piano bench was open and empty, except for a few of my Chopin exercise books and a few old songbooks, but there was something else missing.

Then I realized what it was. My father had taken the big photograph of Grandpa with him, and mine was gone too. The only picture left on top of the piano now was Gerri's, the one my mother had taken with the Polaroid and put in the white leather frame. It was standing on the piano all by itself. My father had left that one behind.

Seventeen

After my father left, everything went sort of dim. My mother spent a lot of time in her bedroom with the door closed and little things began to bother her that had never bothered her before. If one of us spilled anything, she'd lose her temper and let us have it. Then she'd feel awful and spend half an hour apologizing to me or to Gerri. We couldn't afford Mrs Shrub any more, so my mother and I took turns vacuuming and I helped her change the bed-sheets and lug stuff to the basement laundry room. If I took Gerri down with me I'd have to watch her every minute or she'd pour a half a box of soap in someone else's machine or go up to anyone and give him one of her out-of-the-blue-sky hugs. Gerri was finally getting used to the elevator, but if it lurched, or too many people got on, she'd want to get out right away; she once scared the day-lights out of a couple who were visiting someone on the fifth floor by letting out a shriek when they tried to roll a baby carriage in.

Her head-banging got worse after my father left, and pretty often my mother would fall asleep in Gerri's room with Gerri on her lap and I'd find her sitting there asleep in the morning. Now, aside from the telephone calls neighbours made to complain, and their pounding on the walls, we'd get notes slipped in our mailbox or under the door. The notes were full of awful words.

Finally, one afternoon, Mr Parrish called. My mother was out shopping with Gerri because Gerri needed sneakers; my mother had promised to buy her any pair she picked as a reward for learning how to tie her own shoelaces.

Just hearing Mr Parrish's voice on the telephone again was enough to give me the glacier chills. If he wanted to talk to my mother this time, I knew it had to be about us leaving the apartment. If he was calling to tell us to pack up and get out, where would we live?

I supposed I could go live with my father, but where would my mother and Gerri go? My father called pretty often and he always wanted to know if I was playing the piano and was I practising enough? I didn't even tell him I'd stopped taking lessons; I just told him the good news, which was that I was playing more than ever. It was the truth; I did like fiddling around at the piano if I didn't have to do scales and all the boring études. After I'd gotten 'You Have a Lovely Baby Boy' down pat, I taught myself to play the Battle Hymn of the Republic – which was the best of the numbers Wendy Wellington was going to be playing in the Follies – and when Gerri climbed up on the piano, to tell the truth, as long as she took off her shoes, I just let her. She'd sit up there not bothering anybody, just to listen, and she seemed to like my playing a lot. It was the one time you could bet your life she'd be quiet and not get in anybody's way.

On the day Mr Parrish called, in she came, wearing her new sneakers, which were really cool, and looked a lot like a couple of the flags of the world I have all over my notebook (Italy and Great Britain), only better. My mother looked pooped but she was smiling: Gerri had learned two new words – *shoe* and *sock* – and had practised saying them all the way home. Gerri sat on the couch next to my mother and looked really pleased with herself.

102

She smiled down at her sneakers and said, 'Shew, sock, sock, shew. Sock sock shew shew.'

She looked much better these days because my mother made her sleep with two wool scarfs tied around her head so the bumps would stop bumping out no matter how hard she banged. She was almost all healed up and her hair was growing in, and when it was all combed down flat and her face was clean, she looked something like Jane Reilly, who is playing Betsy Ross in the Follies and got the part because she is so pretty.

I wanted to put off telling my mother about Mr Parrish, but I couldn't. I knew she'd boggle like I did just hearing he wanted to come up to talk to her, and sure enough, she got up from the couch and began walking around the room, not really looking at anything, just rubbing her elbows as if she were putting cream on them, and pacing from the windows to the door, and back to the windows again.

I wanted her to tell me it would be all right, that if Mr Parrish didn't want us living in his building we'd find another place just as good, but she had a look on her face that said I-don't-want-to-talk-about-it. I guess she was thinking what I was thinking. If a good guy like Mr Parrish didn't want Gerri in his building, who would?

When he came up to the apartment this time, it was after dinner and we were watching television in my mother's room, so it was no problem keeping Gerri out of the living room. She had her eyes glued to the TV because she loves to watch people dance and sing, and luck was with me; channel four had a great musical review rerun and she wasn't taking her eyes off it.

I left her in there and stood in the hall near the door to the living room where I could hear what was going on.

Then right away I was sorry I was listening because I didn't like any of what I was hearing.

'You know I'm sorry, Mrs Oxley,' Mr Parrish was saying. I heard the rustle of paper. Was it the lease? Was he going to tear it up into little pieces and throw it out the window like confetti or do some other marble-hearted thing?

It wasn't the lease, though. It was a petition. I heard him tell my mother, 'Eight tenants have signed this petition, Mrs Oxley,' and I heard my mother cry out like she was having a bad middle-of-the-night dream, 'I can't send her back! I just can't!'

To which Mr Parrish said, 'There isn't much I can do.'

I couldn't see my mother and I couldn't hear her very well either. She did say something else, but I don't know what it was. As for me, I felt like a wrecking ball was swinging at my life.

Eight people in the building had passed around a paper asking Mr Parrish to get us out, not let us live in our own apartment any more, *get rid of us*. I imagined them passing the petition from door to door, getting everybody to run around looking for a ball-point pen to sign it with, happy to be doing something that would help rid the building of a pest like Gerri, like she was a termite chewing up the foundation.

I stood there in the dark hall and no kidding, I felt that hitting the wall with my head wouldn't be enough: I wanted to kick everything in sight, write rotten words on the walls, break windows like some of the East End kids did every day of the week. I wanted to grab Gerri by the hand and drag her around through the building and show everybody that she was no termite and was learning new stuff every day – like not getting the toothpaste all over the sink and always remembering to flush the toilet and eating cheeseburgers without waiting for applesauce.

If I couldn't take her around from door to door, at least I thought I could show her to Mr Parrish, ask her to say 'shew' and 'sock', and make sure he saw that she wasn't pulling down the curtains and the curtain rods or screeching in the elevator any more.

When I heard Mr Parrish telling my mother that he was going to ask us to be out by first of next month, I figured I had to drag Gerri out there to show how far she'd come, what a good citizen she was turning into, and how if people would only give her a chance, they'd see she was a person like everybody else even if she was a bit of a variation.

I ran into the bedroom and grabbed her hand. 'Come on, Gerri,' I said, 'I want you to go in there and say "shew" and "sock" to Mr Parrish.'

Would you believe she wouldn't budge? A bunch of ladies with coloured umbrellas were doing Japanese dances on channel four and Gerri wasn't going to move away from the set and miss a bit of it. She was sitting there with Woodie on her lap, her eyes glommed on the screen like she'd never seen anything in her life this interesting. I just stood there thinking how I'd like to give her a nice punch, or one killer-karate chop – *whap*. That would get her really moving fast. Or I could zap her with one of her own sneakers. Mum would never have to know.

Hey, sneakers. I eyed Gerri's new ones, which she'd slipped off her feet when she sat on the bed to watch the show. I scooped them up and ran out of the room with them, intending to show Mr Parrish how my mother had worked and worked to get her to make a knot and tie a

105

bow and finally gotten her to be pretty good at it. I arrived in the living room just as Mr Parrish was leaving. My mother was slumped into a chair staring at the floor, and he was about to go to the front door when I flew in with the sneakers.

'Look, Mr Parrish,' I said, and I held them practically up to his nose in the foyer so he could see how well Gerri had tied the knots and how even she'd managed to get the laces. 'My mother taught my sister to tie her own shoe-laces,' I said. I was out of breath from the dash I'd made and at first I thought Mr Parrish hadn't understood what I'd said. His face stayed sort of blank as if he were watching a movie with the sound turned off and wasn't getting it, so I told him again. 'My sister learned how to tie these all by herself,' I said.

He had heard and he had understood. The bad news was that he didn't really care that Gerri had learned to tie her own shoelaces. He didn't get it, how Gerri was on her way up.

He had that petition in his hand and I guess his mind was set, fixed, and frozen against us. He said, 'That's very nice, Neil,' in an I'll-be-polite voice, and then he turned away from me, leaving me standing there with the sneakers hanging in my hand like a couple of too-small fish I had to throw back in the river.

'Shews, shews,' We both spun around. I guessed the Japanese ladies had stopped dancing, because Gerri was shuffling towards us, smiling from ear to ear, heading right for Mr Parrish and saying 'Shews, shews.' Then, just as she was practically on top of us, she did the most incredible thing!

She walked right up to Mr Parrish and held out her hand, waiting to shake!

No kidding, shake hands instead of hug!

When had my mother finally gotten it through Gerri's head that she wasn't to throw her arms around and squeeze everybody she ran into? When had she taught her that shaking hands was polite and grown-up and civilized and didn't scare people out of their wits?

I guess that really surprised Mr Parrish. He just held out his right hand and Gerri took it and they shook and it was very serious and solemn, like they weren't just shaking hands, but making a big-time deal.

All of a sudden his whole face changed; he looked like someone on the highest diving board who suddenly gets too scared to make the dive. Then he said something about losing his job but having to live with his own conscience, and – would you believe it – he took the petition in his two hands and tore it straight across once and then twice, and he handed the pieces to Gerri, and he patted her hair where it had grown back in, and without another word to me or my mother, he turned and walked out of the apartment.

My mother and I were so relieved that Gerri had saved our apartment again, we just took one look at each other and burst out laughing, especially my mother, who needed three tissues to wipe her eyes and blow her nose.

I went over and shook Gerri's hand all over again and promised to teach her to say thank you and how to play a C scale, but as it turned out, 'thank you' was too hard for Gerri to say, and teaching her to play a C scale was impossible because when I got home from school a couple of days later, the piano was gone.

Eighteen

Dad had the piano removed when my mother let it slip I'd stopped taking lessons. She said it took a whole morning and part of the afternoon for the men to take it apart and lift it out of the windows. In a way I'm glad it happened when I was at school.

I admit it, I missed the piano. School had turned worse than ever because now I wouldn't even speak to Joe/Jason. I figured that any kid who had blabbed to Beef about Geraldine was not my friend, even though he tried to tell me about a zillion times that it had accidentally just slipped out of him to two East-Enders in science class, when the teacher was talking about extra chromosomes. I thought I might forgive him in five or ten years, but I wasn't ready to forgive him now; I just wandered around school alone most of the time, feeling like a flea without a dog.

Until one day when I wandered into the auditorium right after school. It was empty, there was a gorgeous concert grand piano just standing there waiting for someone to play it, and I was in no hurry to get home to look at the big empty space in the living room where our own Bechstein had been.

I sat down and did a few scales just to get my fingers limber, and then I slid into a few chords, an arpeggio, and on into the Battle Hymn of the Republic, and I guess I was halfway through when I realized I had an audience.

A whole bunch of kids from the music/drama group had come into the auditorium, probably to rehearse for the

Follies, and had been standing there listening to me play without my even realizing it. Of course, I stopped cold and just sat there feeling like I was winning a blushing contest, not knowing what to do and not knowing what to say.

'Hey, don't stop now!' somebody called to me from the back, and no kidding, I'm not sure what came over me, but not knowing exactly what else to do, I just started again where I'd left off and went through the whole piece better than I'd ever played it, with only one baby mistake that no one but Wendy Wellington could have picked up.

She was there too, of course; I saw her watching me from the stage exit and when I finished, she started the applause. By this time I felt like my face had gone to the colour of tomato soup, so I jumped up from the bench and said, 'I gotta go now,' and I ran out of there past all those kids like I had to rush off to be on time for an appointment with the President of the United States. As I ran out of the auditorium, I heard Joe/Jason's voice call after me, 'Neil, hey, Neil! Come back here, willya?' but I kept running and running until I was out on the street and by myself, where I guess I felt I belonged.

That night, Dad picked me up in the ord and drove me out to Lake Alfred for the weekend. We had a great time fishing Saturday and I caught one small and one pretty good-size rainbow trout and a sunfish we had to throw back. On Sunday it rained most of the morning, so Dad and I sat in the cabin after breakfast looking at the rain run down the windows, and I guess it made us both sad, because Dad got into one of his silent moods and I didn't feel much like talking either.

When it let up after lunch, I said I was going for a little hike around the lake to look for early raspberries. I was hoping Dad would come with me, but he was sitting in the living room rocker with yesterday's newspaper in his lap and said to go right ahead, he'd see me when I got back; he'd just stay here and take it easy. I set off with a tin can and didn't give it another thought, because I never expected the surprise that was waiting for me when I got back.

The whole hike was pretty much of a disaster, not only because it turned out to be much too early for raspberries, but also because when I'd gotten halfway around the lake it started to rain again. It rained hard enough to get me soaked through to the skin and kept me busy trying to avoid stepping into mud puddles that looked bigger than moon craters, and the whole hike took about three times longer than I'd expected it to.

Dad wasn't in the living room when I got back, and he wasn't on the porch either. I went into the bathroom to dry off and I found an open razor lying on the sink. I was really puzzled because Dad doesn't use anything but an electric shaver. It scared me a little too. I guess I've seen a thousand horror movies that use razors for bloody murder and suicide weapons and it got me jittery and wondering – where was Dad, anyway?

'You back, Neil?' His voice came from the kitchen, sounding safe and unmurdered. A minute later his face appeared in the doorway. 'Did you get caught in that downpour?' he said.

I nearly jumped a foot. Good, grey grief, Dad had shaved off his moustache! No kidding, I was speechless. It was gone. His face was back, and it was the last thing I expected. Dad had really loved his moustache. I'd seen him at the mirror a hundred times trimming it and brushing it, smoothing it down and even shampooing it. It had taken him so long to get it full and thick, the way he wanted it.

110

'Why'd you shave it off, Dad?' I asked. 'How come?'

Dad sort of shrugged the way he does when some little thing goes wrong, like a fuse blowing or the fishing line getting tangled around the rod, and he said, 'It was uncomfortable, Neil, darned uncomfortable. It was getting on my nerves so I thought, why not get rid of it? and I found this old razor up in the medicine chest and – *fffft* – no more moustache, see?'

It took a while getting used to a moustacheless Dad, but by the time he got me home I decided that although I liked his face better with a moustache, it wasn't bad plain either. He stopped in front of our building, and now that he was doubleparked, he got talkative. He said he was sorry about taking the piano but he really needed it. He said he'd finished 'Firecracker' and wanted me to come to his new apartment to hear him play it. Then he got very serious and said he wanted me to think over moving in with him as soon as possible. All the while he was talking I kept thinking that now that his face was so different maybe he'd come home again to live. I guess all along I'd thought that his moving out wasn't going to be forever and that one day when I woke up in the morning, he'd be in the living soom sitting on the piano bench like always.

'I wouldn't really want to leave Mum and Gerri,' I said, and my father turned away from me and looked through the windshield, although there was nothing out there to see.

I thought that maybe I should tell him how my mother sometimes does the same thing, stands looking out of the window for an hour at a time at nothing at all, and how she burst into tears for no reason day before yesterday when she dropped a bottle of shampoo in the bathroom and it broke.

Instead I said, 'Gerri is learning to talk. She can say

111

"shoe" and "sock" and she can count to two. She can say "one, two".' I had taught Gerri that myself yesterday and she'd picked it up fast. By next week I figured I'd have her counting to five.

Dad did not seem to be listening to me. 'Look, Neil,' he said, 'Gerri will never get better. She'll never have any real sense.'

It wasn't that Gerri didn't have any sense, it was just that she had her own kind of sense, but Dad didn't understand that.

A car had driven up behind ours and was honking, so Dad said I'd better get out and that he'd call me soon. I was sort of glad to leave because I didn't want to talk about Gerri any more. I wanted to get up to the apartment and tell my mother about the neat fish I'd caught. I'd tell Gerri too. If she didn't understand, I'd just show her a picture of a trout in the encyclopedia. Maybe I'd teach her to say 'trout'.

Dad rolled down the window to say good-bye when I'd gotten out of the car, and all of a sudden, I thought of what he'd said about his moustache, how it was uncomfortable and got on his nerves, so he'd decided to get rid of it – *fffft* – and no kidding, it was like being hit with an icy wind when I realized that the way he felt about his moustache was exactly the way he felt about *us*.

'Remember, if you change your mind about moving in with me, call me any time, will you, Neil?' he said.

I said okay, but I didn't really think I'd change my mind. I didn't have any intention of moving out then, of leaving. I couldn't possibly guess that in a week's time, I'd be packing my own suitcase, saying good-bye to my sister, and dialling my father's number to tell him to come and get me, fast.

112

Nineteen

As soon as I walked in the door, my mother gave me the good news and the bad news about Gerri. The good news was that she'd slept through the night all night Saturday for the first time without banging her head. The bad news was that she'd wet her pants again, this time in public, at the zoo, when the elephant trumpeted and scared her out of her wits.

Other news was that Joe/Jason had called twice and wanted me to return his call as soon as I came home.

I was in no mood to dial Joe's number. 'Aren't you going to call him?' my mother asked twice. 'Too tired,' I said. I didn't want to go into it about Joe. 'Where's Gerri?' I asked. I wanted to tell them both about the fish.

'She's asleep. And you know what else, Neil?' my mother said. Her eyes opened really wide, like she was going to spring a biggie surprise. 'When I was giving her a bath tonight after she messed herself up at the zoo, she started to sing the Battle Hymn of the Republic, can you believe that? She sang it all the way through. Well, she did put her own lyrics to it, but you know what, Neil? She never went off key, not once!'

'No kidding, Mum?'

'No kidding.'

Joe/Jason came to my home room to see me first thing next morning. 'Why didn't you return my call, Neil?' he said. 'I have some colossal news.'

'You won an Oscar.' I tried to get my voice sounding real ex-friend cool. Who knows how many more people he'd educated about Geraldine and what colourful yarns he'd spun all over school about her?

'Please, baby, I told you it was a slip of the lip about your sister. Can't we bury it?'

'Okay, it's buried. Now what's the news?

'We all want you to play the Battle Hymn of the Republic in the Follies. All the kids who heard you Friday, that is. Everybody thinks you're great.'

'What are you, putting me on? What happened, did Wendy break her fingers in a game or what?'

'She didn't break a thing, baby. She just thinks you'd be great doing that one number, that's all.'

'What'd you do, pay her off or something?'

'Would I do that?' Joe/Jason said, and right away his ears flamed up pink as rose petals. I couldn't even imagine what he'd promised Wendy to get her to give up that plum piece in the show. A sterling silver candelabra for her piano?

Or – aha! – I just remembered I'd heard she was flunking maths. Joe/Jason was a star in maths and knew all the algebra ropes, didn't he? 'It's too late,' I said. 'The Follies is this Friday night, isn't it, Joe... er... Jason?'

'Listen, you've got it down pat already, so what's the problem?'

'How long did you promise to tutor Wendy?' I wanted to say, but I didn't. I didn't want his charity, no kidding, but all the same I did. I kept thinking how Dad would come to the Follies, and maybe sit in one of the front rows and applaud like crazy when I'd finished the piece, and how everyone in the school would see me up there too and stop overlooking me all the time. Most of all, I'd become part of the music/drama group and have some-body to sit in the cafeteria with and walk through the halls with and just plain hang around with. I wouldn't have to be a singles act any more.

'Can I practice on the school piano? Our piano is – hmmm – out of tune,' I said. No point in telling Joe/Jason *that* whole story.

'Sure, any time,' Joe/Jason said, and he looked so relieved, I felt like I'd almost done him a favour.

I guess I never worked so hard in my life as I did that week. Although I knew the piece pretty well, knowing I was going to have to sit out there and play in front of two million people (well, a couple of hundred, anyway) gave me a headache that spread from my scalp right down to my knees.

Every day after school I'd sit working at it in the auditorium and still worry I might mess it up Friday night. Joe/Jason and the rest of the music/drama group were really in there for me, and everyone said I was putting real glory and hallelujah into it and it was going to be the highlight of the show.

By dress rehearsal I was pretty confident I'd do a fair job. I guess if I live to be two thousand I'll never forget how to play that piece, I'd played it so many times.

My number came just as Joe/Jason came downstage and announced he'd won the election and four girls danced out and threw red, white and blue confetti all over him and sang 'Congratulations, President Pierce!' 'You'll stop the show!' a couple of the kids told me.

My mother had arranged for Mrs Shrub to sit with Gerri so she could come to the performance, and of course I'd told Dad to come too. He sounded really pleased and said he'd pick Mum and me up Friday night and drive us to school very early to make sure he and Mum would get good seats up front.

My mother let down the sleeves of my old blue jacket that had got too small and sent it to the cleaners and bought me a new blue tie with little white musical notes on it, and left me a note in my room saying 'Don't forget to shine your shoes!'

Gerri was still blamming her head against the wall, but now she skipped a night here and there, and her performances were down to about three or four blams per night. The night before the concert, I just lay awake waiting for her to start and that night she never did, but I hardly slept anyway.

I was jumpy all day Friday too and so was Joe/Jason – he said his mother was going to slip him one of her tranquilizers before show time – and the rest of the music/drama group was jittery too. Today for the first time, I sat with them in the cafeteria at lunch and even if I was no rajah, it was good to be in on everything and feel like part of a bunch.

My mother made my favourite casserole for dinner, but I hardly ate a bite. My eye was on the clock and so was my mother's. 'Where is Mrs Shrub?' she said a couple of times. 'It's not like her to be late.'

She hadn't arrived by the time my father came and buzzed from downstairs, signalling he was double-parked and wanted us to come down right away.

'I'll have to wait for Mrs Shrub,' my mother said, frowning. 'You go ahead with Dad, and I'll follow in a taxi as soon as she gets here.'

When I got downstairs and told my father, he said he'd hold a place for my mother but we'd better hurry or the best seats would be gone. He said he liked the way I looked and especially admired my shined shoes. He thought they'd be wasted under the piano and kiddingly suggested I plant them right on top where everybody would see them.

Everybody was in a frenzy of panic backstage. Joe/Jason was practically green with fright under his stage make-up because his mother had changed her mind about the tranquilizer and had given him milk with a shot of vanilla in it instead, which he said made him even more nervous. The only really cool performer was Wendy Wellington, who had tied her hair some crazy new way on top of her head, which made her look like her own older sister and gave her the look of someone without a worry in the world.

I took a peek out at the overflow audience through the side of the curtain and found my father, who had an aisle seat in the third row, but the seat he was saving for my mother was still empty. What if Mrs Shrub didn't come? My mother would never get to see me play!

But there was no time for worry; it was show time!

The orchestra struck up, the curtain opened, and Joe/Jason marched out on the stage to do his opening number. He was great, he was terrific, he was better than he'd ever been, and his first number practically brought the house down. I peeked out and saw my father applauding, looking as if he was really enjoying the show. The seat next to him was still empty.

Now Wendy Wellington stepped out and walked to the piano like performing was something she did twice a week, and played, 'Congratulations, Mrs Pierce,' and I did hear her make one or two little mistakes but I think the audience missed them, because she also got a great bunch of applause when she was finished.

By this time I was a trembling wreck knowing I'd be on right after the next number, and starting to feel cramps that jumped from one part of my body to another. One minute I'd get this tight feeling in my neck and the next minute it jumped down into my wrist, then it landed in my fingers.

'Neil, you're on!'

I walked out of the side stage door to the piano, and right away Rich Whitefield, the kid in charge of lighting, turned the pink spotlight on me. My legs felt like a couple of paper drinking straws that might fold right up under me in any old direction. I don't really know how I made it, but here I was, sitting on the piano bench in the middle of the pink spotlight, the whole place quieter than the public library, everybody in the audience waiting for me to begin. I was to start playing and the action would begin onstage after I'd played eight bars, but now I felt as if ten million eyes were on me, ten million ears were tuned in my direction, ready for me to hit the first note. The auditorium was dark, so I couldn't tell if my mother had arrived, but it was too late to worry about that now.

I began to play, concentrating with every spark plug in my head, letting my fingers remember each plink and plunk, getting the horsepower into my hands, and, like Dad had told me, going easy on the right pedal. I relaxed ... it was working! My fingers took over and zipped along like they belonged to someone else, maybe Tchaikovsky. The keyboard felt like velvet and the tempo was perfect. The cramps disappeared; I was really proud of myself.

118

Then!

I heard a laugh from the back of the autitorium. *Ha, hee, hi, ho yeeeeeee!*

NO!

It was like someone shot me me right in the stomach with an icicle.

YeeeeeeEEEEEEEEEEEEE!

The spark plugs exploded in my head, the horsepower went dead in my hands, the plinks and the plunks turned into blangs and blongs. Gerri was somewhere out there (had my mother lost her mind, bringing her here?), and although it was dark and I couldn't see, I went cold as a corpse thinking she was headed this way – was going to try to – oh, good, grey grief – climb on this piano?

Sure enough, the sound came closer. *YeeeEEEEE!*

My fingers died on the keys. The audience stirred. Someond laughed.

I heard my mother's voice, whisper-calling 'Geraldine! come back here!'

More laughter. Feet scraped. People began buzzing. I heard Joe/Jason's voice snapping at me from behind the curtain. 'Play, Neil, play!'

I couldn't play. I could hardly breathe.

'Geraldine!' cried my mother's anxious voice. Shuffle/shuffle footsteps came nearer.

Now I could see her dim form shuffle/shuffling right towards me. No hand from heaven was coming down to grab me, nobody was going to save me from this here-and-now, real-live nightmare.

'Play, Neil, for pity's sake, play!' Joe/Jason sounded pretty hysterical, but my fingers were finished and useless, like a steam-roller had just gone over them.

The audience was now out-and-out laughing,

119

snickering, scraping their feet, even clapping.

Geraldine was practically at the piano. I saw my mother weaving through the standees in the aisle, trying to get at her to grab her.

I heard her say, 'Come back, Geraldine!' and then – rock bottom – Gerri yelled, like an echo in the mountains, 'Gelldeen. Gellydeen. GELLYDEEN!' and it didn't take more than two seconds for three or four East-Enders in the first two rows to pick it up and yell, 'Jellybean! Hey, Jellybean:' and pretty soon somebody from the back joined in and then it was all you could hear, *Jellybean, Jellybean, HEY, JELLYBEAN!* until the whole auditorium was in pandemonium.

That was it. My mother grabbed Gerri just as she reached the piano, and Mr Peck got up to restore order, but it was all over for me.

My hands were shaking like ashes in a wind, and Wendy Wellington had to come to the piano to finish the Battle Hymn of the Republic. The show must go on and the show did go on, but it went on without me. My sister had finally learned to say her own name, sort of, but at that point even if she'd recited the Declaration of Independence I wouldn't have cared.

I hardly remember how I got out of the school and into the car. My father drove us all home, and no one said a word except my mother, who explained that Mrs Shrub's back went bad on the way over to our house and she called from a phone booth to say she was sorry she couldn't come but she was going home in a taxi to lie on a board. My mother apologized five times for bringing Gerri, but said she just couldn't miss the show. She said she'd warned Gerri about behaving and that she'd stayed way back and held Gerri's hand but that when Gerri saw me she went wild and tore away from her and practically whizzed down the aisle, squeezing between people who were standing there and squiggling through to where my mother couldn't reach her. My mother said she'd never forgive herself, *never*, and then she was quiet too, just looking out of the window of the car as if she was letting the quiet and the dark sift right into her skin and bones.

That night, Gerri's head-banging was worse than it had been in weeks. While I was lying there listening to the thumps, I realized Dad had been right all along: I'd be better off living with him, and the sooner I moved out of here, the better. I couldn't face going back to school Monday anyway. Or ever. I'd call Dad first thing in the morning to tell him to come and get me as soon as possible. Right away. *Now.*

Twenty

I never did get to sleep that night. I just lay awake until it got light, watching my room go from black to blue-black to misty-grey, thinking and thinking, waiting for it to get late enough to call Dad. Just as he said, there was no use trying to stay here with Mum and Gerri. Who could predict what more crazy things Gerri might do to wreck my life? She hadn't stopped the head-banging, so Mr Parrish would probably be back again with another petition (maybe even the police next time) and the neighbours would keep right on hating us, people would go right on staring at her in the streets wherever we went, kids would probably go on throwing pebbles, maybe even rocks, at her when they saw her in the park, the way they did the one time I took her, and other mothers would keep their children as far away from Gerri as they could in the playground, as always.

If I moved in with Dad, it might even be easier for Mum. One kid is easier to take care of than two, and Mum could give Gerri my room and turn Gerri's room back into a dining room.

At five sharp, I slipped out of bed, got dressed, and went down to the storage room to get my old suitcase. It was dark and spooky down there and for a minute I was tempted to wait until it brightened up, later, but my mind was made up. I didn't want to waste time. Without waking a soul, I brought the suitcase up in the elevator, let myself back into our apartment, and went to my room to get ready.

As early as it was, I wasn't alone long. How could Gerri have heard me creeping around like a mouse in my room? I'll never know. All I know is that she suddenly appeared in my doorway, the wool scarfs still tied around her head, with that clean-slate expression on her face that looked as if she was still in the middle of a dream.

'Go back to sleep, Gerri,' I whispered. I didn't want to wake Mum, not now.

Gerri just stood there, mouth open, head to one side, watching me open drawers, take out socks, shirts, and underwear, reminding me of the way she'd watched Dad when he was packing to leave.

'Go back to bed, willya?' I whispered again, but she wasn't leaving. Her eyes were just following me and watching every move like she couldn't believe what she was seeing.

'Willya stop staring at me, for pity's sake?' I said, and Gerri said, 'Blixen, vixen, Gellybeen,' and a little saliva stayed in the corner of her mouth.

I thought if I ignored her, she'd pretty soon get bored watching me and go back to bed, but no luck. She took a step into my room and then another step and then – believe it or not – she started to *un*pack my open suitcase, take out the socks, the shirts, the underwear, and try to stuff them back into all the wrong drawers!

'Cut it out, Geraldine!' I hissed at her, 'Just stop it!' but she wouldn't listen. Out came all the stuff I'd put in, the shirts, the belt, two of my photo albums, and the camera, and all the time she was shuffling around undoing all my work, her nose was getting redder and redder like she'd been out in a snowstorm and was catching a terrible cold and was going to sneeze up the place in about a minute and a half.

It made me good and mad that she wouldn't listen, although I'd told her to get out and leave my things alone about ten times, so I grabbed her by the shoulders and stuffed her into a chair and looked at her with real murder in my eye and ordered her not to dare get up or I'd have to get real tough.

That did it. She just sat there, not daring to move, watching everything I did, too scared to say a word and looking as if I'd already punched her in the nose.

I repacked the suitcase, and closed it. Half my stuff was still lying around my room, but I guessed Dad would come and pick it up for me later. For now, I had enough to see me through a couple of weeks. I was set to go.

I heard my mother stir in her room, heard the bed-springs creak, and held my breath. Had all the commotion waked her? But no, she'd probably just turned over in bed; being up half the night with Gerri usually meant she'd sleep late, especially Saturday mornings.

It was almost six, still probably too early to call Dad, but I'd try anyway. If he knew I wanted to come live with him, he'd pick me up right away, I was sure.

I closed the kitchen door and dialled Dad's number. He didn't answer for the longest time; ten rings, then eleven. What if he wasn't home?

'Hullo?'

Of course, he'd been fast asleep, and his voice sounded like it was coming through a tunnel from the centre of the earth.

I told him to come and get me, but I had to tell him three times before he understood. Finally he caught on.

His voice got a bounce in it. 'I'll be right there,' he said, and he told me to meet him out front with my suitcase. Then he said, 'I'll hurry, Neil. I'll be right there,' and hung up.

I went back to my room. Gerri was still sitting in there where I'd left her, slumped in the same chair, looking like a bunch of old clothes somebody had left in a pile to go to the laundry, staring at my suitcase like any minute snakes were going to pop out of it.

'Cheer up, Gerri,' I said. I went over and took the wool scarfs off her head. 'I'll visit often, no kidding.'

Gerri didn't answer.

I went to my desk and wrote a note to Mum and stuck it on my dresser, where she couldn't miss it and Gerri couldn't reach it. After what happened last night, Mum would understand.

Then I picked up my suitcase and tiptoed out of my room.

I crossed the living room and walked to the foyer practically holding my breath.

I heard a sound and spun around. Gerri had followed me. She was standing right where the piano had been, in the empty corner, not daring to get closer.

'Go back to bed,' I whispered.

Gerri's mouth opened wide, it closed, it opened. Then Gerri said, 'Neil.'

Or was I hearing things?

'Neil.' She said it again, clear as anything. 'Neil'. She'd learned to say my name. 'Neil, Neil.' No kidding.

Well, so what?

Learning a simple name like Neil was no big deal.

'Good-bye, Gerri. Thanks for learning my name, but I'm leaving,' I said.

I walked out of the apartment, got in the elevator, and relaxed. I would not be meeting Mr Rasmussen at this hour of the morning; none of the other petition-signers was likely to be on the elevator either, giving me the evil eye or making remarks. The floors slid by – five – four – three – two. At each floor, I could swear I heard Gerri saying it again, as if her voice were following me all the way from upstairs: *Neil, Neil, Neil.*

The elevator stopped, the door slid open.

I picked up my suitcase and walked across the lobby, through the glass doors, and outside, onto the sidewalk. It must have rained during the night, because the sidewalk was damp around the cracks and there was a puddle in the gutter. The air smelled like laundry soap and the sky wasn't blue yet, but it looked like it was trying.

I saw the ord coming down the street, slowing down. It pulled to the curb right in front of me. My father, without his moustache, smiled at me.

'Do you need a hand with the suitcase, Neil?' he asked.

Suddenly I could hardly see my father, the damp sidewalk, the sky, or anything; everything blurred up like somebody had turned a sprinkler on behind my eyes. I blinked and my father said, 'What's wrong, Neil?' or something like that. I'm not sure what he said because there was interference; it was ricocheting from the sky or my head or from over the rainbow, for all I knew; it was Gerri's voice saying, 'Neil,' and no kidding, it was putting a firecracker right in my heart.

'Neil, what's the matter?' my father asked.

I couldn't say it; it just jammed up in my throat like old rags, that not everybody can have perfect pitch, that even though Gerri would always be strange/different/ funny/weird, she was the way she was, and she was my

126

sister.

The music/drama kids would tear me to shreds because of her Monday, but they're regular kids, so sooner or later even Joe/Jason might forgive me.

Dad curled his fingers around the steering wheel, then he uncurled them. 'You've changed your mind, haven't you, Neil?' he said.

I nodded. I wished like anything he hadn't shaved his moustache. Maybe he'd give it another chance, sometime.

'I understand,' he said, looking straight out the windshield so he wouldn't have to see me standing there sniffing and looking stupid and not knowing what to say. 'Maybe one day I'll change mine,' he said.

'You mean you'll come home?'

My father didn't answer for what seemed like a long time. Then he said, 'Not now, not right now,' and he cleared his throat. 'I'll call you soon, Neil,' he said, and I picked up my suitcase and watched him pull away from the curb. I stood a while, thinking about it. 'Not right now' didn't mean 'never,' did it?

I turned, went back inside, and pushed the elevator button. Almost immediately the elevator door opened and Mr Rasmussen stepped out with his Scottie dog on a leash. At this hour!

'Good morning, Mr Rasmussen,' I said, quaking as usual at the very sight of him.

'Good morning,' Mr Rasmussen said, almost cordially, and as he stepped aside, he held the door so it wouldn't slide closed on my suitcase as I was lifting it into the elevator.

'Thank you,' I said, but Mr Rasmussen kept holding the door, as if he was waiting to tell me something but

127

didn't know how to say it. Finally he said, 'Your sister is really coming along, isn't she?'

I was so surprised I guess I just stood there, half in the elevator and half out of it.

'She brought some scraps to my dog the other day and I really appreciate it.'

'She did?'

'It was very thoughtful, and he loved every last bite. Except–' Mr Rasmussen then smiled. *Smiled*. Showed his teeth, at least ten of them. I couldn't believe it. 'Except the marshmallows. I afraid he's not much for marsh-mallows,' he said.

My sister, now smart enough to push the right elevator buttons, to say my name so anybody could understand it, to bring leftovers to a dog – and getting smarter by the minute. *Really coming along*. Even Mr Rasmussen had noticed it.

My own voice came out of nowhere. 'She's getting there,' I said, proud as anything. She's all right, no kidding, I thought as the door of the elevator slid closed and the elevator began moving up.

A Handbook for
School Governors

E.C.Wragg *and*
J.A. Partington

A Handbook for
School Governors

Methuen

First published in 1980 by
Methuen & Co. Ltd
11 New Fetter Lane, London EC4P 4EE

© 1980 E.C. Wragg and J.A. Partington

Filmset by Inforum Ltd, Portsmouth
Printed in Great Britain by
Richard Clay (The Chaucer Press) Ltd,
Bungay, Suffolk

British Library Cataloguing in Publication Data

Wragg, Edward Conrad
A handbook for school governors.
1. School management and organization – Great
Britain   2. School boards – Great Britain
I. Title   II. Partington, J A
379'.1531'0941   LB2901

ISBN 0–416–71590–7
ISBN 0–416–71600–8 Pbk

Contents

Acknowledgements

The authors and publishers would like to thank the following for permission to reproduce the following material: Heinemann Educational Books Ltd for Figure 2, from *Biology by Inquiry*, Robert A. Clarke, P. Rupert Booth, Peter E. Grigsby, Jack F. Haddow and John S. Irvine (1968) and for Figure 12, from Schools Council Project Technology, Brief 23 (1975); Macmillan (London and Basingstoke) for Figure 3, from *English for Living*, A. Rowe (1976) and for Figure 13, from *Changing the Primary School*, John Blackie (1974); Granada Publications Ltd for Figure 4, from *Royal Road Reader*, Book 1 (1970); The Schools Council for Figure 5, from *The loose tooth*, David Mackay, Brian Thompson, Pamela Schaub and Posy Simmonds (1970); Longman Group Ltd, for Figure 8, from the Nuffield Physics Year 1 (1978) and for Figure 9, from *Reise nach Hamburg*, Eric Orton (1968); Addison-Wesley Publishers Ltd for Figure 6, from *Mathematics for Schools*, Level 1, Book 6, Harold

Fletcher *et al*. (1970); Schofield & Sims Ltd for Figure 7, from *Alpha Mathematics 4*, T.R. Goddard, J.W. Adams and R.P. Beaumont (1979); Holt, Rinehart & Winston for Figure 10, from *Exploring Your Language*, N. Postman (1966); Nelson & Sons Ltd for Figure 11, from *Life in Our Society*, Vol. 2, K. Lambert (1975). They would also like to thank Caron Robinson for the chart on p. 10 and Adam Yeldham for the cartoons in the text.

Introduction

This is a book for ordinary folk who find themselves elected, coerced, co-opted or even, for all we know, tricked by their crafty fellows into becoming a school governor. The contents are based on our experience as governors of schools, and from training sessions we have organised for school governors at our respective universities.

We have found over the years that governors' needs are fairly straightforward, and can perhaps best be indicated by giving some of the questions the new or established governor commonly asks:

How can I help the school?

Where can I find out more about what happens in schools?

What does the LEA expect of me when I am appointed?

I am a parent/teacher/pupil governor. How can I best serve the people who elected me?

1

How does a committee work?

What are governors supposed to do if a really tricky problem emerges?

Where can we turn for help if we don't understand a particular matter?

Can governors actually get something *done*?

We have used these questions as our guide when considering what to write about and how to divide our subject matter.

Some school governors will already be extremely knowledgeable in one or another field, and their expertise can usually be of great help to their less well-informed fellows, though on occasion it may be an obstacle to progress. Teacher governors will know a great deal about education in general as well as their own school in particular. People who have served on other committees will often be very knowledgeable about committee procedures. There may be lawyers, builders, doctors, social workers, bus drivers, mothers or factory workers on a governing body, all of whom know something useful about children, the community, buildings, rights and obligations, curriculum and social problems. Putting one's knowledge and experience at the disposal of one's fellows rather than blinding them with science is the hallmark of the successful expert, and the same applies at however modest a level to a school governor who offers something useful, be it experience as a parent or detailed knowledge of building regulations. The two most important qualities of the effective school governor are:

(a) A concern for the well-being of the children, teachers and others in the school community.
(b) Common sense.

Given these two attributes in sufficient quantity amongst the membership of a governing body many problems can be solved.

Is being a governor a waste of time?

It is, sadly, the case that some governors' meetings are so

tedious and unimportant they make Samuel Beckett's pause-laden *Waiting for Godot* look like *Ben Hur*. At the end members, their brains corroded beyond redemption, resolve to go home and do something really exciting, like counting the pages of the telephone directory.

Sometimes the sense of purposelessness occurs because none of the governors takes any interest in the school. The result is that when matters come up for decision only the head and the teacher representatives really know or care what is going on, and, being as human as the rest of us, feed in just as much information as is necessary to get the rest of the governors to support what they want. Although some heads and teachers prefer that governors should show little interest in the school, most much pefer it when governors take the trouble to inform themselves about what is on the agenda so that they can see all points of view.

It will be seen in Chapter 2 'Being an effective school governor', that there is plenty of scope to help the running of your school. In some ways, the very title of 'governor' is unhelpful, because it suggests that the holder is someone who gives orders to subordinates; it is perhaps this point of view which encourages antagonism on the part of some teachers. In practice governors give very few orders as such: their function is not to control the school but to help to sort out problems and get the best possible deal for their school from all the outside agencies.

Yet there is undoubtedly at the moment a demand that governors' powers should be increased, a demand which was sufficiently strong to persuade the Labour administration of 1974–9 to set up the Taylor Committee which reported on the role of school governors in 1977. Argument usually centres around the issue 'Who controls the curriculum?' In Britain there is no central control of curriculum from the capital city, as would be the case in certain other countries. The head and staff of each school have a fair degree of freedom to use their collective professional judgements in devising a curriculum for children in their school.

When the Taylor Committee proposed increased powers for

school governors the General Secretary of the NUT described the recommendations as a 'busybodies' charter' – an inflammatory statement, but one which illustrates how sensitive is the issue of control over children's education. In our experience the best partnership between professional teachers and interested lay people in the community, be these governors or parents, occurs when it is accepted that decisions about the day-to-day running of the school must be made by the paid professionals, but with proper regard for the views of the lay people concerned. There are countless examples of this mutual respect and trust working well, and rather fewer of it working badly.

On the other hand there is now a legitimate concern for accountability in education as in other spheres. Serious doubts have been expressed about the quality of education some children receive, and issues such as the teaching of basic skills, preparation for adult life, relevance, and standards of achievement are discussed endlessly in the press and at meetings.

Would it help to give governors more power over what is taught? If you look at your 'Instrument' and 'Articles' you will find almost certainly that you have these powers already. A specimen set can be found in Appendices A and B. Although the LEA determines the general educational character of a school and its place in the educational system, the governors are, according to suggested articles of government in the 1944 Education Act, supposed to have 'the general direction of the conduct and curriculum of the school'. The reason why such powers have fallen into disuse is simply that governors in general have often not pondered sufficiently about what is taught, and why, in our schools. In some cases, governors do not even know what is taught, so their ideas in meetings have little credibility. Governors who take the trouble to inform themselves about life in school, and then use their energy and imagination to help the school will not be wasting their own time or that of anyone else.

The purpose of this book

Education has become such a vast and complex business that even those who spend their whole life in teaching cannot hope to be familiar with more than a small fraction of what goes on. Thus no governor, upon reading a single volume, can become an expert in all aspects of school government.

Our hope is that governors who take the trouble to read this book will be a little better able to do their job, will understand more clearly what goes on in schools, and will be able to play a full part in governors' meetings.

In Chapter 1, therefore, we concentrate on how governors fit into the educational system and what they are expected and empowered to do. Chapter 2 looks in more detail at the job of the individual governor, be he parent, teacher or LEA nominee, showing how he can make his contribution to the life of his school. It includes a section on training for governors. We turn to the question of governors' meetings in Chapter 3, explaining how committees work, the importance of group dynamics, and an analysis of dirty tricks (a topic rarely discussed in texts on the subject).

Chapters 4 and 5 are about life in school and current issues in education. It is, of course, impossible to do more than prick the surface of these topics in two chapter, but we hope that reading them will give governors an appetite for discovering more about the problems of learning and teaching in our schools. We suggest some further reading in Appendix C.

Finally in Chapter 6 we analyse some thorny issues which often perplex governors when pupil suspensions, accidents or vandalism are discussed, or when the school is reorganised or threatened with closure.

An optimistic/realistic view

Our principal belief is an optimistic one: that most governors are trying to be helpful. We realise, of course, that some are not, and that certain governors may even be arch-villains, enemies of humanity, but we believe that few come into this category.

Similarly we believe that most teachers work hard for the good of their pupils. We have both visited hundreds of schools throughout the country, worked in several on a regular or occasional basis, and trained thousands of novice or experienced teachers. We have some knowledge of teachers or heads who do give cause for concern, and of schools where all is not well. In general, however, we find most teachers deeply concerned for their pupils' welfare and learning.

We concentrate, therefore, on trying to encourage a *positive* partnership between interested governors and professionally committed teachers and heads, whilst knowing that this will not always occur because we are talking about real human beings, with all their frailties, not identikit Hollywood heroes.

We hope that people reading this book will find education as interesting as we do ourselves. We have both attended our share of conferences where sombre-faced educators proclaim gloom and doom, and have read our fill of papers on education which call toys 'learning stimulus materials'. We have minimised the professional jargon so that interested lay people can read the book for pleasure not penance, and if certain descriptions are in a lighthearted vein, that is because human behaviour in general, and events in school or committees in particular are often funny, pretentiousness and pomposity being especially hilarious.

Four points are worthy of mention. First of all no book about education can be comprehensive or completely up to date. A change in government or in LEA policy can reverse a situation which has operated for years. We describe situations as they are at the time of writing. Thus we address sections of the book to parent, pupil or teacher governors not because of any favouring of some group, nor in anticipation of legislation, but because there are governing bodies which already have several categories of governor, irrespective of the recommendations of the Taylor Committee report or of legislation by the present or any future government. Indeed, at the time of writing, the Education Act of 1980 was almost through its parliamentary stages, and we have mentioned some of its implications on the assumption that they were soon to become law.

Secondly, we use the term 'governor' throughout to cover anyone who may be a member of the governing or managing body of a school. The Education Act of 1980 abolished the title 'manager', which was formerly used in primary schools.

Thirdly, we concentrate on primary and secondary schools in the state system. Much of what we describe will be relevant to colleges of further education, special, denominational or independent schools, but our principal focus is on LEA primary and secondary schools. It would need much more space than we have available to describe adequately the issues covered in all our educational establishments.

Fourthly, in referring to governors as 'he' in the text for consistency and convenience rather than preference, we hope we shall not be misunderstood by the many effective female governors around the country.

To make the book as readable as possible, we have only used occasional footnotes. A number of books are mentioned in the text, and a list giving details of these can be found in Appendix C.

Finally, governors of schools in Scotland and Northern Ireland will find some variations in practice from what we describe, which is the current situation in England and Wales. These differences are, however, often only slight. Readers interested in Northern Ireland should consult the Astin Report. Those concerned with Scottish schools need to read *Scottish School Councils: Policy Making, Participation or Irrelevance?* (HMSO and Scottish Education Department, 1980).

1

How governors fit into the educational system

When governors are appointed it is difficult for them to know how they fit into the national, regional and local system. 'What powers do I have?' 'How am I supposed to do what the LEA expects of me?' 'Does the Department of Education and Science ever come into it?' are amongst several questions asked by newcomers, or even by established governors when they find the powers, responsibilities or duties of governors being discussed or reviewed.

Who's in charge?

This is probably the most difficult question of all on the education system of England and Wales. The basis is a type of power-sharing: no single person or body has supreme authority, but rather a large number of individuals and organisations are consulted, involved and given responsiblity for parts of the system. Even the Secretary of State for Education and Science, the 'top' person in the system, appointed by the Prime Minister and occupying a seat in the cabinet, has only limited powers, and the Education Act of 1944 gives him only the somewhat vaguely defined task of 'promoting the education of the people of England and Wales'.

This intentional sharing of influence and authority is the envy of educators in countries which have more authoritarian governments, and just as much the despair of enthusiastic British reformers who, having been granted a glimpse of their paradise on earth, cannot find the right levers to pull to bring it about. 'You want me to be a dictator', lamented one Secretary of State when challenged as to why something of which his questioner disapproved had not been put right.

Figure 1 shows the educational system in simplified form. In some cases instructions are given by superiors to subordinates, and these are shown by bold arrows. For example the Education Committee of your Local Education Authority* in trying to carry out the wishes of the electorate, lays down policy guidelines which must be followed by you as governors, and equally by the Chief Education Officer or Director of Education as he is sometimes called, the senior employee in the authority's education department.

Just as important are individuals and groups who advise and bring all sorts of influence to bear: these are indicated by the broken arrows. Pressure groups are nowadays very active in several fields. Some, like Parent-Teacher Associations, are local in origin, others like CASE the Confederation for the Advancement of State Education, are national. Many are set up to promote particular causes only to disappear again when the cause is achieved or dead. Some of these attempt to have old schools replaced or outside toilets scrapped; denominational groups will be formed to support schools of their own per-

---

* The local education authority is the County Council (in non-metropolitan counties), the Metropolitan District Council (in metropolitan counties), the London Borough Council (in outer London), or the Inner London Education Authority (in Inner London).

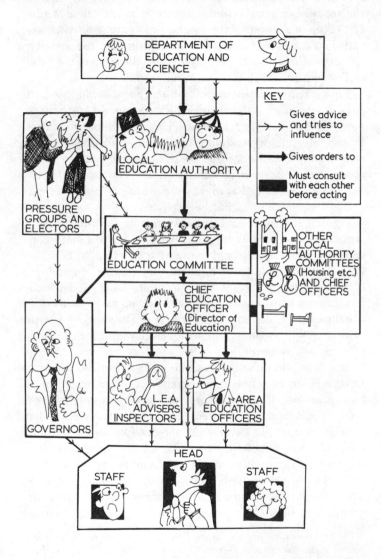

Fig. 1 'Who's in charge?'

suasion. In recent times some groups have campaigned to stop the closure of village schools. It is thus an important part of the system that everybody should have an opportunity to talk to everybody else, and that as many people as possible are brought into the decision-making process. It can be slow, but it often works well.

When the talking is over, most of the major decisions affecting your school will be made by the Education Committee. Yet even that body and the Chief Education Officer do not have a completely free hand, since their freedom of action has been restricted by recent reorganization of local government structure, intended to ensure more effective use of local authority resources.

It used to be the case that the local authority sub-committees set up for various purposes (for example to look after roads, education, welfare, housing and so on) worked more or less independently of each other. Each received an annual allocation of public funds and set about spending it as it pleased. The work of these sub-committees often overlapped: e.g. the people planning new housing developments needed to know of decisions made by the committee in charge of siting new schools: for one to act without the other was wasteful.

People began to argue that it was not the best use of public funds to have one department designing and building council houses and another, quite separately, designing and building schools. Clearly they had much, if not everything, in common, and both of them needed also to be in touch with the authorities concerned with fire prevention. Nowadays, too, the legislation affecting employers in their relationships with employees has become so complex that a separate personnel officer is often necessary to oversee the position amongst all council employees, including teachers and other employees of the Education Committee. Last but not least, a council may decide in one year to spend less on education but more on welfare. It may even be necessary sometimes to divert money at short notice from one sub-committee to another, and a particular project in education may have to be stopped.

It is with a view to providing a constructive solution to these and other problems of communication and consultation that many local authorities have introduced what is called *corporate management*. The effect is that the various committees must work more closely together. Furthermore, the Chief Education Officer is but one member of a Chief Officers' Committee, which can collectively review his decisions and if necessary ask him or her to think again. The leader of this powerful committee, known as the Chief Executive, is directly responsible to the county council. This sort of consultation is shown in Figure 1 by broad bold lines. In short it means that even a Chief Education Officer is not always in the position to give you what you want, however much he may wish to, and however hard you lean on him.

What do all these bodies do?

The Department of Education and Science does not send out *detailed* instructions about how schools should be run, what subjects should be taught and so on. On the other hand it does have a responsibility to the government of the day to see that the government's wishes are carried out and that public money is wisely spent. The DES effectively influences the system through its control of finance. Its permission must be obtained, for example, before schools can be built or adapted. It has often been argued that this financial power gives the DES excessive influence, and there have been occasions when it has, albeit under political pressure, refused permission to build comprehensive schools or grammar schools. In the same way the DES has a profound effect on the supply of teachers into the system, through its influence over the numbers of teachers admitted to training institutions.

The DES regularly issues to the local education authorities various papers. The most potent of these are departmental regulations (officially called *statutory instruments*), and they are part of the law of the land, covering a range of subjects from school buildings to the School Meals Service. Less authoritative are the so-called *circulars* which are meant to reveal current DES thinking and call for consultation. The spirit of these is one of 'This is only a suggestion, ladies and gentlemen, but *do* remember who is making it!'

These circulars have been known to have far-reaching effects over many years. Indeed, comprehensive reorganisation was initiated by a circular, number 10 of 1965, which indicated for the first time that the DES and the government were becoming interested in the actual organisation of schools, a matter which had hitherto been the sole responsibility of local authorities, and many LEAs were initially outraged that the DES was seeking to interfere in the running of schools. The next government issued Circular 10 of 1970 which appeared to put the responsibility back with local education authorities. Finally, there are the *administrative memoranda* which, as the name suggests are concerned with smaller, day to day matters.

From time to time also the DES invites independent reports on parts of the education system. There have been many of these during the last thirty years or so, and ideas produced in them have found their way into schools and the system. Some of the most significant ones appeared in the 1960s: the Robbins report on higher education (universities and polytechnics), the Crowther report on the education of fifteen to eighteen year-olds (sixth formers), the Newsom report on the education of children who intended to leave school as soon as possible, and the Plowden report on primary education. Cynics argued that these reports appeared in exactly the wrong order: there might have been more logic in starting with primary education, rather than finishing with it.

Of particular interest to you as a school governor is the 1977 Taylor report on the management of schools entitled *A New Partnership for our Schools*. It proposed radical changes in the way schools are governed. All such DES sponsored reports are purely advisory. It is up to the government to decide whether to give their recommendations the force of law. At another level it is for LEAs and individual schools to discuss how recommendations can, or should be implemented. You should follow press cover-

13

age of such reports as they will often be in the minds of teachers for a two or three year period.

The DES also gives its support to the Schools Council, an independent body which is charged with injecting new ideas into the curriculum and examinations. It is a body numerically dominated by teachers and academics, and has been responsible for new ways of thinking about particular subjects and teaching them in schools. The Schools Council has sponsored a wide range of projects, in the fields of science teaching, modern languages, reading and many others, and is further discussed in Chapter 4.

Lastly, on a quite different front, the DES has the legal authority to make decisions over disputes which cannot be settled amicably 'further down the line'. It can happen from time to time that the other parties to the system, governors, parents, LEAs, disagree and dig in their heels. As a governor you are perhaps most likely to meet this when disputes with parents arise over which school their child should attend. The parents are entitled to appeal to the DES for a ruling, which, when given, has the force of law.

Usually the DES tries to work through reason and persuasion, and brings out its heavy artillery only when some major issue of principle is involved. Even here, though, the powers of the DES are more restricted than used to be thought. In 1975 the Secretary of State for Education and Science ruled that the Tameside Local Authority was acting 'unreasonably' in going back on a scheme for comprehensive schools in its area which had already been agreed with the DES. When the Local Authority challenged the Secretary of State in the High Court, the judges ruled in turn that Tameside was after all acting reasonably. In the eyes of the law, the DES could not rule that the Authority was acting *unreasonably* if what it really meant was only that it *disagreed* with Tameside.

You will probably have already noticed how often the term *'reasonable'* has been used, and it is characteristic of the way our education system works. It is assumed, rightly or wrongly, that governors, parents, teachers and administrators will work together harmoniously, with the DES as senior partner.

The Local Education Authority provides and runs schools, makes sure that sufficient school places are available, and employs teachers accordingly. About half of the necessary money comes from local ratepayers, and the other half from the government in the form of the annual Rate Support Grant. Needless to say, each side wants the other to pay more, a favourite quarrel being the issue of teachers' salaries, which the Local Authorities sometimes wish to be paid entirely by the government. In theory, Local Education Authorities can do what they want with their own money: the government money comes with policy strings attached. Local Education Authorities also have the task of seeing that children are properly educated, a theme to which we return below.

What do governors do?

Whereas the LEA has to deal with many schools in its area, the governing body and the head of the school are responsible for one school only. The practice of grouping several schools under one governing body, although legal, is undesirable, since it is far better that governors should know one school well than several badly. The system is, fortunately, dying out slowly, and you might be able to help speed its demise in your own area.

Under the Education Act of 1980 the LEA needs the approval of the DES in nearly all cases before schools can be grouped. If Parliament in the future agrees, you will have the right to protest to the DES about a grouping proposal. On the other hand, if your school works closely with a particular school — perhaps all the pupils from your school automatically move on to the other one — then there is probably much sense in asking one or two governors to serve on both governing bodies.

On your appointment as governor you should be given a document containing the Articles of Government for your school. If you are not, then the clerk to your governing body, who is usually a paid officer of the LEA, should be able to put one at your disposal. At the present time the equivalent document for primary schools is called the Rules of Management, but this name will disappear when future legislation converts primary school managers into governors. (The Articles at present in use in Nottinghamshire are reproduced as Appendix B.) Although some of the document will be of necessity couched in rather dull and legalistic language, it is worthwhile to persist with those sections which refer to the conditions under which you hold office as a governor, and the powers and duties you have.

It is important to remember at all times that it is the governing body *as a whole* which has power to do things and *not* individual governors acting on their own. This is why the Articles always refer to 'governors' in the plural. The intention is in no way to squash your keenness or willingness to help as an individual, but rather to see that authority is exercised properly by the group, not by an individual.

It would be wrong, for example, for a parent governor to seek to use his position to secure preferential treatment for his own child at the school, or for a politically appointed governor to seek to have supporters of his party appointed to the teaching staff. For this reason, anything the governing body wishes to do must be decided by a resolution at a meeting. None of this applies to friendly and informal visits to the school which can usually be arranged by talking to the headteacher. Indeed, it is through such amicable contacts that you can become a trusted and respected member of the school community, and discover the ways in which you can best help.

One word of warning, however. Governors are in a privileged position and will often come into possession of information which, in the interests of all, should remain confidential. You may be called upon, for example, to decide what is to be done about the continuing education of a girl who has just given birth at fourteen to an illegitimate child. To talk about the case around your community would be a grave breach of the trust invested in you.

Although common sense suggests that some matters, as for

example the above, ought to be regarded as confidential, it should be borne in mind that *everything* is in fact confidential. There are very good reasons for this. One is that governors would be less likely to speak their mind if they thought that everything they said was going to be reported elsewhere, perhaps in the local press. Sometimes, too, a decision taken by the governors is later shown to be inappropriate when additional information comes to light and obliges them to change their mind. Beware, too, of publicly discussing allegations which may be made at a meeting; quite often they turn out to have been false.

Because of this confidentiality, you are given by law what is called 'qualified privilege'. Like MPs when they are in the Commons you can say exactly what you like without the fear of legal action being taken against you. But this privilege covers you only during formal governors' meetings and not outside; nor are you at all protected if it can be shown that you spoke in malice.

You may perhaps feel that the system is set up in order to gag you: this is a false impression. Anything that the governing body *acting as a group* wishes to make public, it may; and there will be many occasions when you will wish to do so in the interests of keeping in touch with your community. Unofficial breaches of confidentiality are likely to make you very unpopular with your fellow governors and might lead to your dismissal from the governing body. The LEA has the power to do this. We return to this difficult matter in Chapter 2.

Whom do you represent?

All sorts of different organisations nominate governors: the LEA, the churches, and universities are a few. More recently parents of children in the school have been asked to nominate some of their members. Obviously you will feel a degree of loyalty to the group which asked the LEA to put you there.

However, once you are made a governor you are a member in your own right and not a delegate. This means that you are free to vote exactly as you think fit as an individual charged with the best interests of your school, even if on occasion this might run counter to the group which put you there. In practice this issue arises most frequently in the case of parent governors, particularly where you may have to represent as many as 4,000 parents in a big comprehensive school. Parent governors can find themselves pressurised by articulate groups of parents with a particular view of what should happen; or even be lobbied by two opposing camps. The task of the parent governor is to speak up for parents as a group, not for only a few of them.

Finally, if ever you are obliged not to support your own group's views at governors' meetings, do not let threats of being 'unseated' tempt you to break the rules about confidentiality, or you risk alienating your group, your fellow governors and the LEA.

What is in the Articles?

The Articles make it clear that 'the Governors shall have the direction of the conduct and curriculum of the School' provided that they act in conformity with the general policy of the authority, and that the headteacher 'shall control the internal organisation, management and discipline of the School and shall exercise supervision over the teaching and non-teaching staff . . .' (see Appendix B, Article 6(a) and 6(b)). A word of explanation is necessary here, since what happens in practice has come to differ considerably from the theory.

The fundamental principle has always been that the head and his staff are the acknowledged experts on how to teach. The governors, however, may be seen to be an important link between the school and the world at large, and as such have worthwhile things to say about what should be taught. Although some heads do feel threatened unnecessarily when governors intervene in matters such as curriculum, it is only reasonable to point out here that to change the curriculum of a school might involve decisions you cannot, as governors, make. For example, it is the local authority not governing bodies,

which employs teachers in all maintained schools, except those which are voluntary aided (Appendix B, Article 9(c) (iii)), so that you cannot decide to appoint a teacher of, say, Indian ceramics without permission. The LEA would have to determine whether such an appointment was feasible.

In recent years, too, local education authorities have been appointing professional advisers in the main areas of the school curriculum, and frequently their advice, properly given to the Education Committee, becomes converted into 'the general policy of the Authority' mentioned earlier, thus seeming to cut the ground from under governing bodies. An example of this might be where it is decided that primary schools should teach French. If you were a secondary school governor in such an area, you would find it virtually impossible to have, say, Russian, Spanish or German taught to first years in your school. Children who have started French should not be obliged to give it up merely because you prefer another language.

Nevertheless, despite all the complexities of curriculum change, it is today as true as ever that many schools welcome informed suggestions from intelligent and interested lay people, be these parents, employers, local worthies or their own governors. It is regrettable that local education authorities sometimes think only of their Advisers and the Schools Council, to which they collectively subscribe, when ideas about the curriculum are needed.

There are good reasons why the headteacher should be given ultimate control over the internal workings of the school. Not only is he or she the experienced senior professional, but the efficient running of a school requires a series of on-the-spot judgements; if every decision had to be referred back to the governors, chaos would rapidly result, since for most of the time they are not present, and governors' meetings usually take place only once or twice each term.

It is, however, not unreasonable for governors to ask the headteacher about decisions he has made, and, moreover, the headteacher is required by the Articles to tell the governors about certain matters: when pupils are suspended, for example (Appendix B, Article 6). The price the head pays for the high degree of discretion guaranteed him by the Articles is that he alone is responsible if something goes wrong through internal mismanagement. The head's discretion is not unfettered, but it must be wide enough for him to assume complete control of all matters concerning internal organisation, management and discipline. If he fails to use this discretion, he is accountable.

Here are some of the things that governing bodies are called upon to do. The list is not exclusive.

(1) *Consult and listen to the views of the teaching and non-teaching staffs of the school.* Usually this takes place through the headteacher or representatives, but it is a good idea to have an occasional get-together (preferably informal, perhaps over tea and cakes in the Domestic Science block). This is a good way for any governor to get the 'feel' of a school, and meet both teaching and non-teaching staff.

(2) *Decide on means of consulting parents and the local community about matters affecting the school.* To some extent this will happen already if your school has a parent-teacher association, but do not forget that many parents who could have useful things to say may not be members of the PTA. Even if all parents are technically members of the PTA, many might prefer to talk to

you or the school directly. This matter is discussed again in Chapter 2.

(3) *Discuss any reports about the school, either by the headteacher or the local education authority.* Occasionally the school may undergo an inspection by Her Majesty's Inspectors of Schools (HMIs) or LEA Inspectors. The governors should be asked for their views while the Inspectors are preparing their report, and the final version should be discussed at a governors' meeting.

The headteacher usually prepares a report for each governors' meeting as a matter of course, but it is quite in order for you to ask in advance for information to be included on matters which interest the governors particularly, and which otherwise might not come up. Nor is there any reason why you should not ask for special reports from time to time, provided these concern topics of genuine concern and importance, and are not just a means of satisfying your personal curiosity. Preparing a report takes valuable time from the head and teachers which might be better spent working with children.

If you are discussing matters connected with the curriculum or general conduct of the school, you may well feel the need of outside advice, in addition to that offered by the headteacher. One person to approach here is the Chief Adviser to your local education authority. He works in the education department and may well be prepared to come to one of your meetings. In certain circumstances also, your local HMI may be willing to help, and his office can usually be found in the local telephone directory under Department of Education and Science.

You may well also be asked to prepare reports yourself. The local education authority might ask to know what you propose to do about, for example, vandalism of the school buildings both during and outside school hours. Usually it is the Clerk to the governors who actually writes the report after the discussion at the governors' meeting.

Your local authority will also expect its governors to keep it informed about the current state of the school buildings and furniture, which, incidentally, includes any decoration which becomes necessary, and the quality of the heating, lighting and sanitary arrangements (Appendix B, Article 7). When you hear that large-scale building is taking place near your school, it will be up to you to ensure that the local authority is both aware of what is happening and is planning the extra school places necessary.

(4) It may be possible for you as governors to control the *letting of the school building when it is not in use for normal school activities*. This is a good opportunity to encourage links with the community and various social groups – and it might be possible to divert some of the proceeds from the lettings into the school fund (see Appendix B, Article 18(b)(ii)).

(5) From time to time you may be asked for your views on what the *catchment area for the school* should be. This usually happens only when it seems that the school is likely to become overcrowded, either because it is very popular with parents or because of a rise in the number of children in the area. This is an issue where governors' local knowledge is indispensable, particularly in gauging how the community will react to various possible proposals.

(6) Governors are usually also involved in *making appointments* to the school staff, along, of course, with the headteacher and possibly a specialist Adviser from County Hall. This is a most important assignment and we shall therefore discuss it at greater length. There is no need for you as a lay governor to feel that you have nothing to offer the experts. By the time things get as far as the interview, applicants with unsuitable professional qualifications will usually have been sifted out, and the appointment will probably turn around which candidate is likely to fit into the school and make the best contribution to all aspects of school life. Here a well-informed governor can have as much to contribute as the professional experts. On occasion, you might even score a point or two. On one occasion a lay governor, in private life a housewife, asked a very highly qualified applicant for a post teaching Domestic Science why the subject was taught in school at all; after all, wasn't it up to parents to teach their children to cook at home? The candidate appeared not to have faced that basic question before and

floundered badly, yet none of the experts present saw fit to ask it.

In making appointments, governors are in fact only advising local authorities whom they would like to see appointed, since it is the authority which hires and fires teachers. In the vast majority of cases the authority acts on that advice, but once in a while an appointment is not ratified, often because further information has come to light.

'Hire in haste, repent at leisure' is an old saying in the appointments business. A teacher may be appointed after an interview of no more than half an hour. He may spend the next twenty years doing untold damage to your school and your hopes. Time spent on the careful selection of a teacher is not wasted.

In general, it is a good thing that governors should be closely involved with new appointments. It is, for example, one way in which you can become involved with what is taught in your school and how. Equally importantly it provides an excellent way of getting to know the teachers. There are unfortunately a number of horror stories around of governors who ask idiotic questions or ride roughshod over the views of others, and such behaviour when it occurs embarrasses all concerned. There is no law or regulation generally which requires governors to be present at appointments, and some LEAs leave them to the head acting on his or her own.

During the 1980s it is inevitable that there will be a sharp fall in the numbers of children in secondary schools in particular, and consequently there will be too many teachers for the schools. In order to ease the problems of redundancy, LEAs will do their best to fill teaching vacancies with teachers displaced from other schools within the authority. This could perhaps give you a headache. When a head is told that he must reduce his staff because of falling numbers he will not be keen to lose his best teachers first. He might even be glad to be rid of someone who can be traded off to another school. On the other hand, when the LEA is forced to close down a whole school, you might be able to pick up teachers who will be a real asset to your own school.

Whether the LEA can force you to accept a transfer to fill a vacancy at your school depends on local circumstances. Look carefully at your Articles of Government, and remember that your first responsibility is to the school you govern (see Appendix B, Article 9(c) (iii)). There seems to be little point in giving yourself a problem simply in order to solve one of the LEA's! In particular, take the matter up with your clerk, and look at the teachers' Conditions of Employment or the Staff Code for your LEA. We return to the question of school closures and falling rolls in Chapter 5.

When a vacancy occurs. If you are asked to assist in the appointment of a new teacher, you should first discuss with the head what the vacancy actually is, and find out his ideas on the sort of qualifications and person he would like. Your options might be limited: if the need is to replace the one and only teacher of knitting, because pupils are half-way through an examination course, then there is no room to manoeuvre. However, if the vacancy is within a large department it might be possible to work in something new – say, Computer Studies in the Mathematics department, or Russian in Modern Languages. You might even find it possible to start a new out-of-school activity with the assistance of the person you appoint. Teachers in primary schools are usually generalists, i.e. they teach a range of class subjects. In secondary schools they are usually subject specialists teaching History, Science and so on. In our rapidly changing society it is often important that teachers should be flexible, and an ability to teach as part of an integrated studies team in Humanities or Environmental Studies may be very useful.

You should also find out any other factors involved in making the new appointment. The school may need, perhaps, more women teachers to even up the burden of those school duties which can be done only by a member of a particular sex, though unless the work can only be carried out by a person of that sex, the Sex Discrimination Act does not allow employers to appoint or reject people on the grounds of their sex alone. The post

24

might be more suitable for an experienced teacher if it involves difficult children, otherwise a keen young teacher straight from college or university might be just what you want. Perhaps the department needs some vigorous new ideas injecting into it, and so on.

Candidates for appointment always appreciate being given the opportunity to have a good look at the school and their prospective colleagues before they take a post. The best method is usually to hold interviews later in the day, and make it possible for the interviewees to spend the earlier part of the day looking around and generally talking to people. This arrangement pays handsome dividends, since some applicants who might have accepted the post on interview find that your school is really not for them and save everybody much wasted time.

Finally, look through the application forms of those to be interviewed in advance. Remember that they are personal and highly confidential documents, and intended solely for the interviewers. If you are in doubt as to what parts of them mean, ask the head to explain.

Do's and Don'ts at the interview. Here are a few suggestions. Allow the candidate to talk, and don't talk too much yourself. Find out what else, apart from his main subjects, the candidate has to offer your school. Games? Chess? Producing a school play? Stay away from discussing the candidate's politics or religion. Of course, if you are appointing a Religious Education teacher in a voluntary school (or, indeed, any teacher in a denominational school) it is permissible to question a candidate about his religious opinions and practice. Remember the Race Relations and Equal Opportunities Acts make it illegal to consider the racial origin or, generally, sex of applicants. Ask the candidate what he makes of your school after looking around. If he has nothing to say, he may either be not very wide awake or, worse, a creep.

Find out what he has discovered about the school in general before he came to interview. This will give some indication of how interested he is in your particular post.

Ask him to talk about his achievements in his present post. Ask him to say why he thinks his subject should be taught in school instead of, say, learning to drive or snake-charming.

If the candidate has had several posts, ask why. Perhaps he has conscientiously set out to gain wide experience, which is a good thing, particularly if you are looking for a senior appointment. On the other hand it may mean that he never stays long enough to be rumbled, and may well leave you quickly too.

Watch out for outdated qualifications. A 'Distinction' on a college course, or a first-class degree mean little if the holder has done little since he gained them ten years ago or more. Teachers, like doctors, should keep up with new developments in their field through further training courses, which are readily available if teachers are willing to invest their time and show interest. Beware of the 'I'm far too conscientious to leave my pupils to go on courses' argument: if top surgeons took that view many of us would now be dead.

Read the references supplied carefully. It is often worthwhile to check that the most obvious people have been asked to support the application. Although an applicant is perfectly free to ask whomsoever he likes to act as his referee, it is clearly odd, for example, if a teacher quotes only the pub landlord and his uncle in ICI. If you have doubts on this score, ask the applicant during the interview.

Ask what the candidate would do in your school if he had a free hand. Ask him how he would provide in his teaching for the cleverest and the weakest children. Find out his attitude to punishment and incentives for children.

Finally, always allow sufficient time at the end for the candidate to ask you any questions he may have. Appointments are a two-way process, and the candidate is entitled to interview the school, although people who do this too aggressively often irritate the interviewers.

Remember that if you are asked to take part in an appointment it is one of the most important tasks you will have to do as a governor. Remember, too, that the people coming for interview are usually highly trained professionals who may have to uproot their family if you appoint them, and who may have travelled a considerable distance to attend for interview. Interviews should be searching but sensitive affairs.

(7) *Cases of problem pupils* will also come your way, and the headteacher will value any assistance you can give. If a pupil has disrupted your school, has got into trouble and now been suspended for misbehaviour (Appendix B, Article 6(b)), perhaps the governors can help him move to a more suitable school. Another approach might be to throw the governors' weight behind a formal approach to the parents. A pupil whose attendance at school is erratic might be dealt with in the same way. It is important to remember not to get involved with these difficult cases on a personal, individual level: such a relationship would make it impossible for you to sit in judgement later if the question of expulsion were to arise.

(8) Although under Common Law it is the teaching staff of the school who are required to take reasonable care of their pupils, the responsibility of local authorities and governors to care for the wellbeing of both has been extended by the *Health and Safety at Work Act, 1974*. It is not yet clear, however, just how this Act will affect the management of schools, but it is a matter which governors should take up with County Hall to obtain clarification. Governors of aided and independent schools, because they are employers, have particular responsibilities.

(9) From time to time you will need to check that the arrangements for dealing with *fire at school* are satisfactory. It is common practice for schools to have firedrills, and you should check that these are recorded in the headteacher's report to the governors. The head will usually tell you of any problems here, and how long it takes to get all the pupils out of the building.

(10) Occasionally you will be called upon to decide on grievances which are put to you. As employees, assistant teachers and heads have *a procedure for settling grievances* which is part of their conditions of service. Briefly, when a dispute is formally notified to you in writing, you must hold a meeting within ten days, and invite the people involved to attend. You must come

27

to a decision on the basis of what they tell you, and any reports or other documents you receive.

(11) You will from time to time receive reports about the way the system of *'school dinners'* is operating (App B, Art. 12). Your school will in all probability have a separate staff to cook and serve the meals: there will be a cook supervisor in charge. In many schools the head takes care of the dining arrangements but in very large schools it may be the case that the system is administered directly from County Hall and the head has little to do with it.

Your job as a governor is to see that all is well with the system, and particularly to ensure that the premises are adequate. If they are not, you should press the LEA until they are. There are detailed building regulations which specify how much room is to be used for school meals. The Clerk will have information on this.

At the time of writing it is proposed that only needy pupils whose parents receive supplementary benefit or family income supplement will be automatically entitled to school meals or refreshment; other children may have school meals if your LEA chooses to provide them. This is a considerable change from the former position whereby all children were entitled to meals. Furthermore, your LEA will have to provide facilities for pupils who bring sandwiches or other refreshment to school for lunch.

In the last few years difficulties have arisen over the supervision of pupils at lunchtime. At one time these duties were carried out by the teaching staff of the school and there was a general assumption by all that this was a normal part of teachers' duties. The courts then decided that this was not after all the case, and such duties are now voluntary, a free meal usually being provided for the teachers on duty.

Opinion in the teaching profession is divided. Many teachers take the view that a break at lunchtime is their right: in practice the free time is often taken up anyway in preparing for the afternoon session. Others take the more extreme view that the social need for the whole school meals service has now disappeared, since malnutrition among children is largely a thing of the past. They object to being treated as child-minders while mothers are relieved of a cooking burden at lunch-time, or go out to work. Others are prepared to see the school lunch as part of the social life of the school, a chance for the pupils to meet children other than their classmates.

Since these duties are now voluntary, despite the fact that many teachers do still volunteer, LEAs employ so-called 'supervisors' to look after the children at lunchtime.

The position in law here is at the moment obscure, and, hopefully, it will not take a nasty accident to a pupil to cause the matter to be decided in the courts. Because the courts relieved them of 'duties connected with school meals', some teachers argue that they are free of all duties at lunchtime and may, for example, leave the premises if they wish. On the other hand the common law 'duty of care' towards pupils extends for the whole period that pupils are on the school premises. Since schools are open by local regulation all day, and do not close at lunchtime, one would therefore expect a system of supervision to operate similar to that which operates at other times during the day when no teaching is taking place, e.g. morning break. What is perhaps more worrying to parents is whether the supervision by kind-hearted part-timers is as efficient as that by trained teachers.

As with many other aspects of school life the successful functioning of the school meals service depends heavily on goodwill from teachers, parents, supervisors and pupils. When in 1979 some teachers withdrew their goodwill as part of industrial action in pursuit of a pay claim, no one was anxious to rush to the law courts for legal rather than commonsense solutions.

(12) You will from time to time have to consider the matter of *staff absences* (see Appendix B, Article 9(f)). The LEA will usually have clear policies about whether their teachers may have time off with pay in order to attend conferences or deal with urgent domestic matters and so on. It often happens that teachers are absent for reasons which are outside the policy as laid down, but which might seem to you nevertheless to be very

29

good ones. In such cases you would pass a resolution at the meeting that the teacher should be paid. There is no obligation on you to do so, however, and you must judge each case on its merits.

(13) In some voluntary schools the governors have responsibility for *admission*, and approve the lists of new entrants (see Appendix B, Article 10). In county schools admissions are controlled by the LEA, although it is usual for governors to have a say in the case of unusual admissions. These could include, for example, children whose parents would like them to start school before the age of five, and those who live outside the school's usual catchment area. The latter are sometimes known as 'extra-zonal' or 'out-county' admissions.

Perhaps no other single issue affect governors quite as much as parental pressure to get their child into a particular school, and it is worth knowing what the legal position is. The 1944 Education Act states:

> *Section 76. Pupils to be educated in accordance with wishes of parents.* In the exercise and performance of all powers and duties conferred and imposed on them by this Act the Secretary of State and local education authorities shall have regard to the general principle that, so far as is compatible with the provision of efficient instruction and training and the avoidance of unreasonable public expenditure, pupils are to be educated in accordance with the wishes of their parents.

In fact, despite its cheerful wording, this section is not as helpful to parents as it might seem at first meeting. It certainly does *not* mean that parents must be given what they want at all costs. The LEA must 'have regard to' parents wishes, but may 'have regard to' many other things as well — such as whether there is room for the child, and whether admitting the child will entitle him to free transport from the LEA. Similarly, it is not a reasonable use of public funds to build, say, a Roman Catholic school, if only a handful of parents, however devout, want a Catholic education for their children. The LEA in law must do no more than provide a place in school appropriate to the pupils' age and ability, which in practice tends to mean a place in the local primary or secondary school. Under the 1980 Act parents will have a new right of appeal against LEA or governors' decisions to special local appeal committees, about which your Clerk will tell you. About 1000 appeals are currently made each year.

Governors faced with difficult decisions about admissions should consult the DES 'Manual of Guidance – Schools – No. 1.', published in 1953. Although now withdrawn, it gives detailed guidance about the principles you should consider.

A further proposal of the 1980 Act is that LEAs be required to publish their admissions policy in order to make clearer to parents the principles by which they admit children to schools. There must also be an agreed policy for each aided and special agreement school and governors may well be involved in drawing this up.

Generally speaking, a parent must be granted his choice of school unless, to quote the 1980 Education Act, his choice '. . . would prejudice the provision of efficient education or the efficient use of resources' – a seemingly rather vague and woolly principle. Nor will he be given the school he wishes if to do so would be to upset any arrangements about admissions already made between the LEA and governors of aided schools; and obviously a parent cannot choose a school which has an entrance examination unless his child also passes that examination.

Governors of voluntary schools will find that their duties are rather more extensive. In simple terms these are schools which are not set up by Local Authorities, as county schools are, but which do receive most of their financial support in one way or another from the local authority or the DES. County schools used to be called 'provided' schools, and voluntary 'non-provided' schools; the older titles were probably more use in understanding the difference.

Voluntary schools are the direct descendants of schools which were going concerns before Parliament began to take an interest in education in the late nineteenth century. Although the original buildings, sometimes substantially modernised, may

31

still be in use in many places, there are also many new buildings which have been erected since the 1944 Act. Originally the schools were self-supporting through fees from parents and income from charities and endowments and bequests. As time went by these schools found, like British Leyland, that they needed government money to survive, and the government started subsidies to them in 1833. Since 1902 the responsibility for aiding these schools from public funds has rested with the LEAs. Since a local education authority nowadays has no choice but to provide school places for all children who need them, it is usually very ready to include voluntary schools in its planning for the area, as a cheaper alternative to building its own.

You may find, then, that your school is not owned by your local authority, but by an educational trust or charity, or possibly by one of the bigger religious dominations. Somewhere among the dusty files in the clerk to the governors' office there will be a document called a Trust Deed which, along with your Articles of Government, may well lay down conditions as to how the school is to be governed, and you should make sure you know what these are. It is just not possible here to mention all the things you might find. Most common, perhaps, will be the requirement that the school should teach the Anglican or Roman Catholic faith; possibly you will have to take in children from a particular area, and so on, depending on the intentions of the people who originally drew up the deed and provided the original endowment.

There are nowadays three types of voluntary school, of which the *voluntary aided school* is the most distinctive. In such a school you and your fellow governors are responsible for seeing that the outer fabric of your school is well maintained and decorated and for paying the bills for this – although at present 85 per cent of this money will be refunded to the school by the DES. Similarly, if the decision is taken to enlarge the school, or perhaps even to move it somewhere else, which often happens (say from a city centre to a green belt site), then, as before, you will have to see that the builders are paid and the 85 per cent reclaimed. For its part the local authority will look after the inside maintenance of the building. You could be forgiven for asking: where does the one finish and the other take over? The answer lies in a complicated schedule which will tell you among a thousand other fascinating details that the roof is your problem, but the ceiling the local authority's: a leaking toilet is the local authority's problem, but not if the cause is the overflow pipe which passes through the outside wall which is your property. Of such is the stuff of educational administration made.

As a governor of a voluntary aided school you will have far more contact with the financing of the school. It is possible that some of your fellow governors were appointed for their financial expertise, for obviously in order to meet its commitments the school may well have considerable private funds. You will probably have discussions on how this money will be spent — perhaps on grants to pupils, school prizes and so on. Teachers' salaries are, however, paid directly by the local authority, although teachers are actually appointed and employed by you as governors. The local authority and the DES will have seen to it that your Articles of Government will permit you to appoint staff up to a prescribed number; you may not dismiss staff without the approval of the authority, however (except on grounds connected with the giving of religious instruction), and the authority may, if it wishes, order you to dismiss a teacher. If it is ever your misfortune to become involved in such a matter, you would do well to consult the provisions of the Employment Protection (Consolidation) Act 1978.

A *voluntary controlled school* probably started its life as something very akin to a voluntary aided school, but has found that it cannot keep up its financial commitments. As a result, the local authority will have taken over all the financing of the school, and will also have become for all practical purposes the employer of the staff, as in its own county schools. The task of governing the school will be much more like that of governing a county school, although there may still be some additional provisions to observe in the trust deed.

There are also in existence 131 *special agreement schools*. These

33

were established as a 'one-off job' in the later 1930s, and local authorities paid between 50 and 75 per cent of the cost of establishing them. None has been set up since, nor are any more likely to be established, and the functions of the governors and their duties are very similar to those of voluntary aided schools.

Governors of all voluntary schools are also required to co-operate with the local authority in the medical and dental inspection of pupils, and in the School Meals Service. Usually this entails making such premises and equipment available at the school as the Authority requires.

Finally, the Articles will give you some say in the admission of pupils to the school. Generally speaking, voluntary schools do not have notional catchment areas in the way that County schools do, unless they choose to do so. Since the school is an integral part of the local authority's plan for the area, the actual numbers in the school will however be agreed with the authority. An Anglican school would clearly give preference to Anglican pupils, and so on.

Being a governor of a non-maintained school

These schools are usually referred to as 'independent', because they are almost entirely responsible for their own affairs, and are largely independent of both the DES and LEA. For this reason the governing body and the head carry considerably more responsibility for the success of the school than is the case in state schools.

Much time is spent at governors' meetings in discussing finance, and the governing body will include people highly skilled in such matters. It is up to you and colleagues to find the money to pay for the running of the school on a day to day basis, and to finance new developments and keep the school up to date. Buildings are inevitably perhaps the greatest problem, since they are by now probably fairly old and in need of constant maintenance.

Independent schools find their money through fees paid for pupils, through investments of all sorts, and frequently through appeals to the community and former students for specific projects such as science buildings or sports facilities.

Direct grant schools where they exist have an additional source of income. In return for substantial co-operation with the state system, these schools receive a grant directly from the DES (hence the name). In addition, LEAs pay the fees of many pupils at these schools, either in full or in part depending on parents' income. The fortunes of these schools vary according to which political party is in power. The Labour government of 1974–9 sought to dry up funds, forcing them to become LEA or fully independent schools. Conservative governments tend to support the idea of state-aided places at independent schools. In law independent schools are regarded as educational charities, and are run on a non-profit-making basis. A few are run for profit by their owners, but as such are unlikely to have constituted governing bodies. As with all charities, the ultimate body concerned with keeping an eye on what happens is the Charity Commission.

All independent schools are required to be registered with the DES; and there is a Registrar of Independent Schools. This system is designed to ensure that the school reaches a minimum standard of efficiency. After inspection by HMI many schools are officially regarded as efficient. In extreme cases it is possible for the DES to strike schools off the register, in which case it becomes illegal to operate them. It is also possible for the DES to declare a person to be unfit to teach in an independent school, or to be the proprietor of one. Here again, the DES word is law, although there is of course a machinery for appeals.

Governors of independent boarding schools tend to be less directly involved with parents and the local community than their counterparts in state schools, because inevitably their pupils come from far away, even overseas. This is not true, of course, of public day schools, which have distinctly local connections and are run very much in the grammar school tradition.

Unless governors take considerable care, there is a real danger that the very worthwhile and valuable independence enjoyed by

35

their school might cut them off from possibly beneficial outside influences, which at worst could lead to an undesirable educational isolation. Whereas LEAs run professional courses for their teachers, for example, provision for teachers in independent schools is limited to the relatively few courses run nationally by DES and universities. Similarly the services of LEA advisers are not normally available, although in this respect use can and indeed should be made of local HMI.

Relationships between independent schools and LEA are generally good and it is worthwhile to foster them at all levels. Indeed, one justification of the independent sector in British education is that it can bring more people into decision-making in education if it works well.

How are governors appointed?

Along with the Articles of Government you have received, probably in the same booklet, you will find the *Instrument of Government* (such as can be found in Appendix A), which lays down the details of who is to appoint school governors, and the sort of people who must be chosen. When a new school is started, the local education authority decides on the composition of the governing body, draws up the Instrument accordingly and sends it to the DES for approval. The DES will probably make a few suggestions, perhaps increase the numbers of teacher or parent governors and so on, and then formally approve the Instrument which becomes part of the law of the land.

The procedure for voluntary schools is slightly different. The DES has the ultimate responsibility for seeing that educational trusts and charities, including voluntary schools, are properly run, so it must draw up the Instrument for voluntary schools with an eye to looking after the interests of the endowment. Consequently for a voluntary aided school the charity will appoint the majority of the governors (two-thirds) and the Local Authority the remaining third.

In the case of county schools the Local Authority controls all appointments but for a few, to which we will return later. Voluntary controlled schools are in a sort of halfway-house position: although technically they are most similar to voluntary aided schools, they are utterly dependent for finance on the Local Authority as we have seen, and the way the governing body is put together reflects this. The charity finds one-third of the governors, the Local Authority the two-thirds majority.

The governing body must consist of parents, elected members of the teaching staff, the headteacher (always entitled to be present, but sometimes not a voting member of the governors), possibly senior pupils, and representatives of the Local Authority, who in bigger authorities will not always be members of the county council, since the large number of schools to be governed often means that there are simply not enough councillors to go round. They will, however, usually be appointees on whose support the Authority knows it can probably count in any emergency. Governors are also usually permitted to co-opt a certain number of further members.

Local Authorities usually take care to see that their representatives have a voting majority on governing bodies of county schools, and it is this practice which has led in recent years to demands for a reform of the system. The Taylor Committee's 1977 report 'A New Partnership for our Schools' proposed a formula which offered four equal shares of seats, three to LEA nominees, parents (including pupils if appropriate) and teaching staff, who would co-opt the fourth group members of the local community, possibly selected from an LEA list of people willing to serve.

The arguments for and against a voting majority of LEA members have been strongly put. The job of the DES is, as we have seen, to ensure that Local Authorities carry out the government's policy for education. To do this, Local Authorities must in turn be able to rely for help on their school governors. A local authority would find itself in a very difficult position if it were being pressed to do something by the government and its governors refused to agree. In the vast majority of cases this does not occur, but it becomes more likely on highly controversial issues. In the later 1960s for example, when the government of the day was leaning heavily on local authorities to make their secondary modern and grammar schools into comprehensive schools, it was not uncommon for governors, particularly of voluntary schools, to try to use their powers to thwart the local authority's wishes.

Local authorities argue also that governors spend public funds (for example, see Appendix B, Article 7(b)), and should thus be accountable to the public for what they do. If we think that our local councillor has been an incompetent school governor and has not spent taxpayers' money in the way of which we approve, we can always remove him at the next election. Although it is often said that education should not be politically controlled, it is hard to see how it could be otherwise. Education is closely tied up with the distribution of resources in adult life, and with social ideas such as fairness or equality of opportunity, which is what politics is supposed to be about. Furthermore politicians often see social changes as something which can be brought about through schools, sometimes to the irritation of teachers or parents.

The opponents of a voting majority for LEA nominees on the other hand believe that it leads to many unsatisfactory appointments. Local authorities are often hard pressed to find the bodies necessary to form voting majorities on all governing bodies, and may, as a result, choose some representatives who have little interest in the schools. Attendance at meetings is then poor, unless the local authority lets it be known that a vital issue is to be debated, whereupon ghostly figures who have rarely been seen dutifully appear to record their vote.

It is further argued that the number of issues raised at meetings which divide the political parties is so small that it is really not worth the effort local authorities put into ensuring that the balance of parties on governing bodies is the same as on the county council.

Despite the voting strength of the local authority, it is not always the case that its representatives have the most influential things to say. If there is a university or polytechnic in the area, lecturers will probably serve on the governing bodies of secondary schools and they may well be able to give advice which is all the more valuable because it is independent both of the local authority and even of the community served by the school. Similarly, representatives of local industry and commerce should know something about local employment opportunities and advise the headteacher accordingly. Parents can advise about such matters as the impact of new school rules, and on how the school is seen in and by the community it serves.

Nowadays it is becoming more common to involve pupils in the governance of their schools although there is no requirement in law to do so. The technical difficulty here is that to be a governor is to hold a public office, and it is uncertain whether, at the moment, it is legal for a minor to hold such office. This makes things difficult for a school with only a handful of pupils, if any, who are of full age, although some LEAs have introduced Instruments of Management permitting pupils of sixteen, or over, to become governors. This action has not been challenged in the courts, and a definite ruling has not, therefore, been given. Certainly, as the law stands at present, a minor may not become a governor of a school where the governors have financial responsibilities (e.g. voluntary or independent schools). Some local authorities get round this difficulty by arranging for pupil observers, who may attend governors' meetings but not vote or speak.

Teacher governors (but not the headteacher) and pupil governors or observers usually leave meetings when certain matters are being discussed. They would not normally be involved in matters of staff promotions, staff policy or disciplinary matters, nor of course anything in which they may be seen to have a personal interest. One way of bringing this about at meetings is to have the agenda for the meeting in two sections: the first for the full governing body, the second without the parties concerned. If some very serious matter is to be discussed and governors are of the opinion that even the headteacher should be invited to leave the room, this must be done as a resolution put to the vote and recorded. Some local authorities insist that any resolution of this importance should have unanimous approval of the governors.

Finally, but by no means least, the clerk to the governors. Apart from servicing governors' meetings and producing agenda and minutes, he will deal with all the governors' correspondence, particularly with the local authority. It makes much sense, therefore, to have as clerk someone who is known to the authority and understands how to get things done. County schools usually appoint as clerk a representative of the Chief Education Officer, probably the Area Education Officer or his deputy. This can apply to voluntary schools as well, although some of these will also employ a second clerk to look after the business of the charity or foundation separately. Sometimes the governors may elect one of their own members to act as clerk.

The clerk is a man of considerable influence, since governors are amateurs and the clerk probably a professional administrator of schools. He will know what the view of the local authority is likely to be on most things that governors discuss, and will advise you accordingly. Remember that your clerk can only advise, and that the very reason for having lay governors is that they can bring a wealth of commonsense, worldliness and know-how, which in many cases can improve on straight professional advice.

Occasionally a clerk may manipulate the governors by suggesting that a perfectly acceptable course of action would not be permitted. If you suspect this is happening you can ask the clerk to write to the appropriate officer for a written ruling on the issue. Usually, however, the clerk is an invaluable source of professional help and guidance who can save a great deal of time and effort by suggesting the most effective course of action in any dilemma. We return in Chapter 2 to the roles of various governors and how these may be performed effectively.

County Hall

As you emerge, perhaps very confused, from your first meeting you will probably remember hearing people say: 'I wonder if

County Hall will agree to that?' or 'Perhaps we ought to ask the Director'. Probably, too, there will have been general grumbles about the all-important 'Works Department', which hasn't sent a man, despite all your requests, to repair the window in Classroom 3.

In Great Britain education is part of the machinery of local government: your local county council has an education sub-committee just as it has a housing sub-committee, a finance sub-committee and many others. In day-to-day usage teachers and officials tend to refer simply to the 'Education Committee', but in fact the education committee, like the others, is respons-ible to the full county council, and in the last resort may be overruled by that council, though in practice this rarely happens except over contentious issues.

The Education Committee appoints a Chief Education Officer – some authorities use instead the older title, Director of Education – to manage the system in the area. The job is a very difficult and complex one, and not easy to define. He or she is not the slave of the committee and required to do no more than carry out policy decisions. Parliament has decreed that each local authority shall have a Chief Education Officer, even if it thinks it can manage without one. Moreover, the DES takes a close interest in who is appointed to the job.

The Chief Education Officer provides the top leadership in a system containing hundreds of schools. Education is the largest of the social services, and in your area may well be spending at the moment well over one million pounds every week. On the one hand the Chief Education Officer will work within LEA policy, and from time to time generate considerable steam if that policy is not carried out further down the line. On the other he has great influence on the shaping of policy through attend-ance at meetings of the Education Committee and his relation-ship to the chairman, with whom he works closely. Together they must ensure that the resources necessary to keep the system running are available. Yet formidable as this team might seem to be, they are far from being dictators, whether they wish to be or not. The Chief Education Officer has to keep abreast with the

41

almost daily flood of administrative memoranda, circulars and statutory instruments from the DES which land on his desk, not to mention sizeable, possibly acrimonious correspondence with heads, governors, teachers' unions or parents. For their part, politicians have to keep an eye on the wishes of their electors and interested pressure groups, of whom of course governors should rightly be one.

There is never enough money available for education, and it is probably fair to say that most Chief Education Officers and their committees in recent times have been less concerned with progress and pushing forward into new fields than making the available resources stretch thinly to cover areas of desperate need. Much time is inevitably spent on deciding priorities, and this is where you as a governor have a role to play. Should your very popular and overcrowded school have an extension built, or should someone else's school, twenty miles away, still working in a building put up in 1862, be completely replaced? Should the buildings to complete the plan for a local comprehensive school be started next year, or should the money be used to get rid of all the outside toilets which freeze up in winter, many of which are a health hazard?

There is no simple answer to any of these problems, and none that will please everybody. It is up to you and your fellow governors to bring whatever pressure you can to bear. Imagine that there is, up at County Hall, a long list of jobs waiting to be done: where your job appears on the list may well be up to you. Remember, too, that even if a list of priorities has been agreed, it will be reviewed at fairly frequent intervals. Find out when it is to be reviewed, and if your efforts meet with no luck now, you may well get somewhere in a few months.

The job of the Chief Education Officer and his staff could thus be described as getting the best educational value for money, and encouraging and supporting the best practices in schools and teaching.

County Hall staff

If in the course of your duties you have to visit County Hall for the first time you are likely to find the experience traumatic. As you wander the long anonymous corridors past the peeling splendour of the Alderman Harry Ramsbottom Committee Room, clutching your petition, compass and thermos flask, you half expect to turn a corner and trip over the dusty skeletons of some other ill-fated governors' expedition which never quite made it to U.R. Smith-Jones of Buildings and Special Projects, not, of course, to be confused with R.U. Smith-Jones of Staffing and Salaries.

In practice, most of your dealings with County Hall will be by letter from your clerk to the appropriate office. If, for example, an item appears on the agenda for one of your meetings about whether Mr Boreham of the French Department at your school should be paid for a day when he was absent, your clerk will know who can pronounce on official policy. On the other hand, it is certainly worthwhile to know how the Education Department at County Hall works, and there may well be instances when you would like to talk face to face with the official concerned: this could happen perhaps on site when additional buildings are being discussed.

43

It is easiest to think of the education staff at County Hall as falling into two separate groups, the professional team of advisers, and the administrators, both of which are directly responsible to the Chief Education Officer. In New York it has been decided that educational administrators should live where the action is, so they are mostly to be found in various schools rather than in a central palace.

The advisory service

Just as managers of industry need to keep themselves and the workforce in touch with new developments in order to survive economically, so it is obviously in the interests of the education service for the LEA as employers to endeavour to keep the service up to date.

Most LEAs now appoint Advisers who are concerned with what is taught in schools and how. In the case of primary schools, Advisers are usually interested in the work of the school as a whole, for secondary and middle schools there are Advisers in individual subjects such as Maths, Physical Education or Modern Languages. Generally speaking they work as a team under the leadership of the Chief Adviser.

As their title suggests, it is the job of Advisers to advise, though in some areas they are now called Inspectors and are given a more investigative role. They advise the Chief Education Officer of new developments, and through him or her of course, the Education Committee itself. If, for example, schools are turning to new Science courses in the sixth form, then the Committee will be faced with additional expenditure on new and expensive equipment. Perhaps social problems in inner city schools suggest strongly that resources should be diverted from other areas to the schools there.

Advisers should be in and out of your school fairly regularly, talking to heads and teachers about new ideas and developments. Often they hold so-called 'in-service' courses, perhaps even on your school premises, at which teachers gather to talk about what they are doing. Because they know the schools and the teachers in their area well, they are often useful members of appointments committees, and can tell you as governors which of the people who have applied to be in charge of music at your school are likely to be good value. If a young teacher has arrived at your school straight from college or university and is having difficulties, it is likely that the appropriate Adviser will soon be involved.

Relationships between schools and Advisers are usually friendly and informal, and governors too are free to talk to them about any developments in school which are of mutual interest. The informality is very important and one of the strengths of the service. Advisers do not usually act as Inspectors in any formal sense except when there is a special monitoring exercise, or when a school is in trouble. A hundred years ago and less public elementary schools were given tightly prescribed syllabuses by the then Education Department in London, and teachers were required to stick closely to them. Inspectors were sent round to test how well the children had learnt their lessons, and the government grant to the school depended on the Inspector's report. That system, called 'Payment by results', led to much bad educational practice and to bad relationships between teachers and Inspectors. Advisers are sensitive about their relationships with schools, and they usually make it clear to teachers that their advice does not have to be acted upon but at least seriously considered. Teachers often find their help extremely valuable, though there are sometimes grumbles that they do not spend enough time in schools, which is partly explained by the many other commitments they have to undertake.

The administrative staff

It is not possible to generalise about exactly who works for whom at County Hall, since each Chief Education Officer will have personal ideas about the best way to organise his staff. The senior staff below the CEO and his deputy usually carry the rank and title of Assistant Director or Assistant Education Officer and one of them will usually be at the head of each section. It will be worth your while to find out the names of your section heads. The sections are usually:

Further Education, dealing with courses for pupils beyond the age of sixteen. Not only the colleges of further education are involved here, but also technical colleges and in some areas sixth form or tertiary colleges. Adult education figures here also. Apart from administering the institutions themselves, this section is responsible for the payment of grants to eligible students to cover tuition fees, maintenance and so on.

The universities and polytechnics are national rather than local institutions, since in general their students come from a wide area of the country. They are not administered therefore from County Hall, but there may well be a section there with the title *Higher Education* to which queries about, for example, grants to undergraduate students may be made.

Schools. This section will be divided up into primary and secondary divisions. There will also probably be a division which looks after special schools, for children with learning difficulties or emotional disturbances, and for those who are officially recognised as educationally sub-normal.

The work here is concerned with the staffing of schools, deciding how many teachers a school should have, and paying teachers' salaries. It will deal with queries about the allocation of pupils to schools, and general matters in the day to day running of schools.

Common Services. This is usually a big section dealing with all those services one can too easily take for granted in the running of schools. Its responsibilities include looking after playing fields and supplies of all sorts to schools, from books to equipment. It looks after the maintenance of schools, school caretakers, and administers the School Meals Service. It also has a host of smaller responsibilities such as the provision of school transport where needed, road safety and so on.

Development. In addition to looking after existing schools, local authorities must also have an eye to the future. Housing estates, even new towns, spring up and require new schools or extensions to existing ones. It takes years to get a school from the point at which the decision is made to build to the moment when the first pupils arrive, and, since pupils have a statutory right to a school place, local education authorities cannot afford to be caught out. For the same reason, they have to keep well informed about movements in the child population, which of course, may not go hand in hand with new housing. At the same time, fashions in education change, and local authorities need to gaze into the crystal ball to ensure that the schools they build now will serve the needs of the future. Will schools in twenty years' time be generally the same size as they are now? Will they still have classrooms as we know them? Will there be more learning from machines? Above all, will the schools be in the right places? And is the right place in a town centre or in the green belt? The Development Section copes daily with these nightmares.

The Area Education Officer

The original local authorities for education one hundred years ago were countless so-called School Boards, some tiny, some, such as London, obviously very much bigger. In general though they had very much a grassroots local flavour. In 1902 they were largely taken over by the then new local authorities based on counties and county boroughs, and education became, as it is now, part of the machinery of local government. Since that time political and economic changes have reduced the number of local education authorities to the small total of authorities we have today.

The bigger local authorities have grown, so they have had to take care not to get out of touch with what is happening at the community or local level. For this reason they usually set up Area Education Offices locally, headed by the Area Education Officer. Their principal function is to act as the eyes and ears of

County Hall and to liaise between it and schools.

Beyond that the actual duties of the Area Education Officer vary between local authorities: almost certainly he or his deputy will be acting as the clerk to your governing body, and will thus handle most of your correspondence. He will also be involved in making staff appointments at your school, particularly the senior ones, and his office will be in almost daily contact with the head and school secretary over a whole host of routine matters. He is your best source of information about what is happening in your area in the field of education.

Her Majesty's Inspectors of Schools

HMIs, as they are usually called, should not be confused with the local authority Advisers we referred to earlier, although in many ways their functions are similar. The essential and traditional difference is that they are an almost entirely independent body and give the help and advice they think is called for in any given situation, and are not necessarily bound by the dictates of local authority policy. Indeed it is one of their strengths that they can, and do from time to time, criticise local education authorities and the way their schools are working.

The title 'Inspector' is slightly misleading nowadays. Until fairly recently teams of HMIs used to visit schools at intervals, and as many as ten or twelve in some cases would spend a week or more sitting in classes, talking to heads and staff and generally shining bright torches into dark corners. Afterwards they would prepare a full report on what they had seen, and submit it, without fear or favour, to schools, governors and LEA for their action. There was no power to order anyone to carry out their recommendations, but the influence of these reports was nevertheless enormous on everyone. The language in which they were traditionally written was often the source of some amusement. Rarely, if ever, did they say 'Mr Jones is a fool': instead they would say 'The red-haired man with one ear and leg who teaches Latin to Form 2 is . . .', and consequently the game of 'Guess who that is' was very popular in staff rooms when reports appeared.

Such full inspections, as they were called, are less common today, though they still occur. HMIs keep in touch with schools through the courses they run for teachers, and you will hear, at meetings, of teachers asking for time off during term to attend them. Such courses are usually very popular indeed, since HMIs know what is going on in the country as a whole, far beyond the limits of your county area and this is reflected in their courses. Although you may not actually see much of them, they are very influential behind the scenes, particularly in dealings between local education authorities and the DES in London. They are often called in whenever, sadly, a crisis point is reached somewhere.

HMIs are led by a Senior Chief Inspector, and have their headquarters at the DES in London. They have local offices also and there will almost certainly be one or more HMI there with a brief to watch over your school. The local offices are not at County Hall, but as mentioned earlier, can be found in the telephone book under Department of Education and Science.

Visiting County Hall.

Your link with the thinking at County Hall is the clerk to your governing body, and he will see to it that matters of concern automatically appear on the agenda for your meetings. However there is something to be said for keeping yourself as a governor well informed directly. You can do this by attending meetings of the Education Committee of your local authority.

One advantage of doing this is that you will get advance warning of what is happening in the area, and to some extent this will combat the feeling that governors sometimes have that everything has been finally decided before they even hear about it. This does not mean that local authorities are deliberately secretive about what they do. Since education committees have to have their decisions approved by the full County Council before they are implemented, the Chief Education Officer cannot act until he has that approval. He may not act in a hurry, therefore, in case that approval is not given.

You can obtain details of Education Committee and County Council meetings either from your clerk, or from County Hall directly. By Act of Parliament (the Public Bodies (Admission to Meetings) Act, 1960) the public must be admitted to meetings. It is a sad fact of life, though, that not many members of the public take up their rights in this respect.

Sometimes these meetings are held without the press or the public being admitted, but it must be stressed that this is the exception rather than the rule. Indeed Parliament has made it deliberately more difficult to do that. The committee has to pass a formal resolution to go into secret session, and must give the reason in the text of the resolution. This means that it is possible afterwards to see if the committee had good reason for its actions. Incidentally, such a resolution has to cover only specific items on the agenda, and cannot be used to exclude the public from a whole meeting.

2

Being an effective
school governor

If a governing body is to be effective then a group of individuals, some of whom may never have met before, must become a team and set out to work for the good of the school and its community. This implies keeping up to date about what is going on in education generally and in the school in particular, and pooling the talents and knowledge of politicians, parents, teachers and others in the locality to facilitate the successful running of the school. In this chapter we consider the roles of various kinds of governor, how governors can be trained, and what they can do to help schools.

Political nominees

The governor chosen by a political party to serve as a local education authority nominee can be in a difficult position. Most people directly involved in schools — parents, teachers, pupils —

do not see education in political terms at all. Although this can be said to be a naive view of life, it describes the vantage point of a sizeable chunk of humanity. Whether political party X or election manifesto Y is for or against some educational proposal is largely irrelevant unless it affects their own school.

Consequently a political nominee may be viewed with some suspicion by other governors for several reasons. He may be seen as a 'professional' governor, serving on several schools' governing bodies whilst not especially committed to any one of them, whereas parent or teacher governors see themselves as concerned only with the one school. He may be regarded as an outsider, perhaps not even living in the area and therefore not knowledgeable about local problems. Worst of all he may be perceived as 'lobby fodder', blindly following the national or local party political line on issues irrespective of the arguments surrounding them.

The political nominee is thus in a similar position to the member of parliament, elected by perhaps less than half his constituents, yet duty bound to represent all of them whether they voted for him or not. He faces exactly the same kinds of dilemma. A member of parliament may find himself voting against his party after some important debate because his own constituents might suffer if the proposed measure became law. A governor may discover that his party's line on an educational issue is in sharp conflict with what his judgement tells him to be appropriate for his particular school.

The strength, on the other hand, of the politically nominated governor can be that he has often accrued great experience of local government, understands the workings of County Hall, and may be a member of some of its key committees, has served on other governing bodies, may have considerable local, regional and national knowledge on certain issues, and has been democratically elected to serve the people, albeit sometimes after a low poll. There is no universally agreed blueprint for success, but the following pieces of advice may be helpful to politically nominated governors.

DO — Use your knowledge of local government to help your fellow governors. If you are also a member of other local government committees, help your school there as well.

— Try to treat each school as special, even if you belong to more than one governing body. Empathise with parents and teachers who are totally committed to 'their' school.

— Attend regularly, not just when something controversial is under discussion.

— Admit you are not too familiar with some issues under consideration, even if you have been on the education committee for years. Councillors who feign great wisdom about everything are rapidly rumbled; those who are willing to learn, no matter how experienced, are greatly respected.

DON'T — Blind your fellow governors with procedural wizardry. Most are amateurs at committee work and do not like to feel humiliated if they speak out of turn or do not understand committee ways.

— Toe the party line blindly. Think about each move. If you were elected on a 'save money' ticket, remember that education does cost money, and help to avoid waste rather than squash every initiative. Don't jump to conclusions about what 'waste' is. Find out!

— Fight the governors higher up. It is two-faced to be silent at a governors' meeting and then oppose their proposal at the education committee or elsewhere. Speak your mind at the governors' meeting, then if you argue against the issue subsequently people will respect your openness.

— Over-play the caucus by always voting as a block because you and your colleagues have decided to stick together on every issue on a 'LEA versus the rest' principle.

53

— Constantly compare the school unfavourably with others you know. It is unfair when few people present can verify or refute your statements. There is a diplomatic way of letting fellow governors know what other schools of your acquaintance do in similar circumstances to the ones under discussion.

Parents

Parent governors have often been elected by the body of parents, many of whom may not know their nominee even by sight. It is quite a good idea for parent governors to give some thought to this problem. For example, there is no reason why parent governors should not be introduced at meetings of the parent teacher association, if there is one, or at a parents' evening. It simply requires the person running the meeting to ask the parent governors to stand up and be seen. We are all used to seeing a couple of self-conscious beetroot faces surface briefly and then subside amid good-natured and curious banter. 'So that's him, then. Don't like his tie' is just one of the hazards of being, however modestly, in public life.

"....AND I KNOW THE HEADMASTER WILL JOIN ME IN CONGRATULATING MR. BASHER ON BEING ELECTED PARENT GOVENOR"

Similarly a recent photograph and the name of each parent governor can be put on a poster and displayed prominently when there is a meeting of parents. There is no point in having parent governors and then not knowing who they are.

Representing the parents' point of view when any school's parents may support all conceivable views under the sun on any issue is not straightforward. It is helpful, therefore, if parent governors try to get around their 'parish' making sure they listen sympathetically to opinions which conflict with their own. Parent governors who speak only for themselves or for the benefit of their own children become notorious. A parent arguing strongly for favourable treatment of one group may, by implication, be arguing for less favourable treatment of another. For example if the parent of a keen gymnast pressed for classes of four in gymnastics, the parents of dance enthusiasts might find their children in a class of forty.

One way of communicating with parents is to ask the governors to agree to the school distributing a newsletter to all parents whenever they send out a mailing. Schools often send letters home about plays, concerts, open days or parents' evenings and one extra paper can easily be added. It can be translated into other languages if the school serves a multiracial community. A brief chatty letter might read something like this:

Dear Parent

You may be interested to know one or two things which have been happening at governors' meetings recently. At our March meeting the headmaster explained about the new options system being introduced in the 3rd and 4th years. There will be a meeting for all lower school parents early next term to discuss this.

One of us was part of a deputation to County Hall earlier this month to see if we could get the building of the changing room accommodation at Top Field speeded up. We were assured that this would be completed before next school year starts.

Some parents have mentioned the dangerous crossing at

the corner of Milton Street near the school entrance. We have raised this and been told that road alterations will soon make it much safer, but that in the meantime a lollipop man has been employed.

We should like to remind parents about visits to the parents of new children in the summer. Last year 25 parents volunteered to visit the parents of all children coming into the school to see if they could answer questions and it was very successful and much appreciated. This year we take in a lot of children from the West Exchester estate, and it would be helpful if about 30 parents could help. Mrs Tripp, chairman of the Parents' Association, will be asking for volunteers early in the summer term.

Finally we should like to give you early warning that we both 'retire' at the end of this year, and so anyone wishing to be a parent governor should volunteer when the note about elections comes round. We have enjoyed the work and found it interesting, and we should be glad to tell anyone wishing to stand for election what is involved.

Yours sincerely,

Eileen Chandler
David Evans.

Remember the point made in Chapter 1 about confidentiality. Make sure that your fellow governors know when you are discussing issues with parents so that no confidences are breached. One further point to remember when soliciting parents' points of view is that it is too easy to report only the views of one's own circle of friends. It is often said that only middle-class parents volunteer for this kind of responsibility, which is partly, if not entirely, true. Thus anyone elected from the posh end of town ought not to report only the views of Rotary wives or opinions gleaned from Tupperware parties or the golf club dinner dance. There is much to be said for parent governors being chosen from different parts of the school's catchment area, and it should be possible for the people elected to be sensitive to views from all sections of the community.

DO — Become known to your constituents.

— Send an occasional newsletter.

— Represent all sections of the community not just your own friends.

— Involve other parents in your work beforehand, not merely tell them about it afterwards.

DON'T — Overplay the line, 'Well my son is in the school, so I got the inside story'. Nudge, nudge, wink, wink.

— Press you own children's case, either openly or craftily, at the expense of others.

— Be afraid to speak if the meeting is full of apparent experts. You are there as the voice of parents, not as Britain's leading authority on curriculum development. Good professionals welcome a clearly expressed non-expert's point of view. In any case many parents are far more expert in their knowledge of children's learning and well-being than they realise themselves. On the other hand don't pretend you're an expert if you are not.

Teachers

Teacher governors can also find themselves in an awkward position. They should become members of the team like everyone else, but they are inescapably employees of the local authority, and may be seen by other governors to be biased in favour of their colleagues whenever anything to do with teaching comes under scrutiny.

Furthermore, as they are also professionally knowledgeable in education they may be tempted to overawe fellow governors with their expertise, and nothing will kill discussion or arouse hostility more quickly.

If he has been elected (and wherever possible teacher governors should be chosen by their fellows) his colleagues will expect to know that their views are represented, and to be consulted about key issues. It is not a bad idea, therefore, for a note to be displayed permanently on the staff notice board giving the name of the teacher governor, so that all, especially newcomers, are clear who is acting in this way for them. The same section of notice board can display notes of information for colleagues about what is happening in governors' meetings, though confidentiality should not be breached.

Anyone volunteering to stand as a teacher governor should be clear from the outset about the pressures which may ensue. On a particular issue, for example, the majority of his colleagues may hold one view, which he is duty bound to report, and the head may hold a different view − so already the teacher governor's loyalties are divided. He may himself hold a third view, which he should be as free to express as any other governor present.

As suggested in the section on parent governors above, he should respect confidentiality and try to discover the view of all his colleagues on matters, not just those of his personal friends or like-minded individuals. One way of doing this is to raise appropriate matters at staff meetings, so that both he and the head can try to interpret staff's views. Whilst it is not a bad idea for the head and the teacher governor to consult before governors' meetings, it is not advisable for there to be such powerful collusion that the rest of the group feels threatened by a professional conspiracy.

The teacher governor should not be made to feel by the head that blind unswerving loyalty is demanded irrespective of his own views, and that any mild dissent is a serious breach of professional etiquette. On the other hand the teacher governor should not seek to embarrass the head deliberately, nor to win victories in the governing body denied to him in staff meetings, unless there is a serious problem of disharmony and lack of confidence in the senior people within the school.

When matters to do with individual members of staff are raised teacher governors often withdraw. It is as well to minimise the occasions when any governer has to withdraw, so that the group can act as a team; and indeed it is an important aspect of professional life that people have to learn to keep a confidence, act fairly and humanely, and not press their own special interest at the expense of their colleagues.

On the other hand when a teacher governor's own affairs or a matter of direct concern to him are being discussed, he should always, in his own interests, be asked to withdraw. Just as a teacher governor should not be granted special privileges because of his position on the governing body, so too he should not be any worse off.

The following summarises some of the points made above:

DO — Keep all your colleagues reasonably in the picture, using notice boards and meetings as necessary.

— Represent all views when asked, not merely those of friends or people with whom you agree.

— Express your own point of view, even if it conflicts with the majority view of your colleagues; you have that same right as anyone else present.

— Discuss first with the head any issue on which you suspect you may wish to disagree with him. You are entitled to hold contrary views but out of courtesy you should let him know if possible.

DON'T — Dazzle fellow governors with technical jargon. Better to carry your real or imagined expertise lightly. This means avoiding phrases like 'Research has proved that . . .' (it rarely has).

— Feel threatened if one of the parents has a child in your class. Carry on normally.

— Press your own, your best friend's or your department's case unfairly when other colleagues are not present to put a contrary point of view.

— Dismiss the views of the lay people on the governing body. They may be contrary to current orthodoxy, but they should be listened to.

— Feel you have to justify everything the school does. Good schools constantly review their practices.

Although other governors might be alarmed if you never had any confidence in what the school was doing, they will understand that issues in education are not always black and white, and that honest self-doubts can sometimes produce healthy changes.

— Serve for ever. Allow colleagues to have the experience, even if they wish to re-elect you. It is good for the job to be shared amongst several teachers over the years.

The Head

The Articles of Government prescribe that the head is entitled to attend throughout every governors' meeting unless, as we have seen above, he is excluded during the discussion of a particular item of business. In this capacity he attends as the principal educational officer of the governors so that his advice may be available to them, and he is able to pick up from discussion the trends in governors' thinking which lie beyond their actual decisions. As an officer he is not a governor, and does not have a vote. It is quite different when the head is also a governor ex-officio, or has been elected as a teacher governor, for in such cases he attends meetings both as an officer and as a governor, and has to remember which hat he is wearing every time he takes part in a debate. The difference is rather like that in industry between a general manager and a managing director. Some heads have made the mistake of unnecessarily standing for election as teacher governor even when granted full voting and attendance rights, and occasionally, to their embarrassment, have not been elected by their colleagues, who see it as a ruse to get rid of the teacher governor principle.

Heads have a vital role to play in any board of governors. Poor relationships between the head and the governing body can affect the running of the whole school and are, fortunately, relatively rare, being usually a symptom of some deeper problem when they occur. There is everything for the school, and indeed the whole community, to gain when relationships between head and governors are good.

The head's report is often an important part of the meeting, other governors being very dependent on him to keep them up to date with what is happening. Governors appreciate honesty here, being unconvinced at hearing nothing but games results when everyone knows there are problems elsewhere.

Most governing bodies look to the head for a clear lead on almost every issue which occurs, and it is as well not to be too defensive and try to prevent governors asking searching questions. The 'clever' head who approaches meetings too slickly, because he believes governing bodies are a nonsense and only need proper handling to make them totally innocuous, does himself and his school a disservice. Successful heads involve their governors in the life of the school whilst not for one moment ducking their own responsibilities.

The balance between the paid professionals, hired to take front-line responsibility for running the school, and the governors, unpaid amateurs charged with certain responsibilities and expected to show interest in the school in general, is perhaps a difficult one to strike, but many heads have done it to the satisfaction of all concerned, and without the need for an elaborate rule book or demarcation procedure.

In summary:

DO — Be open and above board about successes and problems, it will usually be appreciated.

— Establish good rapport with the chairman in particular.

— Express your own point of view, even if it conflicts with that of the rest of the staff.

— Encourage governors to be actively involved in the school in some way, not just attend meetings.

DON'T — Dazzle governors with technical expertise.

— Blackmail the teacher or parent governors by looking hurt if they disagree with your policies.

— Feel threatened if governors offer positive suggestions. If they are bad explain why you cannot use them; if they are good seize them with alacrity. No individual has a monopoly of wisdom.

— Boast to your colleagues that you have your governors sewn up; they may grass on you!

— Deride councillors and lay governors. They are trying, in the main, to perform a public service, and are often delighted to be asked for help.

Pupils

Pupil governors where they exist often have observer status only, and the chief complaint voiced about them is that they rarely join in discussions. Clearly there are difficulties when an inexperienced adolescent finds himself amongst adults, including his own teacher and head and several leaders in the community.

Nevertheless pupils can and do perform a useful function, and much of what is said above applies to them: that they should try to speak for their fellow pupils not merely give their own point of view, that of their friends or their own age group, and that they should keep other pupils informed about what goes on at governors' meetings, except when this involves confidential matters, although usually they will not have been present for such business.

Teachers should take seriously the role of pupil observer or governor and, without reducing the pupil's role, help him to do the job properly by explaining about procedure, giving relevant background information and letting him produce a newsletter for the notice board. Handled well the experience can be a piece of sound social education, both for the pupils directly involved and for the whole student body.

Chairman

The chairman of governors sits in a very important and influential position. He is reponsible for setting the tone at meetings, and can be an important lubricant, establishing communication between himself and the head, and between the governors and the LEA. The role of chairman is dealt with more fully in Chapter 3.

Co-opted governors

Some governors are recruited because of a special role they play in the community. They may, for example, be experienced in the world of industry, the church, farming or the social services. They can bring a dimension to the governing body which other members cannot readily give.

It is important that they use their strengths for the benefit of the school. It is useless if someone co-opted from local industry never shows interest, or merely turns up to meetings to air time-honoured prejudices about education. On the other hand someone who forges links with the world of work, advises about building, financial matters or careers, can be a treasure. Employers of co-opted governors can help by allowing their employee some time off and by not docking his pay on the few occasions he may need to take a little time off work for school business.

Administrators

What has been said above about teachers and heads applies to professional administrators, such as Area Education Officers, who attend governors' meetings acting as clerk: they should not overplay the role of 'expert'; not evade issues by exploiting their knowledge of committee procedure or the complexity of County Hall; not dress up their own prejudices by falsely claiming them to be county policy. And they *should* report practice at other schools, not to disparage a particular school but to inform discussion.

Training for governors

There are several ways in which governors can be trained to do their job effectively. Many local authorities now run workshops for governors, some lasting a half or a whole day, others spread over a residential weekend, or comprising a series of sessions spread over a long period. Courses are sometimes put on for governors over a whole region, or mounted specifically for one or two governing bodies.

There is a great deal to be said for a carefully thought out policy on governor training. Amongst basic principles might be the following:

Involve the profession. Heads or teachers might occasionally be hostile to training programmes if they fantasise that a squad of muscled heavies will descend on them bristling with expertise and tactical weaponry. If one involves heads in the training not only can they see what is happening, but they can give valuable advice.

Make it practical. Let governors see curricular materials, tackle real cases which have come before governors, and role play imaginary meetings. Use problem cases, like those in Chapter 6.

Bring in as many as possible. Training courses which only allow one person to attend from each governing body will take an age to spread and will never reach most people. If possible regional courses should be mounted for two or three representatives from each governing body, and local courses for a larger group of people from each school.

Provide back-up material. Often people go to training courses and then find they cannot recall the details. A small resource booklet or pamphlet summarising the conference, a set of guidelines, letters of information or news sheets will give people a useful record of proceedings to which they can refer at leisure.

Follow through. Often courses are put on and then forgotten about. Governors who have been to an induction course in the early stages of their governorship may have an appetite for something more exacting after a year or two. Furthermore it should be remembered that hundreds of new governors are engaged every year, in many cases for the first time in their lives. Thus a course run one year might have to be repeated every year or two to cater for all the newcomers.

A sample programme for a one day induction course might look something like this:

9.30	Introduction: Governors and the LEA Mr J. Thomas, Deputy Chief Education Officer.
10.15	Governors and the Law Mr B. Davies, Exchester University
11.00	Coffee
11.15	Working groups (lists on notice board) Each group to deal with case studies A, B and C
12.30	Chairmen to report back
1.00	Lunch

2.00	Split into two groups for primary and secondary governors
	A. Recent developments in primary education
	     Mrs A. Bowles, Head of South Exchester First School
	B. Recent developments in secondary education
	     Mrs C. Jackson, Warden of Exchester Teachers' Centre

3.00	Discussion groups
4.00	Tea

Heads, university and college lecturers, advisers and experienced governors might act as group chairmen, and the case material provided can be fictitious items based on real events, involving pupil suspensions, teacher misdemeanour, parents appealing against governors' decisions and so on.

Follow-up sessions might subsequently deal with various new curricula, legislation affecting schools, an introduction to County Hall, important national reports like the Bullock

Report on language, the Warnock report on handicapped children, and any new Education Act.

In addition to courses by LEAs, governors can inform themselves about new developments relevant to their job by showing a lively interest in what is written about education. This point is further developed in Chapter 4, and suggested reading is given in Appendix C.

Helping the school

We asked a number of heads how governors had been particularly helpful to their school. We heard many stories of good support, and this was particularly marked when governors, despite their different backgrounds, acted as a supportive team rather than as a set of disparate individuals.

They told us of parent governors who mobilised other parents to visit the houses of new pupils; of industrialist governors who persuaded their colleagues to provide work experience, raised money to help finance pupils' projects, or helped arrange mock interviews for older students about to enter the job market; of political governors who took on County Hall and their own political party; of governors who came along to school-based in-service courses to see what was new in education.

The other side of the coin is equally illuminating. Governors spoke appreciatively of heads who kept them in the picture, of local authorities who put on interesting courses, of teachers who were open and honest about successes and problems and did not put obstacles in the way of governors trying to do their job.

Sadly there was also a negative element. Heads told of governors who rarely appeared and then torpedoed whatever was suggested; of the governor who opposed the head's release for an in-service course on the grounds that heads should already know all there is to know; the one who stormed into the school announcing she had just been made a governor and had come to inspect; the governor who insisted on helping in the classroom and bored the class to tears with long-winded stories; the one who, because he was a lawyer, claimed expertise on everything on the agenda; and a number of bad chairmen who ruled autocratically, failed to take advice and were insensitive to nervous parent or pupil members.

Unhappy stories from governors concerned, for example, the head who constantly reminded them that they knew little about education and that he was really in charge, or who said he would consider each suggestion and then quietly forgot about it; the teacher governor who saw every proposal as an attack on the profession, and the administrator who never gave an opinion, but always said he would have to consult his colleagues or the great Chief Education Officer in the sky.

In general, however, there were many happy stories, a few miserable ones and some total catastrophes. The greatest enemy appeared to be apathy. Fairly frequently people reported that their governing body had got into a cosy rut, turning up for tea, cakes and chat, and going cheerfully on their way, uncertain why they had met, and sometimes feeling the only purpose had been to plan the time and date of the next meeting and hear yet again that the boys' toilets needed repairing.

There is an important and valuable function for school governors to fulfil and it is the collective duty of all the governing body, not just the head and chairman, to see that the job is done sensitively, constructively and effectively. Whilst common-sense and goodwill alone will not ensure this, they will certainly lay a sound foundation. Anyone uneasy or uncertain about what the governors are doing can always ask the chairman if he would allow a discussion of how the governors can best conduct their business to be a central item on the agenda.

3

Governors' meetings

What is a committee?

'Through you, Madam Chairman', 'Is there a seconder for the motion?', 'I'm sorry but I must rule that out of order'. People joining a committee for the first time are often surprised and even intimidated by the formality of language employed by members who, a few minutes earlier, were perhaps convulsing each other with risqué stories, or calling one another Sid, Dick and Mary. There is thus a need for members of a governing body, particularly those who have not been in such a group before, to become familiar with committee procedure.

A committee is a group of people who meet occasionally or regularly to discuss matters in a certain field. It may be *executive*, i.e. able to make and possibly enforce decisions, or *advisory*. Most committees have been set up by some larger group of people and are therefore accountable to that group. Like governing bodies of schools they may be both executive and advisory, given delegated powers to make some decisions without reference back to the larger group, in this case the LEA, but frequently acting in an advisory capacity. It is often when a committee exceeds its powers that problems are created.

This pattern can be extended still further. Most committees will at some time set up an even smaller group of themselves as a *sub-committee* to do a particular job for which the larger group might be too cumbersome. The sub-committee will then report back to the main committee. In governing bodies this typically happens over matters like staff appointments.

Certain assumptions are made about committees. They are not always fulfilled but can be described as general unwritten hopes when committees assemble. First of all it is assumed that business will be conducted in an *orderly* manner. Anyone who has ever been to a chaotic or acrimonious meeting will know how important orderliness can be. A committee will usually, therefore, have certain agreed procedures to ensure the smooth transaction of its affairs. It will have an *agenda* listing items of business, sometimes with supporting papers giving members background information; a *chairman* who will organise the meeting, call on speakers, give a ruling where necessary, sum up, decide when to pass on to the next item and so on; and a *secretary* to make the notes which will eventually constitute the record of that meeting.

Secondly, because decisions often have to be made, it will be assumed that after discussion a *consensus* of members' views will be sought. If there is some doubt it may be desirable to put the matter to a vote. Again the common assumption is that members will agree to abide by the majority decision and that if there is deadlock the chairman will give a casting vote.

Thirdly, there should be a sense of *collective responsibility*, that is an agreement that, once a decision is made, members will not thereafter publicly dissociate themselves from it, but rather support it as a group, even if they themselves were against it in discussion. This convention is frequently broken, especially when an individual member feels especially strongly about some matter, or is mandated by the group he represents to advocate a particular point of view. If, for example, many parents press a parent governor to raise an issue which is subsequently defeated when put to the vote, it would be most unfair if that governor had to pretend that he totally approved of the decision. On the other hand, in the interest of group cohesion he should not be publicly aggressive about his disagreement, otherwise the governors cannot function as a unit, only as a collection of individuals or pressure groups.

Other conventions are also broken at times, for either good or bad reasons. Someone wishing to undermine a group may seek to have business conducted in a *disorderly* manner by constant interruption, refusal to accept the chairman's rulings, or by speaking at excessive length. This kind of roguish inability to accept reasonable chairmanship is quite rare, and when it does occur sometimes suggests that the chairmanship has been unreasonable.

Committee procedure

To avoid people quarrelling with each other across the room remarks are normally addressed 'through the chair'. This can sometimes reduce acrimony. For example, the angry exchange:

Speaker A I never said you twisted the account of the last meeting.
Speaker B Yes you did, you liar.

might, in strict committee language, go something like:

Speaker A I wonder, Mr Chairman, if Mr Bloggs could clarify what he felt was wrong with the version of events just given.
Chairman Mr Bloggs, could you tell us a bit more about your objection?
Speaker B I felt that minute 234 was not entirely accurate and should have read . . .

Skilful 'Black Belt' committee members can still use committee procedure to generate hostility, anger or to scapegoat, and no amount of formal chairmanship will ever make a miserable group happy or a divided group cohesive. The question of formality is discussed again below.

In order that members may make their decisions and recommendations in the best possible circumstances, certain features of committee work are essential. First of all the location is important. Frequently meetings take place in dismal or cramped conditions, and it is impossible to avoid an air of seediness about the whole affair. Governors should be able to sit in reasonable comfort, neither perched precariously on infant-sized stools nor submerged in the sumptuous and sleep-inducing armchairs of the Alderman Harry Ramsbottom Committee Room.

The room should be decently lit and ventilated, so that members do not have to share the same limited supply of oxygen, and they should agree not to have dined too well beforehand. Those who do so may lapse into slumber, which is not good for the chairman's morale, and they should be awakened unless elderly, frail or more effective asleep than awake, as their eventual loud snore might turn out to be the decisive vote on an important item.

Certain bits of paraphernalia go with meetings. Most important of these are 'the papers', a twentieth century form of magic, which incorporate the business of the meeting.

Minutes and Agenda

Two vital pieces of paper are needed at each meeting. First of all there are the minutes of the last meeting, the record kept by the secretary of business transacted, usually in numbered form:

Minute 234   Headmaster's report

The headmaster reported on the period 1st April to 31st July (copy filed with minutes). Members noted with pleasure the growing interest in charity work and asked the headmaster to convey their congratulations to the pupils and teachers involved. There was some discussion of the amount of time

71

required to administer the new 5th year examination. Governors expressed their regret at the low take-up of science options in the current 3rd year, but were glad to note that the staff were very concerned and were taking action to see that more information would be given to pupils and parents about the options system.

Minutes of meetings are kept together as a permanent record of the life of the school, and some schools have accounts of such meetings going back for hundreds of years. Consequently it is important that the minutes should be accurate. Governors should not hesitate to point out inaccuracies, unless these are tiny and immaterial, but it is not fair for members of a committee to insist that each of their own contributions and every brilliant turn of phrase be logged in. The minuting secretary has a difficult task encapsulating the spirit of perhaps twenty minutes of discussion into five or six lines without being harangued for omitting 'the bit where I said how important it was for the locker-room cupboard to be installed by Christmas'.

If everyone wants his own name in lights the minutes become not a record of the meeting but a literal transcript of it. A word for word transcript of a two hour meeting could run to 20 or 30 pages, would invade nobody's bestsellers list, and would lead to even more Norwegian forests biting the dust to provide the paper. The best one should expect from a set of minutes is a brief and accurate account, giving the flavour of a meeting and recording any decisions taken.

The agenda for a meeting represents the batting order of items to be discussed. Certain time-honoured features regularly appear. A typical agenda, missing out the middle might look something like this:

EXCHESTER COMPREHENSIVE SCHOOL

A meeting of school governors will be held on Thursday April 27th at 7 p.m. in the quiet reading room of the school library.

1. *Apologies for absence*

2. *Minutes of last meeting* (February 10th)

3. *Matters arising*

   (a) *Minute 234* Outcome of staff meetings on 3rd year options (Headmaster to report)

   (b) *Minute 236* Deputation to County Hall on March 13th (Mr Jones to report)

   (c) *Minute 241* Delays to cloakroom extension in south wing (Chairman to report)

4. *Headmaster's report*

5. *New housing estate in West Exchester* Governors will know that planning permission has now been granted for Messrs. Botchett and Scarper to build 75 three- and four-bedroomed houses in West Exchester. A paper from the Chief Education Officer explaining possible implications for the school is attached.

   . . . etc.

12. *Date and time of next meeting*
    Thursday July 13th at 7 p.m. is proposed.

13. *Any Other Business*

Usually the chairman will begin by asking if members agree that the minutes of the last meeting constitute a correct record of events. He signs the filed copy when this is agreed, having made any necessary alterations first. 'Matters arising' allows the chairman or any other member to update colleagues on the latest state of whatever was discussed last time. Sometimes certain matters for report are already included in the agenda, and members are then invited to comment on other relevant items as they wish. Unless there is a particularly pressing 'matter arising' the group normally passes fairly quickly on to the main body of the agenda, otherwise the meeting can never get itself moving ahead.

Newcomers to committee work never understand how the agenda is assembled. Some secretaries or chairmen of committees circulate members in advance asking if there is anything they wish to raise, others assemble the agenda themselves. It is wise to make known how members may introduce an item, the deadline date for typing and distribution and so on, otherwise a sense of frustration develops, or else thorny issues are introduced unexpectedly under 'any other business'.

If you, as a governor, wish to raise an issue it might be helpful to provide a short paper to support the case. People are sometimes unnecessarily inhibited when asked to provide a paper, assuming that a great literary masterpiece is essential, or alternatively that a lengthy document with footnotes and tables is required. A supporting paper is often quite brief, and serves simply to let other members know in advance what the item is about. For example if an item appears as:

6. *School uniform*

no-one knows what is involved. Is there some move to abolish it? Do people wish to change the style of uniform? On the other hand if the item appears as:

6. *School uniform* (paper from Mrs Jenkins attached)

and a short covering note in simple, plain language from Mrs Jenkins is available, like the one below, governors both know what is to be discussed and can find information or think of ideas in advance.

School uniform

At a recent PTA Meeting the question of the high cost of school uniform was raised. Parents were not against school uniform, but were worried at the expense involved, particularly to parents with two or three children at the school. The headmaster and staff were very sympathetic, and we agreed that it should be given some thought before next year. One possibility was that any red cardigan or jumper should be allowed, not just the expensive ribbed one. Another suggestion was that we might somehow help parents buy second-hand uniforms from each other. One person thought that a grant was available to help parents with a low income, but no-one seemed sure. Knowing that one governor was a social worker and another a teacher at a school that had tackled the problem already, we thought it would be a good idea if I, as a parent governor, raised it at a governors' meeting. Both the headmaster and chairman have agreed to this so I hope we can spend a few minutes on it. The headmaster and PTA committee have said they are quite happy to look at any suggestions which come from this meeting. Perhaps the pupil governors could tell us what pupils feel about it.

Edna Jenkins

For similar reasons when items come from the head or the Chief Education Officer they frequently have a paper attached, and governors should become familiar with the background to each item before the event. The only situation worse than a meeting where some members have clearly not even glanced at the papers, is when the chairman is in this position.

Sometimes the item 'any other business' does not feature in an agenda. This is because members may in the past have raised controversial matters under this heading late in a meeting, with no-one in possession of the appropriate information. If a member wishes to raise something, whether under this heading or not, after the agenda has appeared, it is customary to ask the chairman's permission in advance. He may then rule whether it is appropriate to take it at such late notice or whether it should be deferred until the next meeting. In fairness to all other governors, members should try their best to have all important items put on the agenda in the proper way and in good time. If someone tries to bring up an important matter under 'any other business' when several members have already left, propose that it be deferred until the next meeting. Some LEAs have been known to leave 'any other business' off their agendas so that the ruling party caucus can discuss their 'line' on all matters before governors' meetings. Object to this loudly and longly!

Reaching decisions

Some items on the agenda need a decision and others merely require an airing. When a firm decision is needed it is common for the chairman to interpret the mood of the meeting. Where there has been clear agreement the chairman will often ask 'Do we agree then that . . .?' or 'Am I right in assuming that no-one is in favour of . . .?' Where the feeling of the meeting is not clear-cut a vote is usually taken.

Formal procedure over voting can sometimes become a little complex. Normally members will be told what they are voting on, and if anyone is not clear what the issue is he should ask for a statement from the chairman. Normal committee procedure requires one member to propose a motion and another to 'second' it. Once the wording has been agreed the chairman will ask for a vote: 'All those in favour please show . . . all those against . . . abstentions . . . I declare the motion carried by 12 votes to 8 with 2 abstentions.'

Life becomes complex when members disagree over the wording of a motion and wish to propose amendments. Thus someone may say, 'I disagree with the motion as put, could we vote on an amended version and add the phrase "provided he has not made a request during the previous twelve months"?' If a seconder is found the chairman will usually put the amendment to a vote first to see if it is acceptable or if members prefer the original motion, and then ask for a vote on whatever version is agreed. This final version, as amended, is called the substantive motion. It is up to members of a committee to make sure that such constitutional matters do not become silly. Most governors want to discuss issues of concern, not to train as barristers.

It is the chairman's duty to make sure that any formal proposal is clearly worded, not saturated with negatives and ambiguities. Most people operating at sub-genius level would not be certain what a 'Yes' or 'No' vote means with a motion such as 'we deplore anyone refusing to do nothing'. It is far better to vote on a positive version of a motion so that those voting 'for' or 'against' are crystal clear about what they are supporting.

76

Once a vote has been taken the strength of the voting is often important. A group will have more confidence if the vote was clear cut than if it was close. When the voting results in a tie the chairman may give a second, or casting, vote. Some chairmen always give a casting vote *against* any change on the grounds that a tie does not constitute a majority in favour of change and things should therefore stay as they are. This stance is only really justifiable, if at all, if the chairman has no strong feelings on the issue. The chairman is usually an important person and if he has any views at all he should not hesitate to air them. The risk that some unpopular issue might become widely known as having been approved 'only on the chairman's casting vote' is one of the hazards a chairman must occasionally face up to when agreeing to take on the assignment. He can be reassured that chairmen universally have to take on such responsibility, and that it is relatively rare for the casting vote to be needed. No-one should castigate a chairman for exercising his duty to resolve a dead-lock.

Group dynamics

There is something about the chemistry of a group of people meeting together which defies perfect explanation, even though a great deal of work has been undertaken studying such groups. Studies of group dynamics are far too numerous to mention here, but some aspects are of interest.

Small group dynamics are different from large group dynamics. In larger groups people will often have less time to speak and there will be more silent members. Some participants will be under pressure to utter views they do not really support because they are aware that it is sometimes more important to have been seen to state a point of view than actually to believe in it. For example a parent governor might have to voice 'the parental view' whilst privately disagreeing with it. Smaller groups are usually much more informal and decisions are negotiated more casually. Few family breakfasts involve someone proposing and seconding a motion of censure on whoever buttered the toast.

Studies of groups have shown that people frequently play a regular and predictable role in them. There is often a social welfare person who switches on lights, turns heating up or down, suggests it must be time for coffee or that a window needs opening. A joker can help relieve tension by making people smile, or occasionally heighten it when his funnies misfire. A guardian of the nation's morals may remind members that doom is around the corner, that levity will not do, and that sombre faces should be the order of the day. An aura of perpetual sin hangs round such a person, contaminating the rest of the group who feel guilty without being able to say why. A brisk and businesslike efficiency expert may always be hustling the chairman on to the next item. There are many other stereotypes.

Similarly in some groups people regularly have an expectation of time, and often fill it with remarkable accuracy. If eight people meet regularly for an hour, one may talk for twenty minutes, another for ten, yet another remain silent. If for some reason the twenty-minute person is silent for the first half hour he is then under considerable pressure to dominate the last half hour and obtain his ration of talk.

Position in the room or around the table is also a feature of many groups. Without realising it people who disagree with each other frequently choose places opposite one another and avoid adjacent seats, on the grounds that it is very difficult to sustain an argument with someone sitting at your left ear. Similarly those who share views often sit together and a concerted and sometimes orchestrated set of arguments for or against an issue will appear stronger coming from a cohesive group of three or four people. On the other hand super-shrewd operators sometimes deliberately seat themselves in different places around a table so that an impression of general group agreement on an issue is created.

Why some groups manage beautifully and others never get off the ground is very difficult to explain. Certain features which kill groups stone dead are well known. One very aggressive member can spoil meetings and sensitive individuals subjected to a personal attack from such a person may never reappear or rarely speak thereafter. Amongst killers of good group interaction are the following stereotypes. Although caricatures, they are alive and well and often do not readily respond to hints, though you could try circling the appropriate description in this section of the book and leaving it open at the culprit's seat with a note signed 'A friend'.

The bad listener never hears what others say because he is only waiting for a gap in the discussion to enable him to make his own contribution. This frequently is a repetition of what someone has already said.

The 'expert' can be a pain in the neck, particularly if he is not really an expert at all. The person who once built himself a back porch should not pronounce loftily on all building matters, particularly if it fell down. One governing body had to suffer the pontifications of an elderly lawyer. As the sole university graduate in the group he constantly spoke inaccurately on 'O' levels, 'A' levels or further and higher education from the basis of hopelessly out of date memories of his own early days. Even real experts can inhibit discussion by appearing to rule on every topic, but fortunately many genuine experts carry their learning lightly and do not overpower their fellows. Perhaps some of the worst offenders, unwittingly, are governors who are teachers at another school, and seek to make the school a replica of their own. A good and sensitive 'expert' on the other hand, whose views are valued by others, can be absolutely invaluable.

The Mona Lisa. People who sit silently throughout meetings wearing an enigmatic look simply put pressure on others to do all the talking. It is refreshing to have members who do not waste words, but governors who never say a single word on any issue for meeting after meeting are often making little contribution unless they are active behind the scenes. Better is an occasional well thought out statement at the appropriate time.

The windbag can be a serious problem because he prevents others from speaking by enjoying his own contributions so much that he never shuts up. All governors may make a lengthy contribution or series of statements at some time or other, but this is not windbaggery. What distinguishes the windbag is that his speeches are repetitive and tedious, often rambling off the point. Skilful chairmen have a number of strategies to handle the situation, but even 'May I just interrupt you a second and ask you to sum up?' can spark off another fifteen minutes.

'Little me' uses disarming statements like, 'Well, of course, I don't really know anything about these matter', and then, having spent all night in the reference library, goes on to reel off DES statistics for the last twenty-five years.

'The Hear! Hear!' Usually half asleep. Says it indiscriminately, often inconsistently, nearly always after someone has spoken loudly.

"I'LL PUT MR. JONES DOWN AS AN ABSTENTION ON THIS ONE"

Finally it should be said that when group dynamics go wrong it is the duty of every member of the governing body to make the group work. Rather than sit back lamenting about what a poor meeting it was, not speak because the level of debate is too low, or grumble about the boring agenda or lack of action, every member can help make a group a success. It should not be left to the chairman alone to reduce acrimony, curtail rambling discussions or handle difficult members. If every person present exercises self-discipline, cares about the group and the school it serves, and acts unselfishly and in good faith, there will be few insoluble problems. Indeed it is a testimony to the basic commonsense of the human race that most governing bodies are friendly and informal. The only reason that there is some concern in this section about problems is that happy groups will run themselves and problem-ridden groups need help.

The Chairman

The role of the chairman in any committee is crucial. He sets the tone of the meeting, decides priorities, steers the group through the business and liaises with the head and LEA. No-one should agree to take on chairmanship of a governing body unless he is willing to work hard to make a success of the job. It is also for stayers and not sprinters.

Many of the problems described above are avoided by skilful chairmanship, yet there are as many different styles of chairing meetings as there are chairmen. The first aspect of chairmanship which should be of concern is that it offers considerable power to use or misuse. Thus the effective chairman should be seen to be fair. That is not to say that he may not hold personal views, perhaps strong on some issues, but rather that his personal prejudices should not prevent him from listening to all sides of an argument and giving everyone a chance to contribute.

An autocratic style of chairmanship irritates members considerably. One powerful chairman, whose style made Attila the Hun look like a moderate, once took a vote on an issue. There were twenty people present. 'All those in favour?' he asked. Nineteen hands went up. 'Well I'm against it' he rejoined, and passed on to the next item.

One important choice for the chairman is whether meetings should be formal or informal. If there is likely to be strife it is usually better to be formal and insist on contributions 'through the chair'. More often in governing bodies, however, an informal style is preferred. People frequently know each other

"WELL, I'M AGAINST IT, MOTION DEFEATED"

already or feel more welcome in an informal atmosphere, especially if they are lay people unused to committee work. On the other hand informality does not imply sloppiness. If decisions have to be made and recorded then a certain formality of procedure is necessary; one cannot rely entirely on folk memory.

A good chairman can perform several useful services. These include the following:

Pacing. If an agenda has ten or fifteen items he can consult with the headmaster and clerk, using his judgement to see which seem to be important and which seem more trivial. Thus he might start by saying, 'Looking at the agenda it seems as if items 1, 2, 3 and 4 can be dealt with fairly quickly and items 5 and 8 ought to take a little bit more time. If people agree I propose we spend most of our time on items 6 and 7.' At this point members can indicate if they accord with this view, and someone will be free to suggest some other item as a high priority. The advantage of this approach is that it signals to the group where their effort should be placed, so that they can help

82

the chairman move quickly through trivial items, and then debate more thoroughly the key issues. This avoids the problem of spending so long on early matters that later items which are important never receive proper attention. An alternative to this approach is not to make any decision on priorities but keep a constant eye on the clock reminding people that 'we only have 40 minutes left and still five more items to cover'.

Summing up. Often discussion becomes diffuse and difficult to follow. A good chairman can help his members considerably by giving an economical and fair summary, preferably from notes he has been keeping. He might, therefore, once in a while, say something like, 'Now is this a fair summary of what people have been saying? Most speakers seemed to be in favour of a small deputation to County Hall, but Mrs French was against that because of our experience last time. On the other hand three or four people thought that if we held a public meeting first and then went to County Hall this would be better than last time when we hadn't prepared our case properly.' Other members can correct this version or agree that it is a fair condensation of discussion to date. A good summary at an appropriate moment can often get a meeting out of a quagmire and move the group nearer a decision.

Ruling. There are frequently moments of uncertainty in committee meetings when people look to the chairman for guidance. This requires him to give a ruling on some matter, as when someone says, for example, 'I know we're supposed to be discussing the county document on health education, but can we go back to that previous circular on sex equality or would you rule that out of order?' At this point the chairman must use his judgement. Amongst many alternatives might be:

'No, I think we've spent enough time on that issue.'

'Well only for five minutes at the most as we have rather a lot of business still to do.'

'Yes I think that would be well worthwhile.'

'Would members like to spend a little time on that or should we press on?'

83

'Perhaps the headmaster and the Area Education Officer can advise us on this one.'

'Is there some particular point you wish to bring out briefly about the other circular?'

There are many other possibilities. Provided that the chairman is sensitive to the mood of the meeting most committees will accept a fair verdict, and even go along with an unpopular one, realising that business could never be transacted unless someone ruled on tricky matters. Chairmen who run into difficulties have either been too heavy-handed or unsympathetic in their decisions, or else have dithered endlessly when everyone is quite happy to abide by a decision from the chair.

Manoeuvring

Most committees are clean and above board, some are riddled by chicanery. Sometimes it is hard to draw the line distinguishing socially acceptable manoeuvring from dirty tricks. Amongst many time-honoured tricks of the trade, recognisable and easily rumbled if decently handled, annoying and divisive if malevolently done, are the following:

Lobbying. When a person wishes to press a particular point of view he may rally support for it before the meeting. Usually this is a fairly honest procedure: someone approaches a fellow member saying, 'At the next meeting I'm hoping to persuade members to take some action over what I think is a very pressing problem. If I can just explain the background to you I hope you'll support me.' Occasionally the lobbying is more subtle or even obscure and certain dense, or for that matter shrewd, members of committees can sometimes accrue a fair number of free meals and drinks by not catching on quickly. Indeed, if lobbying were made an indictable offence tomorrow, a sizeable group of exclusive clubs, pubs and expensive restaurants might go out of business. Too much lobbying reduces the spontaneity of meetings and also sometimes embarrasses members who feel

"I SEE THERE'S BEEN A CAUCUS
MEETING AGAIN"

obliged to support people when approached in this way so as not to let them down.

Caucus. When a group of like-minded people wishes to press a particular point of view or secure a certain decision, they sometimes meet as a group before the main committee meeting, and work out a plan of action. This is a fairly common occurrence, but it can be divisive, and it is often better to risk the spontaneity of unrehearsed meetings. For example if the parent governors, the political nominees or the head and teacher governors concert their strategies in advance it will be very difficult for the governing body ever to become a cohesive group. Also there is some sourness when the caucus group is in the majority, and non-caucus members find they have little to offer as decisions have been negotiated in advance.

Delaying. Sometimes people in a committee will delay the meeting deliberately to avoid discussion of a controversial item or to ensure fatigue and/or dwindled numbers when an important point is reached. Occasionally a chairman will allow the group to dawdle over earlier items to cut short discussion of key later ones. It is up to other members of the group to be alert to this and ask if progress can be a little faster to ensure proper

85

discussion of later items. Another common device is to set up a sub-committee and hope the problem will quietly be buried. Sub-committees should be used to do a proper job, not to dispose of something in an underhand way.

Horse-trading. When individuals or groups known to favour certain points of view are in conflict they will sometimes agree to do a deal in advance. One group will soft-pedal on one issue, the other on a subsequent one, thus allowing both groups some success. This is often totally bewildering and annoying to members of neither group who are utterly baffled by the lack of bite over what have previously been controversial matters.

Dirty versions of the above devices are really not necessary in any properly run committee, and indeed they bring great discredit to the notion of democratic involvement in decision making. Judicious use of some of the tactics may be acceptable, but any governing body whose members obtain more satisfaction and pleasure from political manoeuvring than from properly looking after the welfare of a school and its community should stop and question why it exists.

Making effective use of committees

Committees are often so stuck with the standard rituals they fail to exploit alternatives to battling through the agenda for session upon session. There are several quite simple and effective ways of conducting business which involve but minor amendments of normal procedures. A skilful chairman can ensure that variety in practice makes meetings both interesting and enjoyable.

Buzz groups. Some members of a larger group experience frustration at not having an opportunity to speak. One way of releasing this tension is for the chairman to allow the group to dissolve into buzz groups. At its simplest the meeting will be suspended for ten minutes or so whilst people gossip with their immediate neighbours without leaving their seats. Alternatively the chairman may say, 'This is an important matter and everyone should have a chance to speak. Let's split into three groups of about six people and come back in half an hour.

Perhaps one person in each group will report back when we re-assemble.'

Working parties. When a committee has a particular job to do it may set up a working party to guide it in its thinking. Whereas sub-committees tend to be more permanent, working parties offer flexibility. Three or four people can be asked to meet fairly often to devise a solution to a problem or to fashion a proposal. Eventually they can present a report to the main committee at which point, their job completed, they may cease to exist. The ultimate fate of a successful working party is to be made a sub-committee and live on indefinitely, like the characters in Sartre's *Huis Clos* who thought they were waiting to go to hell and eventually realised they were in it already, condemned to spend eternity in each other's company. At their best, working parties can do an excellent job in a way that a full committee never could.

Day conference. Committee members often feel fatigued particularly if they meet at the end of the day. Once in a while it is worth trying to find a whole day if this can be arranged. This can have a freshness about it, and also allow more time for members to reflect on issues. It is also good for group morale. A typical day's programme, using local resources, might look like this:

Theme: Changes during the coming year	
10 a.m.	Assemble for coffee
10.15	*Some changes the school faces* The headmaster
11.15	Discussion in groups
12.30	Lunch
1.30	*Integrating handicapped children* Mr Jackson, Special Education Adviser
2.15	Discussion in groups
3.00	*Falling rolls: how this will affect the school* Mr Thomas, Area Education Officer
4.00	Tea

Brainstorming. One way out of difficulty when a group has a problem and appears unable to reach a solution is to have a brainstorming session. The rules are very simple. Each member must produce as many ideas as possible, no criticism is allowed, and the secretary writes them all down. Finally all the ideas are considered more critically and any useful ones are adopted. The reason why a brainstorming session can sometimes, though not always, resolve a problem is simply explained. Some quite useful ideas often never reach fruition because they are criticised and discarded too early. Furthermore sometimes a great leap sideways is needed and solutions which initially seem silly can often be just what is needed. Think, for example, of all those early attempts to make aeroplanes. They failed because designers were stuck with the notion of birds and flapping wings. The idea of rigid wings or no wings at all would have seemed nonsense to people at the time, but this was precisely the solution needed.

Action notes. Often in meetings decisions are reached but no action ensues. It is easy for the secretary to the committee to devise a simple action note and send it to anyone who was asked in the meeting to undertake some task. This reminds the person concerned what was agreed. A simple example would be:

Action note (minute 234 — large classes)

You will recall that you agreed at the last governors' meeting to write to the Chief Education Officer on behalf of the governors requesting him or his representative to meet a small deputation before the end of February if possible.

Governors' meetings, like any committee, can be tedious, interesting, pointless or fruitful. Given goodwill and a little ingenuity there is no reason why your own meetings should not be both satisfying and worthwhile. Governors have an important job to do, and if they can get the chemistry of their meetings right they are well on the way to doing it effectively.

4

Life in school

Wherever we have organised short courses for school governors, some of the most popular sessions were about life in school. Afterwards several governors who were not teachers commented freely how ignorant they felt about what was happening in schools, and how much they welcomed the opportunity to hear an up-to-date account and be able to ask questions. 'I sit through meetings', said one parent governor, 'knowing little or nothing about several of the things we discuss. You can't very well keep stopping the meeting to ask someone to explain what CSE mode 3 is, can you?'

Indeed several governors with long service on governing bodies or the Education Committee also confessed that, although they had picked up considerable information over the years, the world of education seemed to change so rapidly that it proved impossible for a layman to keep abreast of recent developments.

Even professionals working in schools, teacher training, the inspectorate or advisory service find it difficult to maintain a firm grasp of all that is going on, but there are several sources of help available to both professionals and laymen. First of all many newspapers employ an education correspondent, and most of these, despite the occasional dud, perform a valuable service bringing stories about reports on education, new ideas in teaching or problems in schools to the attention of a wide readership.

Television and radio also report educational matters extensively, and programmes such as *Panorama, Horizon* and *World in Action* will often cover an issue in some depth with well filmed classroom scenes and usually, though not always, with a fair degree of objectivity. It is worth watching some of the many programmes for teachers on new developments in schools, or even occasionally sampling schools' television programmes or radio broadcasts, which frequently mirror the best of what is happening in both the primary and secondary sectors.

A further source of information is to be found in the many reasonably priced paperbacks on education, some written especially for parents or anyone interested in schools. Alternatively certain specialist magazines and periodicals appear regularly, and pamphlets are sometimes produced by various agencies, including the DES and local authorities, to give a pithy digest of some important new development on current issues to the general public. A selection of these is described in Appendix C. You can also ask to see copies of the many county circulars which are sent to schools.

Consequently this and the following chapter are only intended to give the reader a flavour of what is happening in primary and secondary schools, and to describe some of the issues and problems being faced by teachers and pupils. In view of the vastness of the area they can be but a starting point.

Changes in society

Many changes in school represent a response to changes in our society of which there have been many in recent times. Children leaving school in the last two decades of the twentieth century will need more skills than any previous generation of pupils. There are several reasons for this.

One major reason is the disappearance of unskilled jobs on a massive scale. When we read about a multi-million pound investment scheme in industry it will usually obliterate unskilled jobs by the thousand. Tasks that were formerly undertaken by a large cohort of untrained and unskilled workers will in future be done by a small number of highly schooled technocrats, a squad of skilled and semi-skilled personnel, a sizeable group of bureaucrats responsible for paperwork, stock control, ordering and dispatching, and a tiny number of unskilled workers. The total workforce needed after the scheme is implemented will almost certainly be less overall than previously, and although some new posts will be created it is mostly the unskilled and semi-skilled ones which will disappear.

Secondly, it is the case that in adulthood generally more skills will be needed for family and community life as well as for work. Children currently at school will need to leave with considerable reading competence, a sound grasp of number, good social and communication skills, and a proper knowledge of where to find information and how to act on it in our increasingly complex technological and bureaucratic society. Those who do not have these skills may find themselves unemployment casualties, or unable to sustain a satisfying adult life.

Many jobs which used to require very few basic skills now require a great deal more. Some, for example, need a higher reading age than formerly. 'Reading age' is a rough and ready concept to describe competence in reading. If someone has a reading age of 10 it means he reads like the average ten-year-old. Thus a seven-year-old with a reading age of 10 would be well ahead of his fellows, a ten-year-old would be about average, and a school leaver with a reading age of 10 would be severely handicapped in adult life, unable to take in anything other than simple texts such as are used by primary school children. You need a reading age of about 15 or 16 to cope with this chapter; in other words the average school leaver should be able to cope with it, even if he does not understand every word.

Shop stewards who used to negotiate orally now have to have a rudimentary knowledge of legislation covering matters such as unfair dismissals and safety at work. Much of the information about such Acts is written in quite complex language, and a shop steward with a very low reading age could not cope with the necessary reading, and would thus be unable to advise his colleagues appropriately.

A reading age of between 12 and 18 is required for various newspapers, and the mind-blowing complexity of some official forms is beyond the comprehension of most mortals, though this can be attributed to poor writing rather than to a defective human race. Similarly, although the mathematics of everyday life can be simple and repetitive, some of it is not so straightforward. Many quite ordinary people fill in income tax forms, pay interest on loans, run a household budget, make VAT returns or have to calculate speed, distance and cost when undertaking a journey. In some fields of work, such as engineering, the mathematical demands are far beyond what they were in the past.

A further aspect of modern life is the speed and scale of knowledge gathering. A doctor, scientist, businessman or teacher curious about research in a particular field is often astonished to discover how many investigators have worked on the problem and written up their results in journals and books around the globe. One file of research in chemistry alone contains over two million references, and computers must be used to search for relevant reports, the task now being beyond the human eye and hand. Every day thousands of further studies are added to these already vast repositories of information.

Teachers in school, therefore, realising that the extent of our knowledge on almost every subject prevents them from communicating all of it to the next generation of children, have to spend some time on basic skills and knowledge and the rest on equipping their pupils with the ability to find and use relevant information (see, for example, Figure 2).

92

(a) Out of doors, point a light meter directly at the sky above you. Note the reading. Then, if possible, take other readings by pointing the meter upwards, underneath a tree or a bush. Note the readings and consider how photosynthesis by small plants under the tree might be affected.

(b) As before, point the meter directly at the sky above. Note the reading. Now point the meter towards the following surfaces, keeping the meter the same distance from the surface in each case, and note the readings: soil, dry sand, wet sand, concrete, dark paper, light paper, leaf surfaces massed together. If the light source is the sky above, how does the light reach the meter when it is pointed down on to these surfaces? Record your results in a table similar to the one shown, Table 8.2.

Table 8.2 Record of light meter readings

Light meter pointing towards	Reading on light meter
the sky	
dry sand	
wet sand	
concrete	
dark paper	
light paper	
leaf surfaces	

Which of the surfaces reflected most light? Which had absorbed most? List the surfaces in order, from the one which absorbed most to the one which absorbed least.

Fig. 2   Pupils learn to find out for themselves: an experiment to discover how photosynthesis works (from *Biology by Inquiry*, Robert A. Clarke *et al.*, Heinemann Educational, 1968).

Yet another change in society which affects schools is the rapid development of technology. When hand-held calculators became available at reasonable prices, so that many children received them as presents and schools were able to contemplate purchasing sets of them, teachers faced a dilemma. Should they ignore the development and carry on as usual? Should they throw out most of their traditional numerical calculation work and just use calculators instead? Or should they give children an understanding of the relevant mathematics plus some practice in hand-worked solutions, and then show them how to use calculators to solve complex problems quickly and with understanding? Many teachers opted for the last solution.

A similar problem was faced when television appeared on a wide scale in almost every household. Some people saw it as a threat to human life, likely to produce a passive breed of spectator, and therefore not to be used in school, others felt it had exciting potential as an educational medium, capable of showing pupils a brilliantly performed Shakespeare play or an expensively produced film on volcanoes around the world such as no teacher could ever hope to make with limited resources.

Perhaps the most problematic aspect of all the changes witnessed in our society in recent times is that it becomes increasingly difficult to predict what life will be like in the twenty-first century, when children currently in school will be adults, many playing key roles in their community. Some forecasters predict a life of endless leisure with the microprocessor revolution leading to automated factories, and a minute workforce.

Others guess that the revolution will not so much abolish work but rather lead to different kinds of jobs coming into existence. Just as people left the land to work in factories after the industrial revolution, so too they may leave factories to work in an enlarged leisure and recreational industry. As the factory machine became an extension of the human arm, so too the microprocessor might become an extension of the human brain, creating jobs and a life style we cannot accurately predict. If more people work in the leisure industry instead of factories then social skills would be most important, as no-one wants to

Talking Points

1 Discuss Wendy's physical appearance. Does physical appearance give any clues to the kind of person one is? Does physical appearance sometimes influence one's character and behaviour?

2 Wendy said she was fat and short, with freckles and pimples. Why didn't she describe herself in a kinder and more complimentary way? Why do young people often describe themselves in this way? How serious are they?

3 Wendy also tells us she was definitely the brightest girl in the class. Considering her behaviour when she received the invitation to the pool, do you agree?

4 What preparations do you and your friends make when you receive invitations?

Role-playing

Role-playing is similar to acting but less formal and with no written lines to speak. Instead, you try to become the person whose role you take over. Put yourself in his shoes—think and feel and talk and act as that person would.

You will find interesting situations developing between the role-players, often unexpected ones, and your own reactions in your new role may surprise you also.

Role-playing is frequently used by adults to help them understand themselves, and how and why crisis situations develop on the factory floor and in management. It is also used by groups of people who have to live and work together. It helps them to learn to recognise the crisis signals and how to take avoiding action before the danger point is reached.

You can deepen your own understanding of yourself and others if you take your roles seriously. You should also carefully watch others playing their roles.

1 Work in groups. Take Wendy's role, and those of her mother and younger members of her family who watch her preparations and tease her unmercifully. Mother tries to keep the peace . . .

2 Take the roles of Wendy's older brother and parents, and Wendy herself. He is preparing for his first date. Wendy and the younger members of the family tease him. He loses his temper. Mother pleads, but can't quieten him. Then Father comes in . . .

Fig. 3 Learning oral and social skills: discussion and role-playing exercises (from *English for Living*, A. Rowe, Macmillan (London and Basingstoke), 1976).

find his leisure soured by people who cannot get on with their fellows (see Figure 3).

We may conclude, therefore, that schools have responded and must continue to respond to changes in society, whilst not always certain when and how change may come about. Increased demands for greater skill, for preparation for community and family life and the world of work, for a quick response to technological innovation, for basic knowledge and strategies for finding further information, all put great pressure on an over-crowded curriculum in both primary and secondary schools, and it is to some of the questions about what and how we teach children in school that we now turn.

Primary schools*

Primary education covers the 5 – 11 age range, and in some areas which have a first and middle school pattern, can include 12-year-olds. The 9 – 13 middle school is usually, for adminis-trative purposes, regarded as a secondary school.

Common arrangements of schools in the primary sector are shown below. Some schools have a nursery section for 3 – 5 year olds attached to them.

1 Infant (5 – 7 year olds)   followed by junior (7 – 11 year olds)
2 First (5 – 8 year olds)   followed by middle (8 – 12 year olds)
3 First (5 – 9 year olds)   followed by middle (9 – 13 year olds)

The idea of the primary school is that it lays the foundations for education by introducing children to important aspects of learning at a simple level, allowing this to be built upon at the secondary stage. Amongst the things to be learned will be important basic concepts in mathematics, science and humanities, and if all goes well there will be considerable

* We are indebted to Keith Gardner, Terry Dolan and other colleagues at Nottingham University for suggestions in this section.

development of children's language and ability to think.

In view of the shortness of children's attention at this age and the widely held view that they learn readily by doing something rather than being passive, there is usually some emphasis on so-called *activity methods*, which mean that children will be encouraged to discuss, explore and do, more frequently than look and listen. Thus those classrooms with rows of fixed desks, everyone facing the front and all doing the same task at the same time, so familiar in elementary schools earlier this century, have, in many schools, given way to small clusters of children seated around tables engaged in individual or group work.

Most primary schools are small, and this is reflected in the numbers of the various types of schools in England. There are about four times as many primary schools as secondary, and the latter are often much bigger and more complex in organisation. Teachers usually take their own class for most of the day, whereas in secondary schools each subject may be taught by a different specialist. In recent years there has been some movement towards a degree of specialisation in the primary school, and it is now more common for teachers to swap classes occasionally with another teacher so that each can give expert help to more than one group in Music, Art and Craft, number work, language or whatever happens to be his particular interest or specialism.

Buildings are of all shapes and sizes. Although most have been purpose-built over the last fifty years there are many older primary schools, some built well over 100 years ago, with solid walls, high windows and cramped classrooms. In more recent times school buildings have more window space, better lighting and ventilation, and are frequently flexible in design, allowing spaces to be used in different ways. There has been considerable use of transportable classrooms which can be set down temporarily in the grounds of a school with increasing numbers, and moved subsequently elsewhere if necessary. In some older schools the 'temporary' buildings erected fifty or sixty years ago still stand, apparently defying all attempts to have them demolished.

97

Open plan primary schools have few interior walls and can be used in a variety of ways. Many were built in the late 1960s and 1970s and were meant to suit the preferred style of teachers who found themselves spilling out into the corridors of traditional schools. Sometimes there are two or three large units within the school, each containing perhaps 100 or so pupils with three or four teachers. The teachers may work as a team or separately.

The open plan area will be divided up into various sections, subdivided perhaps by bookshelves, cupboards or sliding screens, one part carpeted, another with a vinyl floor covering, depending on the type of activity undertaken there. One area may have books, cassette recorders and headphones, to be used principally for reading and language work. Another part may contain maths books and equipment. A sink and formica topped surface may be found in another area, and children will don their aprons and paint, glue and make things there. There may be a 'quiet corner', a little ante-room where children can read on their own, and for music or noisy activities there will probably be a sound-proofed conventional box classroom so no-one else will be disturbed.

A pupil working in such a school may start his project in the language area, move later to library and resources, go on to the 'messy area' to construct something, retire to the quiet corner for reflection and return to a table elsewhere to finish off. Teachers may be stationed in language or number areas, move freely around answering questions, checking progress and encouraging children, or work with a particular group of children on a certain topic in the more conventional one teacher/one class situation. There are many ways of working in open plan schools and teachers' views about such schools vary considerably from enthusiastic support to great dislike. Similarly the buildings are different, some brilliant in design, others noisy and badly conceived.

Secondary schools

Before the second world war over 90 per cent of children aged 5

– 14 were educated in all-age elementary schools, and the idea of secondary education for all was a dream. After the war the common pattern was for children to be selected at the age of ten or eleven either for a grammar school or a secondary modern.

Provision varied according to the area in which children lived, and it was not unknown for 15 per cent of children to go to grammar schools in one area and 20 per cent in a nearby authority. Over the nation as a whole the range was wider still.

In certain parts of the country, notably London, there already existed comprehensive schools taking children of all abilities, and in 1965 the Labour government of the time issued a circular requesting local education authorities to submit plans for reorganising secondary education in their area on comprehensive lines. Many schemes have been approved, and most local authorities opted to open some new schools and make the best use of existing buildings rather than underwrite the vast capital expenditure which would result from a total rebuilding programme.

Amongst schemes which were adopted were the following, in some cases in modified form.

1 All-through comprehensive (11–18-year-olds)
2 Junior comprehensive (11–14), senior comprehensive (14–18)
3 Junior comprehensive (11 – 16), senior comprehensive for those wishing to transfer at 13 and stay on after the minimum school-leaving age (13–18)
4 Junior comprehensive (11–16), sixth form or tertiary college (16+)
5 Middle school (9–13), senior comprehensive (13–18)

Consequently the 1970s saw considerable changes in secondary schools on a scale never experienced before. Not only did many schools reorganise, but at the same time the school-leaving age was raised to 16, there were increased problems of discipline, especially in inner-city areas, and schools often became bigger and more complex.

Since teachers now had to deal with the whole ability range in

99

the same school many new books and curriculum packages were produced locally or nationally, and different forms of grouping were tried as they strove to find the fairest and most effective ways of teaching. Teachers who had never before taught the brightest pupils and those who had never previously worked with average and slow learners had to develop new professional skills to be able to teach across the whole ability range. Sadly this period coincided with a spell of financial stringency, and most teachers, unable to obtain any release of time to study, plan and reflect, had to acquire these skills on the job.

Secondary school buildings are as different from one another as are primary school buildings. In many local authorities substantial secondary school building programmes have been undertaken during recent years. Some of these have been quite exciting multi-purpose buildings, having leisure centres, libraries, arts centres or a theatre attached to them, thus offering a superb set of facilities to the whole community. There are places where a stranger looking for the school is advised to follow the road signs marked 'Sports forum', and when he arrives he finds an unusual restriction forbidding street car parking during evenings and at weekends, simply because the facilities are almost as widely used at those times as they are during the day.

Inside the concrete and glass of new buildings some are on open plan lines, though not quite in the same way as primary schools. A suite of laboratories may run into each other with few dividing walls, or a maths or humanities block may be similarly open.

Other schools operate in ancient buildings or find they are based in a mixture of buildings. A typical hybrid would be for the lower school block to be of recent vintage, the middle part of the school a converted elderly former grammar or secondary modern school, and the sixth form block brand new and purpose built.

Teachers and teaching

There are well over 450,000 teachers in England and Wales,

and currently people can train for teaching predominantly via two different routes. The first pattern is for 18-year-olds to spend three or four years at a university, polytechnic or college. During their course they both study specialised subjects and learn how to teach at the same time. This is called the *concurrent* pattern, and a student may be required to do teaching practice at any stage of his course. He will usually leave with a B.Ed. degree.

The second pattern is for the would-be teacher to take his degree first at a university, polytechnic or college. Having obtained usually a B.A. or B.Sc. entirely devoted to the study of a single academic subject such as French or Physics or some combination of academic subjects, but not containing any teaching practice or study of education, he will go on to spend a concentrated year devoted entirely to teacher training, at the end of which he obtains his licence to teach, the Postgraduate Certificate in Education. This is known as the *consecutive* pattern.

Until the 1970s it was generally the case that B.A. and B.Sc. graduates were trained entirely in universities, and non-graduates and B.Ed. graduates in colleges of education. More recently the situation has been much more fluid, and each pattern of training can be found in many different higher education institutions, though some aspects of the previous system survive. Although the development of teacher training is difficult to predict, it looks as if in future all new teachers will be graduates possessing B.A., B.Sc., or B.Ed. degrees, and about half will come along the consecutive and half via the concurrent route.

Only about a quarter of teachers currently in post are graduates, however, and with over 300,000 non-graduates in schools, it will be some time before teaching becomes an all graduate profession. It is important not to be misled by graduate status: many non-graduates are outstanding teachers who never had the opportunity to take a degree, and who would probably have been the stars of their B.Ed. or B.A./B.Sc. class had they had the opportunity. Indeed a large number of the most successful

101

Open University graduates were formerly non-graduate teachers, and other teachers have gone on to take a degree from a university or college during their teaching career as mature, in-service students.

Once teachers have qualified there are several forms of in-service work they can undertake. In Britain there is no compulsion on teachers to attend courses, though in certain other countries progression up the incremental salary scale is dependent on the person having attended approved in-service courses. Universities, polytechnics, colleges, local education authorities, teachers' centres, the DES, and a number of other bodies all provide courses of short or long duration.

Teachers can attend anything from one-hour sessions or half-day workshops up to a whole-week, one-term or one-year courses, the longer ones leading to further professional qualifications like advanced diplomas or Master's degrees. Release from school and secondment on salary have been difficult to obtain in recent years, and teachers are usually delighted to have governors' support for in-service training. Although many teachers have been frustrated at wishing to attend courses and not being able to, there is the equally important problem of the teacher who would benefit from in-service work but chooses not to take advantage of it.

One interesting development in in-service training is the school-based or school-focussed programme. Here the teachers will not leave their school to go elsewhere but will work at some problem as a whole unit or as a small group of staff, staying on the premises with visiting speakers, workshops and discussions. The advantage of this pattern is that it allows teachers to improvise something they feel is of use to their community and draw in outsiders as necessary. There are several examples of governors attending parts or the whole of such courses and finding the experience extremely valuable. A typical programme for a one day school-based in-service course, using a mixture of home talent and visiting speakers, is shown opposite:

RESOURCES FOR LEARNING

9.00   *Introduction: recent developments in resource-based learning*
           Mr J. Brown, Senior Adviser, Exchester

9.45   *Adapting and extending the traditional school library*
           Mrs A. Johnson, Head of Exchester West Comprehensive School

10.30 Coffee

10.45 Discussion in departmental groups of implications for various subjects

12.00 Plenary session

12.30 Lunch

1.30   *How children learn from various media*
           Dr C. Smith, Dept of Education, Exchester University

2.15   Practical sessions, each member of staff to join one group

A. Making tape-slide sets	Dr Smith
B. Using tape-recordings	Mrs Johnson
C. Assembling sets of newspaper cuttings and archive material	Mrs B. Phillips, Head of History
D. Making and using television material	Mrs L. Thomas, Head of Biology
E. Use of the overhead projector for individual study and as a stimulus for small group work	Mr D. Naylor, Head of Media Studies, Exchester South Comprehensive School.

3.45   Plenary session

Teaching for many people is a very busy job. Some studies of teachers have shown that they engage in as many as 1000

103

contacts with children in a day, when they ask or are asked questions, praise or reprimand, assign tasks, or respond to demands on their attention. This busy professional life style can extend over the whole year, making 5000 such contacts a week and several millions in a whole career. Put another way, imagine tapping your pet tortoise on its shell every few seconds; the effect on its nervous system would be considerable, the RSPCA would soon pay you a call, and no doubt the tortoise would be pressing its local authority for secondment elsewhere or for some shell-based in-service work.

In addition teachers nowadays fill many roles. In some schools they even find themselves acting as front-line social workers, the first to see a bruised child or hear a family hard-luck story. Below are but some of the roles which teachers may find themselves filling at some time during a busy professional week.

Expert	Helping children learn information, or knowing where to find it in various subject areas, answering children's questions.
Counsellor	Advising pupils about careers, personal problems, important decisions.
Social worker	Dealing with problem families, children from broken homes, liaising with various social services.
Parent	Acting as substitute mother or father.
Jailer	Coping with pupils who would rather not be at school, dealing with truants.
Public relations officer	Explaining to parents what the school is doing, dealing with local radio and newspapers.
Bureaucrat	Filling in registers, forms, returns or orders.
Assessor	Marking books, grading tests, devising and administering examinations, writing references.

Technician	Assembling or dismantling equipment.
Manager	Making decisions about the most effective use of available resources.

It is because teaching is an exacting job and because most teachers are professional and committed to their work that the occasional teacher who is incompetent becomes conspicuous. Any parent will confirm that children who like their teachers skip happily to school, and those who do not have to be cajoled into attending. Teachers themselves are very embarrassed to find as a colleague one of the small number of ill-suited or inept practitioners, and, contrary to popular belief, teachers do not have a licence to teach for life, come what may. Amongst the more thorny problems which occasionally surface at governors' meetings will be found that of the teacher about whom there are serious complaints.

There is not, in England and Wales, a teaching council and a professional code of conduct which, if broken, leads to teachers being 'struck off the list' or disbarred in quite the same way as happens in the medical and legal professions. On the other hand the procedure is not radically different. If a teacher commits a criminal offence or is guilty of serious misconduct he will undoubtedly be asked to appear before the local authority's disciplinary committee or its equivalent, and he may lose his job. Furthermore, the Home Office reports all serious convictions of teachers to the Secretary of State who, after giving the teacher an opportunity to make representations, may order that that person be no longer employed as a teacher. (Car parking offences are not reported!) Such blacklisted teachers may not be employed elsewhere without having been reinstated by the DES.

The incompetent rather than criminal teacher is a different matter, though he too is liable to dismissal. Usually heads of department and heads of schools will make exhaustive attempts to help someone in this position aided by LEA advisers and HMI. If however people are satisfied that all help has failed or been rejected then, provided proper warnings have been issued and proper channels gone through, this teacher too can lose his

105

job. What has been said above applies equally to heads. The reason that a certain popular belief persists that teachers or heads cannot be shown the door is that the process is rightly long-winded and is not undertaken lightly.

We have spent some time on the question of incompetent or malevolent teachers only because when they are encountered they cause the greatest distress to their pupils, their colleagues and the authorities. It must be stressed, however, that this is a small, if problematic, section of a huge community, most of whom are highly professional and dedicated to their job.

Curriculum

The knowledge explosion and changes in society have put immense pressure on the curriculum. Consider these short extracts from history and geography textbooks written in the 1870s when pupils had to learn off by heart a set of packaged answers and repeat these like a catechism. They reflect the society of their day, when an uneducated peasantry received its first compulsory education at the hands of untrained teachers handling large classes. Life in family and society was stern, children were to be seen and not heard, and unquestioning obedience was encouraged and valued.

Q Who was Henry VIII?
A Son of Henry VII
Q What was his character?
A As a young man, he was bluff, generous, right royal, and very handsome
Q How was he when he grew older?
A He was bloated, vain, cruel, and selfish.

Q What is the climate of England?
A Moist, but healthy
Q What is the character of the English people?
A Brave, intelligent, and very persevering.
Q What is the size of England?
A About 430 miles long and 320 broad.

106

In the last 100 years children have been encouraged to assume a less subservient role, a great deal has been discovered about how people learn and fail to learn, and it is likely that the style of much of what is taught in the curriculum in modern schools is to offer pupils more opportunity for individual thought than did old textbooks. On the other hand one will still see mechanical and senseless rote learning at all levels, and some critics feel there has been too little movement away from authoritarian teacher-directed learning.

Primary school curriculum

Primary schools operate various patterns. Some follow a time-table of thirty- or forty-minute lessons, sometimes with the 'basics' in the morning and art, craft, music and project work in the afternoon. Others have what is known as the *integrated day*, which may be based on no formal timetable of subjects at all but allow teachers and pupils to spend the day on a variety of individual and group work. Teachers who operate the integrated approach successfully have to prepare skilfully, and record progress meticulously. Usually each child has a certain set of assignments he must complete, some mathematics, some reading, some written work, and then a topic, often of his own choosing. At its best the system allows a child to pursue each task in his own time and not have to break off at some inappropriate point.

Well organised primary classrooms are a joy to see, there being an air of busy enjoyment around the place. Badly organised classrooms have children wasting their time, spending days over unexacting tasks, and learning little.

A typical daily record of four children from a class taught along integrated lines might look as shown over the page, a tick denoting that the teacher had checked progress in the area.

Reading

There are hundreds of well produced reading books suitable for

	Number	Daily Diary	Project (personal)	Project (class)	Art/ Craft	Reading	Comment
Mary	✓	✓	✓		✓	✓	Now understands fractions very well.
John	✓	✓		✓		✓✓	Moved to red readers but found it hard going.
Colin	✓	✓	✓	✓		✓	
Alice	✓	✓		✓		✓	Beginning to lose interest in water project, must switch tomorrow.

children, some graded for beginners, others beautifully illustrated and in appropriate language for children who have learned to read a little and need to become more proficient through enjoying reading.

Several methods of teaching reading have been in and out of vogue in recent years:

(a) *Phonics* is the best-known traditional method, and involves the pupil in learning to recognise the individual letters and sounds and then blend them into the whole word: d – o – g equals dog. It is more confusing when words like bough, cough, through and iron are encountered, but some books use entirely words which are phonically 'true' and do not confuse the learner in the early stages (see Figure 4).

(b) *Look and say/whole word* is a method whereby pupils learn the whole word as a shape or pattern. The teacher often uses pictures and flashcards at the outset, so that a child might learn to recognise even a complex word like 'television' quite early on. The advantage of this method is that reading matter can be made more interesting, involving sentences like 'John liked watching television' rather than 'The cat sat on the mat'. One disadvantage is that children sometimes fail to distinguish accurately the components of longer words and see, for example, 'television' as tel- followed by a jumble of letters. They might therefore read 'telephone', 'telegram' or even 'telxyzzzon' as 'television'. Thus many teachers prefer to use some combination of whole word and phonics in their teaching of reading.

(c) *Sentence/language experience* A more recent method tries to integrate reading and writing rather than teach them separately. Some schemes provide children with a simple aid to sentence writing. Some 200 or so basic words are already printed on separate plastic strips and the child can add words of his own on blanks. Simple readers based on the basic words are available (see Figure 5), and children can write their own sentences by assembling a mixture of

The Trip

When Pat and I went down to Skegness on a bus trip, it was too hot for us to dig in the sands for long, so we went for a swim. After this, I had the bad luck to cut my hand on a bit of glass that had been left on the sands.

Fig. 4   Extract from a widely-used phonics reader (*Royal Road Reader*, Book 1 (for six-year-olds) Granada Publications Ltd, 1970).

printed words and their own choices on their sentence matter.

Few teachers adhere rigidly to one mode of teaching reading, and most will exploit some combination of methods and use both carefully graded reading schemes, which take children from beginner to fluent reader, alongside suitable children's fiction and books of general interest.

What is often neglected, however, is some work on the higher skills of reading. Once a child can read with a fair degree of confidence he needs to learn the kind of reading skills essential in much of adolescent and adult life. These skills involve the ability to scan or skim, read rapidly, to slow down and read over again a difficult passage, to use a book index or library catalogue, to make notes summarizing sections or recording key points, to discriminate between styles of writing, and to recognise fact from opinion. Some researcher colleagues of ours once studied children in school libraries by taking photographs every few seconds. The only person who ever went near the catalogue section was the librarian lovingly inserting more cards for the children not to consult.

Writing

Before the typewriter, having 'a fair hand' was an important selling point in the job market and a valued attribute in Victorian society, when clerks painstakingly entered pages of beautifully scripted entries into huge leatherbound ledgers. Today although good handwriting is still cultivated in most schools, there is also considerable attention devoted to what children write as well as how they write it. Teaching young children how to write involves their learning in the first instance how to hold the pen or pencil, form letters and write from left to right. They are usually taught the small letters first and capitals later, and normally learn to print first using simple traditional letter forms or one of the italic styles.

We use writing in many contexts and for many purposes in

When I went to bed
I put it under my pillow.

12

In the morning
my tooth had gone.
There was some money
under my pillow.

13

Fig. 5   Extract from a reader which teaches children to read and write whole sentences assembled from a basic word list (*The loose tooth*, David Mackay *et al.*, Schools Council/Longman, 1970).

112

our ordinary lives, so children will learn to write for different audiences. Once having mastered the act of writing they will write stories, accounts of their experiences and reports of work undertaken.

The term 'creative writing' has been frequently used in recent years. For some it represented all that was best in the so-called primary school revolution, after which children were encouraged to express themselves in their own way rather than ape the writings and views of their elders. To the critics it was a sloppy 'anything goes' notion likely to be full of wrong spellings ignored by the teacher afraid to dampen emergent genius.

As ever the reality was that few teachers conformed to either stereotype. Most sought to achieve some spontaneity from their pupils, and corrected spellings and punctuation judiciously, neither condoning errors nor fuming with rage at a missing apostrophe.

Analysis of a primary school child's day might show him writing a diary entry, a letter, a note to a friend, an account of a school trip, a made-up story, copying from a book or blackboard, describing the weather, and compiling a shopping list, all during the one period of 24 hours. Many children in school will write more and for a wider range of purposes than their parents. When the quality of children's writing is poor it is either because they have been given little practice, or because too much of what they write is mechanically copied from books, the blackboard or worksheets.

Mathematics

There is a great deal of talk about 'old' and 'new' mathematics, which often annoys mathematicians who find nothing 'new' about so-called new maths. It has always been there, they argue, it simply was not being taught in most schools.

Recent primary school mathematics teaching has tried to get away from mechanical learning and endless repetition, and move towards letting children understand the mathematics they learn. Children will learn not simply that $5 \times 4 = 20$, but that 5×4 is also the same as 4×5 or 10×2 or $5 + 5 + 5 + 5$ or

113

Fig. 6   An extract from *Mathematics for Schools*, Level 1, Book 6 (for five- to seven-year-olds) (Harold Fletcher *et al.*, Addison-Wesley, 1970).

(3 x 5) + 5. They will learn about shapes and get the feel of their properties by making and extending various shapes, rotating or classifying them. They will also learn the measurement, of time, length and mass (see Figures 6 and 7).

In general they will learn better at primary age by directly experiencing mathematics, so that much of the work will be practical using blocks, counters and other equipment as necessary, or involving children in considering aspects of their immediate environment, like measuring the volume of their classroom, the height of their friends or what they can do in a minute, or finding circle and triangle shapes encountered in everyday life.

Solids   regular solids

A

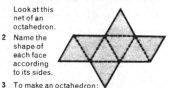

church tower and steeple · funnel · pencil · crossing beacon · spaceship · dice · wall · reading-lamp

1 Name the solids, or parts of solids, used to form the objects shown in the illustrations, e.g. a square prism and a square pyramid are shown in the church tower and steeple.

2 Look around for other examples. Make sketches and name the parts.

B

A regular solid has:
a all its faces congruent
b all its edges of the same length
c equal angles at the vertices.

1 Name two regular solids which you have already made and investigated.

The ancient Greeks, in the 4th century B.C., found there were five regular solids. Later four more were discovered.

The diagram shows another regular solid. It is called an **octahedron**.

Look at this net of an octahedron.

2 Name the shape of each face according to its sides.

3 To make an octahedron:
a use compasses to draw the net, with the sides of each triangle 5 cm long
b cut out the net. Fold it along the dotted lines and join the edges with sellotape.

4 Write:
An octahedron has ☐ faces all of the same size each of which is an_____triangle.

C   Two more regular solids are the **dodecahedron** and the **icosahedron**.

1 Consult a library book to find more about each of these solids.

2 Draw the table and enter what you have found about three of the regular solids: a tetrahedron, a cube, an octahedron.

3 In each case, add the number of faces and vertices and then subtract the number of edges.

solid	number of		
	faces	vertices	edges
tetrahedron			
cube			
octahedron			
dodecahedron	12	20	
icosahedron	20	12	

4 What do you discover from the answers?

5 Now complete the table.

Fig. 7   An extract from *Alpha Mathematics 4* (for nine- to eleven-year-olds) (T.R. Goddard *et al.*, Schofield & Sims, 1979).

Some of the debate about primary school mathematics centres around the teaching of tables, and adults often fantasise that they were themselves mathematical wizards at an early age because they can still chant a nine times table. Critics of primary maths teaching complain that some pupils have to work out 9 x 8 by writing out the number 8 nine times and adding it all up. Skilful primary school teachers recognise that both an intuitive understanding of mathematics and, on occasion, a speedy and accurate response are required, and prepare children for several eventualities, without either boring them to death with mindless repetition or failing to drive it all home after the experience and discovery phase.

Science

A primary school survey by the DES in 1978 was very critical of the science teaching which HM Inspectors saw. Some children appeared to be learning nothing at all about science until they reached secondary school, and only a small number of teachers appeared to be doing worthwhile and exciting work. Yet children at primary school age are immensely curious about their surroundings, and it is a great pity that few teachers preparing to teach the under 11s had any significant science course in their training until recent times.

A great deal of science can be learned from the immediate environment, and children of 3 or 4 often ask important scientific questions. Below are just seven of the thousands of questions children ask their teachers or parents which can lead on to simple work in science or technology:

1 Why do germs make you ill?
2 Why do things fall when you drop them?
3 Where do birds go in winter?
4 Why do we need oil?
5 Why am I out of breath when I run fast?
6 What is electricity and why can it kill you?
7 How does a calculator do sums so quickly?

Skilful teachers use every opportunity to engage children's interest in science. Many toys can be used to investigate basic scientific principles, for example how high a ball bounces on wood, carpet, polystyrene or water. The working of the human body is of concern to children and early health education can deal with tooth decay, a balanced diet or pollution. Elastic bands, lollipop sticks and construction toys can be useful for elementary education in technology.

It is vital for all adults to show an interest in and be knowledgeable about science and technology, and primary school governors should take an interest in what is being done in this area of primary school life as well as the three Rs. It should be remembered, however, that although some primary schools may set aside time for science on a timetable, others may choose to teach science as part of an integrated approach via project work.

Secondary school curriculum

The secondary school curriculum is too vast to describe in a short space, and much of what has been said about primary schools above applies to the secondary sector.

Although most secondary schools still operate a timetable with 40-minute slots there are many variations of this, some of which approach the 'integrated day' notion in the primary sector. Some schools have imported the American idea of 'modular scheduling' based on a 15- or 20-minute unit, so that teachers may ask for one, two, three or more units for a class depending on whether it is for class registration, a games session or a laboratory practical.

Other schools use one hour blocks, and some have gone over to quarter- or half-day units whereby the week is split into 10 or 20 equal length sessions. Occasionally one finds a ten-day timetable which works on a fortnightly cycle, and signs saying 'Day 6' are placed around the school on the second Monday of the cycle to remind people what day's programme is in operation.

117

Again in many schools the timetable looks familiar, there being lessons for all in Maths, English, Religious Education, Science, French, History and Geography with various options for some pupils, like Music or Art and Design, Economics or Spanish. In other schools the decision may have been taken to integrate several traditional subjects in the early years, so one sees Humanities, Environmental Science, European Studies or Combined Science on the timetable.

In some schools brand new subjects have appeared which may not be familiar to parents' and grandparents' generation, or they may be contemporary versions of lessons formerly under a different name. For example, in New York drugs education had to become a major concern at both elementary and high school level, because so many children were dying from using heroin or one of the lethal drugs, or were seriously injuring their health, and parents themselves, never having been taught at school about the effects of various drugs, were clamouring for informed advice to be given to children in good time. In a different context a course called 'integrated craft' might contain some recognisable elements from traditional woodwork and metalwork lessons, but might also deal with leather, ceramics, plastics and textiles, and involve the use of modern power-tools and machinery, as well as traditional craftsmanship.

It would take several books to describe all that is happening in secondary schools so a brief description of certain developments will suffice. As in primary school teaching there has been emphasis in certain secondary school science curricula on discovery learning. Great scientists devise theories which they then put to the test. If successive carefully controlled experiments produce the same findings the theory is upheld. Thus pupils may speculate about what will happen if a current from batteries is passed through several bulbs. Various experiments will be conducted by groups to test out their 'hypotheses'. Finally a principle will be extracted from the results and compared with the textbook versions of scientific laws (see, for example, Figure 8).

In foreign language teaching there has been some movement

29a Experiment
Looking for a law

Take a seesaw and balance it on the wedge at the centre. Put some loads on each side. You should put the loads at the marks so that you know when a load is one step out or two steps out or four steps out from the centre. Don't put a load $2\frac{3}{4}$ steps out because that would make it harder to find out the scientific story of seesaws. First make the seesaw balance with two piles of loads (pennies), one each side.

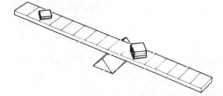

When you have it balanced, the seesaw will tip over to one side and stay there, and it will tip over to the other side and stay there. You will not be able to make it stay exactly balanced in mid-air. That is because it is sitting on top of the support at the centre, ready to fall over either way. But this will be just like 'weighing sweets': when the scales are exactly balanced and you find ever so little more would tip the scale one way or the other.

You have balanced the seesaw with two piles of pennies. *How can you move the pennies and keep the balance?*

Find out what you can about a balancing seesaw, with different loads on it. Make notes in your notebook of what happens. See if you can find out some rule or story that you could tell other people about balancing loads.

29b Experiment
Using your law

Use a large seesaw made from a plank balanced on a brick, and your knowledge of the 'lever law' to weigh your partner.

Fig. 8 Children learn to look for and apply a law in Physics (from Nuffield Physics Year 1, Longman Group Ltd, 1978).

towards stressing oral competence. Instead of the turgid grammar-bound books of yesteryear based on the traditions of Latin teaching, a modern language teacher today may choose from a vast selection of books, flashcards, filmstrips, tapes and audio-visual courses which make use of sound tapes of native speakers and pictures of scenes in the country whose language is being studied. Some schools have had language laboratories installed which offer each pupil a booth containing a tape recorder, whilst the teacher sits at a console and is able to monitor individuals or talk to the whole class. Many courses currently on the market stress everyday life in the country being studied, and children learn the conversation necessary for shopping, travel, family life and leisure (see Figure 9).

English teaching in secondary schools has become very broad, and English teachers may find themselves doing a wide range of children's fiction and adult literature, creative writing, drama, developing oral skills and self-confidence and a host of other assignments. The Bullock Report 'A Language for Life' in 1975 stressed that every teacher was responsible for teaching language, on the grounds that it was better for a Physics or Maths teacher to explain what 'inversely proportional' meant when it occurred in a lesson, rather than opt out claiming that the English teacher would have to deal with it one day. Nevertheless a great deal of responsibility for language development still does fall on the shoulders of English teachers.

For several years there had been a tendency for some English teachers to react vigorously against language work, partly because of the tedious emphasis on clause analysis, punctuation and spelling which had made English lessons unpopular in many secondary schools. Since the Bullock Report time spent on language has tended to increase. More English teachers will now try to teach the higher skills of reading and will attempt to sensitise children to the effects of various language choices. For example a class may study several letters sent to a person, some pompous, some long-winded, some flippant, some insulting, and discover how words are used to convey messages and what impact they have on the recipient (see, for example, Figure 10).

120

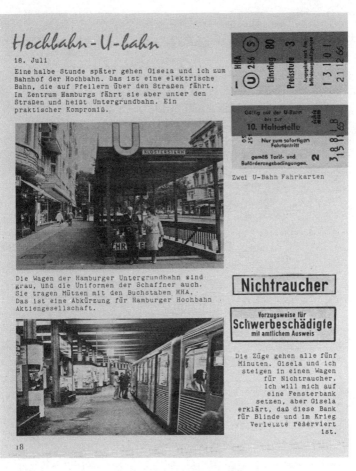

Hochbahn - U-bahn

18. Juli

Eine halbe Stunde später gehen Gisela und ich zum
Bahnhof der Hochbahn. Das ist eine elektrische
Bahn, die auf Pfeilern über den Straßen fährt.
Im Zentrum Hamburgs fährt sie aber unter den
Straßen und heißt Untergrundbahn. Ein
praktischer Kompromiß.

Zwei U-Bahn Fahrkarten

Die Wagen der Hamburger Untergrundbahn sind
grau, und die Uniformen der Schaffner auch.
Sie tragen Mützen mit den Buchstaben HHA.
Das ist eine Abkürzung für Hamburger Hochbahn
Aktiengesellschaft.

Nichtraucher

Vorzugsweise für
Schwerbeschädigte
mit amtlichem Ausweis

Die Züge gehen alle fünf
Minuten. Gisela und ich
steigen in einen Wagen
für Nichtraucher.
Ich will mich auf
eine Fensterbank
setzen, aber Gisela
erklärt, daß diese Bank
für Blinde und im Krieg
Verletzte reserviert
ist.

18

Fig. 9   An extract from *Reise nach Hamburg*, Eric Orton (Longman,
1968).

Similarly they may study different accounts of the same political, social or sporting occasion in a number of newspapers to see
how writers of various persuasions describe the same events.

Other subjects too have seen changes or pressure for more to
be included in their syllabus. Pupils studying History or Geog-

PROBLEM 4

The situation:

You are attending a basketball game with a boy you like very much. One of the players, Ed Shannon, dribbles and shoots equally well with both his right and left hand. Your boyfriend turns to you and says, "I've never seen a player as amphibious as Shannon."

Your language choices:

1) "Amphibious? You *must* be kidding! That means something that can live on land and in water!"
2) "I think you mean *ambidextrous,* Bob."
3) "Yes, he is amphibious, isn't he?"
4) "Yes, he is *ambidextrous,* isn't he?"

Fig. 10 Learning to use language: children choose from various alternatives and discuss the likely effects of their choice (from *Exploring Your Language*, N. Postman, Holt, Rinehart & Winston, 1966).

raphy may do their own survey work, consulting archives, old newpapers, interviewing local farmers or shopkeepers, going on field trips to see industrial archaeology or geographical features. Local history and geography may figure prominently in the early stages of secondary schools, and urban geography – the study of housing, roadways, the location of precincts, factories and supermarkets, has become a legitimate part of some pupils' lessons.

Religious education has often been widened in multiracial schools to include a comparative study of other religious beliefs, or sometimes to include moral education in an attempt to equip

Type of programme	Viewing times, p.m.							
	4/5	5/6	6/7	7/8	8/9	9/10	10/11	11/12
News and talks on current affairs								
Talks on other serious subjects								
Documentaries								
Serious music								
Lighter music								
Pop music								
Opera and ballet								
Serious plays								
Comedy and music-hall								
Serials								
Old films								
Religious services								
Sport								
Quiz and panel games								
Children's programmes								

Fig. 11   Studying media: children analyse and discuss their television viewing habits, using the above documentation as a starting point (from *Life in Our Society*, Vol. 2, K. Lambert, Nelson, 1975).

children with a sense of right and wrong. For other teachers religious education remains exclusively the study of Christianity. Realising that this, the one compulsory subject in school, can be a contentious area, local authorities either draw up an agreed syllabus negotiated between teachers, advisers, representatives of the church and others, or adopt a syllabus prepared by another LEA. Some forms of agreed syllabus are very wide indeed, including several world religions and even permitting reference to communism, always guaranteed to provoke a burst of letters when announced in the press. Special conditions attached to Religious Education in controlled and aided schools, and governors' responsibilities in this instance are described in Chapter 1.

In addition to what might be called the traditional secondary school subjects there are several hybrids or new areas, some of which are described below:

Humanities/Social Studies
Often this combines geography, history and perhaps another subject. Pupils may study a theme like 'transport', 'housing', 'man in society', 'machines and our lives' with reference to our own and other societies, including primitive tribes. Although several commercially produced courses exist many teachers have worked together to improvise their own.

Media Studies
Children will spend hours of their lives watching television, yet until recently almost nothing was done in school to encourage discrimination. Television in particular, radio and newspapers to a lesser degree, inform and shape children's attitudes to a variety of issues, offer heroes and villains and influence their money spending and leisure habits. A media studies course might involve pupils in learning how to make television and radio programmes, understanding how news programmes or newspapers are put together, learning the tricks used by advertisers and politicians to persuade buyers or voters, analysing popular entertainment shows, and seeing how important mass media are in our daily lives (see, for example, Figure 11).

Political education
One of the fears expressed wherever political education is mentioned is that it will result in biased teachers indoctrinating pupils with the philosophy of whichever political party they happen to favour. Most people advocating some systematic teaching about politics do not see it in this light, their intention being rather to look at politics as the use of power in any society including our own. Thus how decisions are made locally, nationally or internationally is of central interest, and party

politics is but one part of this concern. In a true democracy, it is argued, adults must understand the decision-making process. Rather than listen to tedious lectures about Parliament or what rates are used for, pupils may well simulate some local problem, where to build a shopping centre or a motorway, and role play the various parties involved as money is raised, plans devised, votes cast and objections heard. Pupil governors are receiving political education by participating in governors' meetings.

Social education
In some schools departments called 'Personal relationships' have been established and social education is built into the timetable. In others it is not formally scheduled and taught, but is part of what is sometimes called the 'hidden curriculum', a phrase devised to describe the many things schools teach and children learn which are not officially on the timetable of lessons. For example, if one feels a sense of lurking violence on the premises of a particular school, the building is vandalised, pupils barged out of the way along corridors, wall displays tatty, crumbling and defaced and no-one apparently cares, there seems to be a powerful message that human beings do not count, that disorder is acceptable and that concern for others is not to be encouraged. If on the other hand, the school clearly is concerned about the welfare of its members, that children are not bullied, that those of modest ability are not scoffed at, that privacy can be respected or that a craftsman's pride in collective achievement is permissible, then important social education is taking place every time an insensitive pupil is counselled.

Health education
Doctors tell us that adults are often astonishingly ill-informed about the workings of their own body, pregnant mothers unaware that smoking may cause smaller babies, obese middle-aged men ignorant of the consequences of lack of exercise, drinkers not knowledgeable about the effects on the body's vital organs of excessive alcohol, and people on high dosages of amphetamines or barbiturates apparently not realising they have a problem.

125

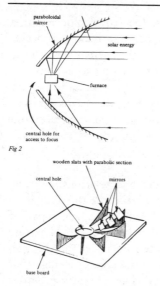

framework of wooden sections each having the required parabolic shape cut in it. See fig 3. On this framework may be tacked an open mesh of, say, chicken wire. To save weight, the space between this wire and the sections may be filled tightly with paper and then the wire covered with wet plaster. When set, the surface may be roughly sanded down.

3 Liquid spun in a shallow rotating cylinder takes up the form of a paraboloid. Mirrors are produced, at a professional level, by spinning thermosetting polyester resins in this way.

Producing a reflecting surface

The surface may be covered with aluminium foil which can easily be kept polished but it should be glued tightly to the surface so that it does not peel off.

Using individual mirrors, the reflecting surface may be assembled piecemeal. Front-aluminized mirrors are preferable; rear-reflecting glass mirrors absorb too much energy during the transmission stage. The mirrors may be made by gluing aluminium foil to small glass plates, the size and shape of these plates depending upon the size of the mirror and the necessity to cover the whole surface.

Supporting the mirror

Fig 1 suggests one possible way by which this can be accomplished. The motors may be connected to push buttons but a more sophisticated arrangement utilizes photocells to sense the position of the sun. These cells would operate the motors via relays.

Fig. 12   Learning to use solar energy (from Schools Council Project Technology, Brief 23, Heinemann Educational, 1975).

Some interesting work on all aspects of health education is being undertaken in many schools nowadays, and whilst information alone will not necessarily prevent abuse of the human body, it may help in those cases where people might unwittingly do themselves a mischief through their own ignorance.

There are many other interesting innovations in curriculum both at primary and secondary level, and it is impossible to describe in such a short space all the work being done in the creative arts, the sciences, technology, business studies and a host of other fields. (An example from the Schools Council Project Technology can be seen in Figure 12).

Curriculum development

Twenty years ago it was possible to be reasonably knowledge-able about the most commonly used teaching materials in a

126

particular field such as junior school maths, backward readers, Russian, 'A' level Physics or 'O' level History. The position today is that no single individual can possibly know all that is produced for schools.

Throughout the 1960s and 1970s thousands of new textbooks, audio-visual courses and multi-media kits were produced in Britain, and several overseas imports from the USA, Europe or Australia added to the mass of available material.

Many of the new ideas were produced by teachers, advisers or teacher trainers who took their ideas to commercial publishers, but others were brought out by teams of developers funded by bodies such as the Nuffield Foundation and the Schools Council. Other groups such as oil companies, other big business conglomerates or private endowments provided finance for curriculum development, sometimes on a sizeable scale. Occasionally a project would begin under the aegis of one body and continue with financial support from another.

The Nuffield Foundation poured substantial sums of money into often quite innovative science and foreign language courses, amongst others, in the 1960s. The scale of funding allowed gifted teachers with sound ideas to be seconded to projects for three or four years, and 'Nuffield Science' with its emphasis on discovery learning, the flexibility of its materials, and inventiveness of its ideas, became a watchword.

Whereas the Nuffield Foundation was a largely privately funded trust based on wealth earned from Morris motors, the Schools Council supported research and curriculum development with money from both the DES and LEAs. Although the Schools Council has often been in the news for its work on public examinations, or throughout its controversial history because of the strong control exerted by teachers' unions, it is best known in schools for its contribution to national curriculum development.

Wider in its scope than any other foundation supporting curriculum development, it has sponsored several major new initiatives, and at any time in its history will be underwriting several more. A few subjects of projects and reports show its wide-ranging influence: mathematics for low attainers, geog-

127

APPLIED MATHS

raphy 14–18, geography for the young school leaver, arts and the adolescent, home economics in the middle years, bilingual education in Wales, effective use of reading, moral education 8 – 13, music education of young children, drama 5 – 11, computers in the curriculum, 'Scope' course for non-English speaking immigrants.

Some of the most interesting curriculum development, however, has been engineered by teachers in their own school. Typically four teachers might work together to devise a home-made course called, say, 'Man in Society'. They will plan a year's work, arrange field trips, make filmstrips, workbooks, invite visiting speakers, using local and national facilities and the resources of the school library or resources centre.

Many schools now have a resources centre, often one which has been fashioned ingeniously and on a low budget from an existing school library. It may contain books, filmstrips, tape-slide sequences which children can study on their own, cuttings from magazines and newspapers, occasionally supplied and catalogued by parent volunteers, as well as videotapes, films and

128

sound tapes. If it has one or two modern duplicating or photo-copying machines it allows teachers to produce booklets and materials of a standard rivalling commercial products, and children to learn from several sources, not merely the teacher's voice and a single textbook.

Postscript

We have several times apologised for the inadequacy of the brief description of some of the recent developments which affect life in school. Inevitably any attempt to encapsulate the vast complexity of what happens in the lessons of over 450,000 teachers in a single chapter must omit a great deal. It would also be wrong to pretend that all the recent developments described above take place in our schools. There are schools which have never changed for years, others which have seen innovation without change (i.e. the introduction of some new curriculum package but with the same strategies used beforehand) and schools dizzy with the whirligig of new courses, changes in organisation and personnel and baffled by their own complexity and fluidity.

Nor would it be correct to say that new ideas invariably ensure outstanding success. We have both in our travels round schools seen brand new audio-visual language courses where the children senselessly and uncomprehendingly chanted French or German phrases over and over again like reluctant conscripts to some junior Nuremberg rally.

Nevertheless despite some poor schools and inadequate tea-chers it is our view that the majority of teachers in both primary and secondary schools have spent a great deal of time and effort attempting to improve children's education in school with considerable success. It will repay conscientious governors handsomely to become as well-informed as they possibly can about what is happening in schools today.

In the following chapter we shall look at some of the issues faced in schools and frequently reported in the press and on television or radio.

5

Issues in education

When in 1976 the Prime Minister of the day called for 'a great debate' about education many lay people outside schools welcomed the opportunity to raise issues of concern or hear others' points of view, and most people inside the system wondered what the fuss was about as a great debate had been going on for years.

This problem lies at the heart of our democratic system. All the matters raised during the so-called 'great debate' which ensued had been discussed exhaustively in school staff rooms, at conferences for teachers, amongst administrators and in national or regional reports for several years previously. Yet people not involved in the teaching profession, parents, employers, tax-payers and ratepayers, had often felt frustration at not being able to take part in such discussions, denied entry to what Sir David Eccles when Minister of Education called 'the secret garden' of the curriculum, accessible only to teachers.

The relationship between professionals and interested but lay parties is in some respects analogous to that obtaining in the medical profession. It would be a bold patient who would instruct the surgeon where to make the incision, but on the other hand he is probably entitled to know whether surgery is the only solution, when he is to be operated on, and to be listened to when describing his symptoms, apprehension or curiosity.

Many of the major issues in education are always with us: what and how shall we teach children? Are we preparing them adequately for adult life? What sort of examination system do we need? Are parents sufficiently well informed about their children's progress? Sometimes, however, it is difficult for governors to join in or even understand the discussion because it may be couched in unfamiliar language.

We are not referring here to the needlessly complex jargon occasionally introduced to make simple issues cloudy by inventing pretentious phrases such as 'learning stimulus materials' (toys), 'materially disadvantaged' (poor), 'endemic reduced placement opportunities' (unemployment) or 'informal decision-making sub-unit' (staffroom bridge four). It is rather that certain changes in the educational system occur suddenly, bringing with them new organisations or terminology sometimes simple in language but difficult to grasp unless one knows the background.

Thus phrases like, 'the school is part of the APU light sampling exercise in science', 'falling rolls could have a devastating effect on our options system', or 'any post-Warnock integration would undoubtedly call for extra resources' are all simple to explain, but might not be fully understood in the first instance.

In this chapter we shall take a number of issues regularly discussed by people connected with schools and sketch a little of the relevant background.

Pastoral care

Looking after the welfare of children has always been a central

131

part of the teacher's job, especially with young children and the phrase 'pastoral care' is commonly used in this connection.

In large schools, where children might easily be lost in the crowd if proper steps were not taken, there is often considerable planning put into looking after children's welfare. Usually the school is broken up into smaller units such as upper, middle and lower school, year groups or houses, and one of the deputy heads may be given special responsibility for pastoral care.

In some schools children have a personal tutor who, if possible, stays with them through more than one year of their career. In others there may be one or more counsellors who spend much of their time advising children about their personal problems, their career or their schoolwork.

The British tradition of counselling is different from the American style. In many American high schools there is a strong and powerful counselling department whose head has deputy principal status. Sometimes there is conflict between the subject teachers and the counsellors about who should advise the pupil on careers or university entrance. On the other hand where the American system works well the pupil has a superb professional service given by trained and caring experts. In Britain there tends to be either no counsellor at all, each teacher being expected to include counselling as part of his repertoire of professional skills, or a single counsellor who works closely with teachers.

The one teacher/one class system in most primary schools allows the class teacher to take full responsibility for each child's schooling and personal welfare. The smallness of a school does not by itself, however, guarantee sound pastoral care, though it is usually there in a natural unpretentious and unsculptured way. Parents usually receive strong messages from their children that teachers either are or are not interested in their welfare.

One problem sometimes arises over records. Schools which pride themselves on good pastoral care may either encourage teachers to keep everything in their heads or to make a detailed record. If, for example, a child has been beaten by a drunken parent and a teacher discovers this he may keep the knowledge to himself. If he leaves, however, a new teacher may not understand why the child is timid and withdrawn. On the other hand if the first teacher, in an attempt to help his colleagues understand the child better, enters a short comment on the pupil's confidential record card, he runs the risk of being accused of biasing his colleagues against the family, or acting on gossip and hearsay. This is a difficult dilemma as one can see problems in any form of record keeping. There is some controversy over whether or not parents should be allowed to see their child's record card. It is arguable whether children's best interests would be served by allowing this on every occasion. In some countries there is a legal requirement that parents be permitted to see such records.

Home and school

Involving parents in school became more fashionable after 1967 when the Plowden Report on primary education stressed their importance. Successive studies of children's achievement in school, both in Britain and elsewhere, show convincingly that parent's attitudes to education are crucial. Irrespective of social class if parents strongly support their children they do much better at school than if they show no interest.

One major stumbling block, however, is that well-meaning parents often do not know how best to help their children. After the Plowden report, a research project at Exeter University involved us in interviewing hundreds of parents about their children's schooling. We discovered great goodwill but massive ignorance about what was happening.

Many parents told us that they deliberately did nothing to prepare their children for school as they had been warned that they might ruin their education. We interviewed teachers to discover what it was that parents did to wreck their children's future. We got only one answer: they taught capital letters and the schools taught the small letters first.

In the light of the interviews several schools decided to write positive letters to parents telling them how they could help prepare children for school, giving tips like 'If your child is interested in learning letters teach him the small ones first', or 'do not push your child to learn things if he does not wish, but many children enjoy helping with shopping, listening to stories, or playing games like picture Lotto, and these are all useful and pleasant ways of preparing for school'.

Other schools put on evenings for parents to discover more about their children's schooling, not in the form of long-winded talks about new curricula, but often based on activity. For example one school showed parents a videotape of a creative writing lesson to demonstrate how children's writing was nurtured. Another put parents into a room set out with junior school science experiments and invited them to pick up a card and do the little experiment on it. Parents spent the evening playing with magnets and iron filings, pouring liquids, discovering about sound and light, and were almost too absorbed to discuss their experiences.

At the end of a year of such experiments at involving parents in their children's education the reaction from teachers and parents was overwhelmingly favourable, and this is a common finding. Many schools which begin apprehensively, wondering if parents will come, are delighted at the response they get.

There are some problems, however. First of all letters of invitation need to be delivered and read. Some children never give their parents the details. In multiracial schools it often helps if community leaders can translate important letters into the appropriate languages, or they may be delivered but not understood.

Secondly the timing must be right. Some parents work shifts and cannot manage a 7.30 meeting, others have small children and a creche or playgroup run by volunteers allow them to come in for an evening or afternoon meeting.

Thirdly the occasion must be worthwhile. The secret of the success of many schools in the Exeter research was that they really involved parents. Even at upper secondary level where the subject matter is difficult some teachers have used the assembly hall, half for the pupils to do their lesson half for the parents to watch and eventually wander round.

One school in an area with massive social problems ran a book club. Children brought small sums of money week by week, and at monthly intervals a good children's bookseller put on a display and they cashed in their savings after school with their parents often in attendance. This allowed high grade reading material to reach children whose homes often contained not a single book. The reading ages of the children climbed spectacularly.

Another school used parent volunteers to collect dinner money, escort children on field trips, help with games coaching and aid teachers building up a collection of magazine articles and newspaper cuttings. With or without a parent-teacher association there is no limit to the ingenuity of teachers who really want to involve parents. The horror stories one occasionally reads of major rows between schools and parents are often, though not always, because parents have not been sufficiently informed of what the school is trying to do.

Almost every parent we interviewed after the Exeter research was full of admiration for teachers, to the surprise of some teachers, who suspected that parents, knowing how tedious and routine school life can be, would be scornful. Parents were full of praise for teachers who coped with thirty or more children when they themselves often struggled with two.

The Advisory Centre for Education (ACE) has sometimes run education shops in shopping precincts and been swamped by enquiries. Despite all the work of the last few years there is still a great deal to be done before parents are fully in the picture, and many schools have already shown the way with good school reports, interesting evenings, easy informal communication and teachers who take the trouble to get to know the district and community where their children live.

Multiracial education

In many city classrooms in Britain one finds a mixture of

children from all sorts of races, from Britain, Europe, West Indies, Asia and Africa. The concept of multiracial education is that teachers will take into account their great variety of backgrounds.

If one looks at what is offered in the curriculum it sometimes has an exclusively British look about it. History, for example, may be about Sir Francis Drake, Nelson and Disraeli; religious education may deal only with Christianity; English may concern itself with Dickens, Wordsworth and Ted Hughes.

Those who advocate multiracial education are not arguing that 'if people want to live in this country they just have to fit in', nor, on the other hand, are they suggesting that the curriculum should be dominated by studies of Islam, the history of black Africa, soul music or the politics of South-East Asia, but rather that there should be some respect for the traditions of various ethnic groups, and that the commitment to mutual tolerance in our society is a worthy ideal.

There are many ways of working towards this objective. Schools often begin by involving parents of all communities in the life of the school as described earlier in this chapter, and by recognising important cultural differences: that certain foods may not be eaten, that girls are not allowed out unescorted at night in some cultures, that families may wish to observe their own religious festivals.

Another possibility is to feature the customs of various groups in some public way, so that children may perform folk dances, sing songs, act plays, read poetry or show and talk about religious ceremonies in their own region. Some teachers will offer options within their course which may be of special interest to certain pupils.

In the United States it was fashionable in the late 1960s to offer 'black studies' or 'parallel history'. When the class studied the civil war or the pioneers there would be some attempt to see what the ancestors of black pupils might have been doing at the same time, to see whether they were in slavery, living in Africa or the West Indies, or enjoying improved rights. Part of the popularity of the television serial *Roots*, which claimed to trace the ancestry of a black American, lay in the nostalgic longing of that ethnic group to learn of its own history.

Some teachers will go even further and attempt to tackle directly issues such as racial prejudice with classes. This needs skilful handling, but if well done can contribute a great deal to harmonious race relations in a community.

Integrating the handicapped

The education of mentally and physically handicapped children is an important matter which has received a great deal of publicity in recent times. Some of the debate has centred around the question of whether such children should be taught in special schools or with the rest of their group in ordinary primary and secondary schools.

One problem which has bedevilled special education for years is the low aspiration which adults have had for handicapped children. For fear of expecting too much they have sometimes expected too little. Those who believe in integration often argue that children's horizons would be raised in normal schools, whereas critics of integration feel that the opposite might occur, that away from the controlled environment of the special school they might become overawed by their high achieving fellows and opt out altogether.

In 1978, after lengthy deliberation, the Warnock committee reported on the educational provision for handicapped children. There had been some anxiety that section 10 of the 1976 Education Act appeared to require speedy integration of handicapped children into ordinary schools. The Warnock report, whilst endorsing that handicapped children can and should be integrated, did not support immediate massive transfer without proper preparation having taken place, and recommended that the DES should first offer comprehensive guidance to LEAs. The report mentions different kinds of integration from permanent ordinary classes but with proper support facilities, to classes containing only special education pupils but with the possibility of social contacts with the other children in the school. It still sees a place for some continued existence of special schools which would 'feature prominently in the provision for children with special educational needs'.

Some countries have already integrated many if not all handicapped children into ordinary schools. It has been done for some time, for example, in Sweden, and there has been some considerable movement towards integration in many regions of the United States, so that one might find over 100 handicapped pupils in a High School of 4000 pupils, some with cerebral palsy or more severe handicap.

If a degree of integration takes place there are several implications for schools. Premises may need altering to take wheelchairs or be safer for the blind, teachers need to learn about mental and physical handicap, specialist teachers need to be available who have been properly trained in the field, and close liaison with medical and social services is essential.

Furthermore the many specialist organisations for blind, deaf and other specific handicaps need to be mobilised. Most people are often astonished, for example, to discover how many books have been put on cassette or produced in Braille editions, and how many aids are available from the various providers, until they encounter a handicapped person for the first time. Although the prospect of a greater degree of integration is daunting and there is no universal agreement about its desirability, those many schools and colleges which have already begun the process have frequently, albeit after an initially difficult period, become very committed to their policy. In schools where significant numbers of handicapped children are to be found it is worth considering having on the governing body someone from the area health authority staff to facilitate communication between the health and education services.

Disruptive pupils

'I don't know what to do with him, but if anyone else tells me he's from a difficult home background I shall scream', said one teacher after dealing with a very anti-social fourteen-year-old boy. This is the dilemma a classroom teacher faces, on the one hand feeling sorry for someone who in his family life is clearly up against it, on the other hand angry at his bullying, vile language or interruption of others going peacefully about their business.

There are several kinds of disruptive pupil and many different ways of dealing with severe disruption. We are referring here not to the mild bit of cheek or inattention one finds everywhere at some time, but to the kind of pupil whose name is on every teacher's lips, and who has the ability, in full flow, to bring lessons to a complete standstill.

Disruptive behaviour is not usually caused by a single factor. For example, one might say that a pupil who does not understand what is happening in lessons will become anti-social, but there will be several others in a similar position who merely stare into space uncomprehendingly. It is usually some combination, therefore, of elements such as boredom, dislike of school in general or a teacher or other pupils in particular, problems at home, and an aggressive or attention-seeking personality, which produces disruption.

Sadly, violent behaviour does appear to run in families, and parents who beat their children have often themselves been subjected in their childhood to brutality by their own parents. A child used to the rule of the fist can be extraordinarily difficult to handle, as school sanctions are far less punitive than what he is used to, and he may simply not know yet how to respond to kindness and interest, having not encountered them before.

One remedy frequently tried is to ignore bad behaviour, but respond favourably and publicly to good behaviour, however unspectacular it may be. In some schools both in Britain and the United States there has been some success with reward systems whereby badly behaved pupils are given tokens for listening to others, waiting their turn, sitting still, getting on with their work and so on, eventually being allowed to cash in their tokens for prizes such as privileges or sweets. Perhaps obesity and dental decay are a fair swap for disruptive behaviour.

Amongst other ideas found in schools is a 'time out' or 'sin bin' system. As some disruptive pupils are hyperactive and quick to lose their self-control, a cooling off period can sometimes help. The pupil leaves the clasroom to go to a special unit with a teacher particularly skilful at dealing with difficult pupils. After a short or longer interlude he returns to his class. This method can work well but it needs extraordinarily sensitive handling, otherwise weak teachers opt out of their responsibilities, and the system becomes a game.

In some schools teachers become very punitive, using the whole range of agreed school sanctions: withdrawal of privileges, detention, extra work or corporal punishment. Although this too can occasionally be effective it can also result in an even more sullen and anti-social pupil, and many teachers prefer trying to win the child's confidence and respect, however wearing this may be.

Indeed some of the more notable successes have been achieved by teachers who have struggeled to get through to very disturbed pupils, sometimes with the assistance of the child guidance service. There has been a significant change in the way many schools psychologists prefer to work. Whereas formerly it was accepted that problem children would be taken out of school and sent to a clinic where the psychologist would work his wizardry, a number of specialists in child guidance, though by no means all, prefer now, wherever possible, to work with the teachers in the school and tackle problems where they occur. When this works well teachers and psychologists find they have a much higher regard for each other, and a better understanding of what needs to be done both to help the disruptive pupil and protect his fellows.

If all else fails there are still some possible lines of attack. A child may be transferred to another school, which, though it often merely passes on the problem, can occasionally give a genuinely fresh start. If a child is judged to be seriously maladjusted he may be sent to a specialist school for maladjusted children or to a school which has a special unit, if one is available in the district.

Should the pupil be in trouble with the police the child's future may in any case be in the hands of the courts if he is to be put into care or sent away into detention. If there is a problem in the child's whole family, there is a new and now well-established tradition in some areas of whole family treatment, using psychiatric social workers if necessary.

The National Association of Schoolmasters has made the suggestion that one way for teachers to be able to gain the respect of really hard-core problem pupils is for them to be together in the kind of residential field centre where there is a great deal to do and a warm sense of team spirit might develop. For teachers robust enough to take on the assignment this is a useful idea and appears to have worked well in a number of cases.

No-one should underestimate, however, the wear and tear on the whole community, teachers and pupils alike, caused by the presence of one or two really disruptive pupils. There are no easy solutions, and the problems of disaffection, violence and anti-social behaviour, especially amongst adolescents of fourteen or fifteen, remain amongst our most pressing social problems.

Formal or informal?

Amongst issues which regularly arouse discussion in the press is the question of teaching methods. Is traditional teaching better than progressive teaching? Are formal methods better than informal methods? The debate was fuelled in 1976 by the appearance of Neville Bennett's Lancaster study in which he found that children taught formally in the primary school did better on tests of basic skills than those taught informally (*Teaching Styles and Pupil Progress*, Open Books, 1976).

Definitions of 'traditional' and 'progressive' or 'formal' and 'informal' are not commonly agreed, but there are some features one can describe. At its crudest a formal style implies rows of desks facing the front, the teacher addressing the whole class, all the children engaged on the same task, no freedom of movement without the teacher's permission, stress on competition and academic achievement, and regular testing.

An equally rough and ready caricature of informal teaching

141

suggests tables placed around the room in no particular order, children working individually or in small groups, the teacher walking around monitoring what they are doing, freedom for children to go to the resources area, to paint, do Maths, pursue their project, or to read as they decide, stress on co-operation and social development, and individual records of each child's progress.

One reason why the discussion sometimes causes wrath is that we all like to believe we were fairly well educated, or at least that what happened to us did us no harm, and that anything different might be an experiment on children, a raw deal for society, or even a needless risk.

As ever the argument often centres around stereotypes which barely exist. Most teachers use a mixture of styles, addressing the whole class when appropriate, sometimes working in groups, allowing freedom of movement in certain phases of the lesson but not others, and determining what children do on some occasions whilst allowing choices on others. Fears that the education system is saturated with way-out informal teachers whose classes never do any decent work are exaggerated.

Estimates of the spread of informal teaching vary between one in six and the one in twenty reported in the DES primary school survey in 1978. Furthermore some informally taught classes work very hard indeed, and in the Neville Bennett study it was an informal teacher whose class showed the highest gains in achievement out of the whole sample.

Teachers can often succeed using any style of teaching to which they are strongly committed. What is critical is not so much the style, but the skill with which it is applied. Informal teaching is very difficult to do well and demands a great deal of the teacher, who needs good class management, great mobility, proper record keeping and considerable inventiveness.

We once did a case study of the informal teacher whose children obtained highest gains in the Bennett study. She had excellent relationships with her class, and ensured that everyone worked hard by getting around to every pupil and sometimes publicly taking stock. She would, for example, review progress

142

by saying suddenly, 'Now you two are doing your maths, and John and Peter you're still working on assembly, Mary I think it's probably about time you were leaving that'. It was a light touch but everyone knew that she had a complete grasp of each child's progress. The work-rate of her pupils was the highest we ever recorded in either a formal or an informal classroom.

It is true, unfortunately, that the lessons of teachers who attempt informal teaching and are not able to handle it with skill can be very unproductive. Children slow-time the teacher by spinning out a half-hour task into a half or whole day, and learn very little else, other than to dislike the school. Equally, however, an unskilled formal teacher can bore children to distraction by talking most of the time and allowing little or no individual work.

At the heart of skilful informal teaching often lies sensitive handling of project work. A project is undertaken either by the whole class or on an individual or small group basis. Thus a primary school class may spend a few weeks doing a project on 'our village', but individuals may opt for something of personal interest like 'horses', 'railways' or 'farming'.

By devoting a considerable amount of time to projects which have captured their imagination children will read and write a great deal, and will have to learn how to find and use information, as well as how to organise their time. A teacher's scheme for a class project on 'our village' shows how wide-ranging the topic can be when properly planned and thought out (see Figure 13).

The formal versus informal debate will continue, but no-one has yet proved conclusively that a way of operating by itself is critical. The Bennett study was based on only twelve formal and thirteen informal teachers, and the superiority of the formally taught group is in doubt not only because of the smallness of the sample, but also because the samples were not properly matched at the outset, the formally taught classes having a higher initial achievement than the informally taught ones.

Nevertheless the Bennett study was a well conducted piece of research, and questions about teaching methods must always be asked by both professionals and the lay public. Such questioning is entirely healthy provided that sensibly worked out new teaching methods, thought to be more effective, or more suitable to changed conditions or improvements in our knowledge, are permitted. Schools where nothing changes are as undesirable as those where nothing is ever the same, and new methods can only prove themselves if given a decent chance to run and if subjected to regular and deliberate evaluation.

Grouping for teaching and learning

'Setting', 'streaming', 'banding', 'mixed ability teaching' are all terms used to describe how children are grouped in schools. Most primary schools use classes of mixed ability, and in recent years this pattern has spread to a number of secondary schools. It is perhaps most helpful to give a short description of the meaning of each of these terms, in so far as there is any agreement about them, and to mention some advantages and disadvantages commonly attributed to each.

Streaming was for many schools the traditional way of grouping pupils. Some indication of *general* ability was sought; it might be an IQ score or, more likely, it would be the child's performance in end of year exams. Thus the brightest children were put into the A stream, the next brightest into the B stream, and so on, right down to the D or E stream, or even the fourteenth or fifteenth stream in a few very large secondary schools. The advantages seemed to be that the teacher, having a thin band of the ability range in his class, could keep children occupied at the appropriate level, stretching the brightest and moving slowly with lower streams. Critics argued that the system was insensitive as some pupils are good at maths, poor at French or vice-versa, and led to the 'self-fulfilling prophecy' whereby children in the D stream, feeling they are the 'sink' or the 'thickies', become anti-social and unambitious. A further problem was the low transfer rate between streams, which meant pupils placed in a low or high stream were probably destined to stay there.

144

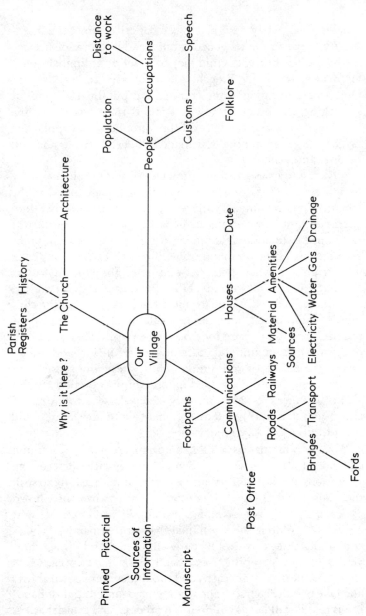

Fig. 13 A project diagram showing how the topic Our Village might be studied (from *Changing the Primary School*, John Blackie, Macmillan (London and Basingstoke), 1974).

145

Setting was partly designed to combat criticism of the insensitivity of streaming by general ability and is a form of streaming by *specific* ability. A child may be in set 3 for English, set 1 for maths, set 2 for French, set 5 for science, and so on. Objectors argue that some children are put in high sets for everything and others in low sets for all their lessons, so the 'sink' mentality and the self-fulfilling prophecy still apply, the bright get better and the dull are given lower horizons and still become anti-school.

Mixed ability was an attempt to give everyone a fair chance by having classes containing the whole ability range found in the school. Thus on intake children will be put randomly into classes all containing a mixture of backgrounds and abilities. It was hoped that this would remove the difficult D stream problem, and avoid the premature labelling of children as bright or dull at an age when poor self-esteem might crucially affect learning. Critics of mixed ability grouping argue that the assignment is too difficult for most teachers, that bright children become bored, and the less able are left behind as the teacher struggles to cater for the average pupil. They also point to the massive amount of preparatory and recording work necessary if the teacher is to do mixed ability teaching sensitively, ensuring each child is engaged in something appropriate to his ability and interests. Most primary school classes are now mixed ability and there is continuing argument about how far it should spread into secondary schools.

Banding is for many schools a compromise between streaming and mixed ability teaching. Sympathising with some of the aspirations of mixed ability enthusiasts, but not wishing to span the whole ability range, they operate usually two or three broad bands of ability. For example a school with an entry of eight classes of children each year may have three bands, band 1 containing three classes of brighter children, band 2 with three classes of average ability, and band 3 having two classes of slower learners. Within each band the classes are of equal ability and take parallel courses. The argument advanced against banding is that is still labels children as A, B or C, and transfer across bands can present difficulties.

Other possibilities. People can be grouped for learning in any way one chooses. For many years children were grouped by *sex* with boys and girls educated separately. We take it for granted that children of the *same age* should be educated together irrespective of their ability, yet in some primary schools 'vertical' or 'family' grouping is practised, whereby 5 to 7-year-olds are put together and there has been a remarkable breed of practitioner in one and two-teacher rural schools who has coped with 5 to 11 or even 5 to 15-year-olds in the same class. In smaller sixth forms 16 to 19-year-olds may be in the same group, and adult education caters for evening classes containing adolescents, the middle-aged and retired people, from 13 or 14 up to 70 or 80.

Amongst other criteria which may one day in the future figure more prominently are:

Personality. It is known that extraverts and introverts learn differently, but personality grouping has rarely been tried, though often advocated. One speculates about the possibility one day of leaping extraverts and a high adrenalin teacher in one room, whilst next door shy introverts hide under their desks and a blushing teacher peeps out from behind a cupboard. It is a more serious issue than this, however, and deserves a serious trial.

Learning style. Some people like a syllabus to follow, work methodically through checklists or pages of sums, others enjoy freewheeling, exploring, rejecting the constraints of a syllabus. Learning style is related to personality and can be said to be a manifestation of it. The day may come when reflective children work in one group and impulsive ones work together in another, though many teachers would argue that the mixture of styles in the same class is an important part of the group's chemistry and children's social education.

Teachability was a term used by Thelen, an American investigator, who put together teachers and pupils who enjoyed being with each other, on the grounds that human relations are important in learning, and if these are right all else may flow

147

from it. It could be embarrassing for a pupil or teacher unloved by anyone, but is an interesting notion nevertheless.

Most of the debate about grouping in recent times has centred on the question of mixed ability teaching, seen by its supporters as the long-term solution to inequality in schools and by opponents as an improper attempt at social engineering. A DES discussion paper based on visits to schools by HMI and published in 1978 was very critical of mixed ability teaching, saying that there was too much whole class teaching, and that only the most skilled teachers were doing it successfully.

Teachers of mathematics and French often opted out of the mixed ability pattern (though a few did not with conspicuous success) on the grounds that these are linear subjects. In order to learn B you must have learned A first, it was said; and certainly it is the case that in most secondary schools which do have mixed ability classes for the first two or three years the mathematicians and linguists are likely to prefer setting from the beginning or after the first year.

Successful teachers of mixed ability classes use a judicious mixture of whole class teaching, individual and small group work, and spend many hours creating workbooks, workcards, and resource material. Almost invariably they keep detailed records of children's work.

There is a shortage of hard evidence about how well mixed ability teaching works because it is an extremely difficult area in which to conduct reliable research. It has been the norm for many years in Sweden and the United States, and in primary schools in Britain. Indeed the reason why some interesting teaching emerged in secondary school mixed ability work was the happy accident that half the nation's primary school teachers seemed to be married to half its secondary force. A study at Banbury school in Oxfordshire found some positive gains for mixed ability teaching.

There can be no hard and fast rule about grouping children for learning; what suits one school is simply not appropriate for another. A key factor, however, is the commitment of those who have to work whatever system your school favours.

Specialisation

By comparison with many other countries the British educational system is very condensed, and this has partly been due to early specialisation which has narrowed choices for pupils at 13 or 14 by asking them to choose between, say, more science, another language and practical subjects. Thus the third year secondary pupil would be making a critical decision which might already be determining whether he will eventually join the Arts or Science sixth form, or what job he may take when he leaves school.

At the 16-plus stage he will probably specialise in two, three or four subjects, (whereas his counterpart in many European countries or in the USA would still be studying in several fields), and at 18 he may go on to complete a three-year degree programme. Meanwhile a similar student elsewhere might at 19 embark on a four-year degree course, or, in Germany for example, on an open-ended university career which might last for at least six or seven years. This early specialisation in Britain produces graduates at 21 as compared with the 23-, 24- or 25-year-old graduates abroad.

Critics of early specialisation have tried to secure a broader curriculum through revision of the examination system. Various sixth form examination patterns have been proposed over the years, some necessitating an Arts/Science mix, others requiring the sixth former to take exams at two levels, say some 'A' levels and further 'O' levels, or, as in the Schools Council proposals made in the late 1970s, three subjects at Normal (N) and two at Further (F) level. Some educationists favour the pattern of the International Baccalaureate, which not only requires pupils to study a wider range of subjects, but has an added recommendation of being widely accepted abroad, particularly in the EEC, in an age when international recognition of qualifications obtained in various countries is becoming increasingly important.

The notion of specialisation is also related to the question of choice in the curriculum. In the light of the many changes in society, the impossibility of learning all there is to know in a

149

field of knowledge, and the lack of central control of the curriculum in Britain, where teachers tend to have greater autonomy than in many countries in Europe and elsewhere, some people have argued for a common core curriculum for all in the early years of schooling, and a pattern of school and personal options.

Some advocates of a core curriculum, for example, propose that all pupils should spend a certain period of the week covering an agreed syllabus in subjects such as Mathematics, English, French, Science and Humanities, this being the core. Individual schools would be free thereafter to teach whatever they wished in these subjects and others, but the core would be covered everywhere. A series of options would be available to pupils to meet the criticism that the next generation was only being programmed with state-approved knowledge. In 1980 the DES produced a consultative paper, 'A Framework for the School Curriculum', which proposed a core containing at least 10 per cent of time in each of Maths, English, Science and a foreign language, as well as some physical and religious education for all. At the same time, a discussion paper written by HMI entitled 'A View of the Curriculum' endorsed the notion of a national consensus about a compulsory core.

One major problem in the debate about specialisation is identifying the elements which affect children's choices. When pupils have to choose at 13 or 15 whether to do more science or take another foreign language they are influenced by several factors such as the quality of teaching in various subjects, their friends' choices, their parents' views, and occasionally some whim or chance, like having scored an A in one subject the week during which the decision is made.

Consequently unexciting science teaching and outstanding English teaching in a school may produce a dearth of science and a glut of English specialists. Similarly strong sex stereotyping, whereby it is subtly suggested that girls ought not to do science, for example, can bring about the situation which has occurred in Britain producing in the late 1970s about 25,000 boys taking 'A' level Physics and only 5,000 or so girls. Yet in other countries girls may take science on the same scale as boys and go on in sizeable numbers to become engineers, technicians or nuclear physicists. The Equal Opportunities Act, which made it illegal for someone to be denied the opportunity to take a subject on offer in the school on the grounds of sex alone, as well as some changes in attitude generally, have led to more girls specialising in science and technology in recent times. The DES secondary school survey in 1979 criticised some schools for offering too many choices and for allowing premature specialisation.

Tests and examinations

The concern for accountability in education often tends to focus on examinations and testing. Tests, it is argued, will show whether or not schools are delivering the goods and there is some support for this idea. Dissenters on the other hand point to the evils of the 'payment by results' system in use before the turn of the century, when schools for poorer children were starved of resources and this served to compound rather than alleviate children's misfortune.

In the 1960s and 1970s there was a massive shift in the public examining pattern. The 11+ examination, designed to help local authorities assign pupils to secondary schools, declined sharply as comprehensive reorganisation spread, but the 16+ increased considerably over the same period. Whereas formerly about 20 or 25 per cent of the age group would take a public examination like the GCE 'O' level, the establishment of the Certificate of Secondary Education (CSE), originally aimed at the next lower 40 per cent of the school population, meant that the position changed rapidly. By the late 1970s about 85 per cent of pupils were leaving school having taken 'O' level or CSE examinations. The 'O' level is graded from A to E, with grade C or above often described as a 'pass'. The CSE is graded 1 to 5, and a grade 1 is accepted as at least the equivalent of a grade C 'O' level. Thus pupils aiming to enter a profession or higher education need to secure 'O' level grades of C or better, or CSE

151

grade 1 passes.

At the time of writing proposals which would affect examining at both 16 and 18 are under discussion. A fusion of GCE and CSE to be called the General Certificate of Secondary Education (GCSE) has been proposed and might come about in the 1980s. This proposal for common examining at 16+ has been supported by many people, but anxieties have been voiced about a single examination catering for some 60 per cent or probably more of the ability range. At 18+ the N and F proposals, as described above, were rejected by the government in 1979.

Any new system, if adopted, would be administered by a smaller number of examining boards than the GCE and CSE system. One problem of having over twenty different examining boards is that syllabuses can vary considerably, and it becomes difficult to keep standards constant from year to year, and between the various boards and different subjects. It is commonly believed, and was reported in the Parliamentary Select Committee report of 1977 on the Attainments of School Leavers, that Physics appeared to be harder to pass than Biology and that one or two boards are thought to be easier or harder than others. It should be said that the examining boards do make great efforts to ensure comparability, though they have been somewhat resistant to suggestions of monitoring by an outside body.

Another major change in public examining occurred when CSE was put more firmly in the hands of teachers than had been the case with GCE which was influenced by universities. At the same time many Germans, used to the strong teacher control of the Abitur, the school leaving examination, greatly admire the British GCE system and often seek to copy it. A new principle, called mode 3, was established when CSE was set up. In CSE and GCE mode 1 is the system most people know: the board determines the syllabus and sets and marks the exam. Mode 2, which existed in GCE but was rarely used, allowed teachers to propose a syllabus but the board would examine it. What was new about mode 3, now available in GCE too, was that teachers could determine the syllabus, the form of examination and do the first marking, subject to outside moderation. At its best teacher-controlled examining allows flexible teaching and appropriate testing; at its worst it can cause anxiety amongst both parents and pupils if they suspect favouritism or bias.

Public examinations are, however, but one part of the assessment process, as local and national monitoring has become more widespread. The DES has established an Assessment of Performance Unit (APU) which is committed to assessing Mathematics, English, Science and Modern Languages by testing a sample of children throughout the country. More difficult areas to measure such as aesthetic, social and physical development are also being considered.

Several local authorities also undertake monitoring exercises, and the Parliamentary Select Committee on the Attainments of School Leavers suggested that two key points at which local authority monitoring might take place were towards the end of the primary phase, and part way through the fourth year of the secondary school. The advantage of regional monitoring is that it can be designed more sensitively to suit local conditions. For example some authorities may wish to use diagnostic tests, that is tests which indicate where a pupil needs to improve, as these can be particularly helpful to schools. In many states in the USA a system called 'minimal competency testing' is employed, whereby pupils in high school are given tests in basic skills as well as in areas useful in adult life such as understanding a bank account or using a guide to a state park. Unless they pass the test they will not receive a high school diploma.

Clearly, too strong an emphasis on testing tends to narrow the curriculum with teachers under pressure to coach exclusively for the test. On the other hand a sensible programme of testing can provide useful measures of the extent to which knowledge and skills are being acquired, attitudes are changing, or objectives are being realised.

The suggestion has occasionally been made, even at government level, that the results of either public examination or local monitoring should be published in some kind of league table, as already happens in some parts of the United States. This sounds attractive on the surface, in that it seems likely to keep teachers and pupils on their toes. It is insensitive, however, to the great differences in school catchment areas. There are schools in areas with difficult social problems, recruiting overwhelmingly children with low ability and poor support from home, which would always be bottom of the league no matter how skilful and hard-working their teachers were, and those with a much more education-conscious catchment area who would be near the top of the league however slowly they cruised. There are some remarkable achievements in many schools in difficult areas which would never show up in any league table.

There have been several new developments in testing in the last few years. Whereas in the past many examinations consisted exclusively of essay questions, current techniques include:

Oral tests	Interviews with pupils, tape-recording of conversations in a foreign language etc.
Multiple choice tests	The pupil has to circle the correct answer from a set of several possibilities, only one of which is correct, the others acting as distractors, e.g.

Britain declared war on Germany in 1939 because:

   A The Archduke of Austria was assassinated by a German.

   B Germany and Austria signed a treaty.

   C U-boats had been sinking British passenger ships.

   D Hitler occupied Poland and refused to withdraw.

   E German planes bombed London.

Continuous assessment	*Pupils' work during the year, such as* projects, tests, written work, and laboratory experiments is included as part of the assessment package.

Graded tests

Like the driving test these are pass/fail tests, sometimes called criterion-referenced tests. Instead of gaining a numerical mark the pupil simply passes or fails and may take the examination again until successful. Music examinations have always been organised like this and the idea is spreading. In French, for example, level 1 might be an indication of the pupil's understanding of simple French, level 2 the pupil's ability to sustain simple conversation on everyday topics, level 3 being able to read French, and so on.

From school to work

The transition from school to work can be a rude shock for pupils who have not been properly prepared, and careers advice has been poor in many schools. Some optimistic features can be noted, however. Work experience schemes have spread, and, though varied in quality, have tended to be beneficial provided pupils have been properly looked after in the factory or business where they are sampling the world of work.

In some areas the development of the tertiary college, often a merged further education college and grammar school sixth form, where all aged 16+ who wish may attend for 'A' levels, day release, or for a wide range of full-time or part-time courses, has led to a healthy rubbing of shoulders between those who are at work and attend the college for part-time study and those who are full-time students.

The development of schemes for teachers to spend time in industry has also been helpful in broadening their horizons, but the reverse scheme, attempted in places like Sheffield, which allowed people from industry or commerce to spend time in schools, has gained only limited support. This is a pity because there is often a poor understanding between teachers, who may react against industry and advise pupils to take white collar jobs, and industrialists who frequently lament what is happening in schools whilst knowing little about them. For example, some employers who complain that school leavers today cannot spell or calculate as well as apprentices of thirty years ago, do not realise that many pupils now stay on for further and higher education, and that the little wizards of yesteryear who used to leave school at 14 would nowadays be in a college or university.

The greatest problem of the school to work transition remains the ill-equipped school leaver with no skills to sell in a world which requires them. This disaffected 10 or 15 per cent, a group called by the Department of Employment the 'unqualified, unskilled and unemployed', presents in Britain and in several other industrial countries the most powerful threat to social order of our age. Numerous job creation schemes have helped alleviate the problem, but especially in areas of high unemployment massive demoralisation and eventual delinquency will be inevitable unless all steps are taken to find such pupils useful and rewarding employment. What is encouraging is that a number of people who have failed in school often become highly motivated to learn once they have a worthwhile job and decent prospects.

It is not a solution to anticipate work in school by having a curriculum entirely to prepare people for work. Schools have a duty to provide an all-round education suitable for adult life in all its facets, including work, family and community life and leisure. Narrow emphasis on gas-fitters' English or the mathematics needed by shop assistants would neither benefit the pupil nor please employers, who look for basic skills, a balanced personality, and an interest in learning the specific skills of the job at the appropriate time.

Falling rolls

Until the late 1970s most people thought that falling rolls were what you got when the baker's delivery boy dropped his basket. They are much more devastating than that.

156

From 1954 to 1964 the birth figures climbed steadily, reaching around 900,000 in 1964. Each year after that they dropped steadily and then sharply, falling below 600,000 in the late 1970s and producing the lowest birth cohorts since the 1930s when some people thought that the British would be extinct by the year 2000.

The consequences are clear to see. When the birth figures drop by over one third in quite a short time the effects are bound to ripple right through the educational system. First of all primary school rolls fell in the 1970s as the leaner years began to enter full-time schooling. Secondary schools reached a peak in 1978 or 1979 but must cope with falling rolls throughout the 1980s. Higher education will be affected in the 1990s. Teacher training was also decimated as fewer teachers were required, and many colleges of education were forced to close or merge with universities or polytechnics.

In primary schools the effects were considerable but manageable, as the one teacher—one class system allowed natural wastage when someone left or retired. In secondary schools, where most teachers are subject specialists, the effects will be worse. Promotion will be harder to come by, the school may no longer be able to offer all it could when it was larger, and early retirement and redundancies may have to be faced.

Falling rolls will have different effects on different schools. If one imagines a secondary school of 900 pupils, in an inner-city area where the population is moving away or being rehoused, it may fall to 300 pupils or be closed down. In a more typical area it will drop to 600 pupils. On the other hand if sited in a new town, near an expanding housing estate or a popular suburb, it may stay at 900 or increase to over 1000. On average the drop in many secondary schools will be a quarter to a third between the early and late 1980s, and it is up to the DES and local authorities to plan effectively. Chapter 6 discusses what to do if your school is affected.

If the birthrate continues to increase during the 1980s as is expected, then rising enrolments will begin to affect primary schools from 1983. Rising rolls usually bring a need for temporary classrooms, more teachers and resources, and more new schools. The system could probably cope with the kind of increase being predicted unless annual births went above the 900,000 mark. Governors will, however, hear most about falling rolls in the secondary sector, and this may be their most pressing organisational problem. Those who are not too old might consider breeding for Britain, on the grounds that each new child will provide employment for a twentieth of a teacher or so, and help look after the rest of us in our old age when all the low birthrate years have to work like two people to pay for our vitamin pills and false teeth.

A school on the run

All the issues discussed above pale into insignificance when a school becomes the victim of adverse publicity and finds itself on the run. The effect on staff, pupils, parents and the whole community can be considerable and the mass media play an important role.

The relationship between the educational system and the media is a curious one. For some reason bad news about schools is good news for newspapers, so that teachers are often dismayed when the local press, having ignored all their exam results, the pupils who painted old people's bungalows, or collected a million lollipop sticks for Oxfam, devote half a page to the cult follower excluded from school for turning up with a safety pin through his nose.

William Taylor, writing about the press's negative reaction in the first years of the secondary modern school, cited many extracts from newspaper cuttings in the early days of these schools which gleefully emphasised vandalism, low standards or pieces of scandal. Comprehensive schools have suffered in the same way, as have informal teaching methods and certain new curricula.

For example, the Neville Bennett Lancaster study was given massive television, radio and newspaper coverage, because informal teaching appeared to do less well than formal teaching, even though only twelve formal and thirteen informal teachers were in the sample. A reading survey by Start and Wells which was not well conducted and was strongly criticised in the Bullock Report on language in 1975, was also given extensive coverage because it claimed to have discovered that reading standards had gone down. Reports finding no change or rising standards merit a fraction of the coverage, presumably because they do not sell newspapers.

One of the present writers was once concerned with an independent enquiry into a school set up in response to huge press coverage of criticisms by a small group of parents. Newspapers had devoted pages to the accusations, TV and radio had covered the setting up of the enquiry and national politicians who had never been within 100 miles of the school were calling for dismissals and resignations. When the report of the independent group was published stating that there was no substance to the accusations and that the overwhelming majority of parents supported the school, no national paper showed any interest and TV and radio were silent. Only the local newspapers carried brief reports.

Consequently it is vital for all schools to have good relations and effective communication between staff, parents, local and regional media and governors. It is quite common for governors, head, teachers or parents to be interviewed when some problem has occurred, and if public strife is fuelled it is hard for the school to recover and for scars to be healed.

When angry people write to MPs or the Secretary of State, demand enquiries, say in the press or on TV that they are 'appalled' or 'disgusted', something has gone seriously awry. It could happen to any school one day no matter how carefully it goes about its business, and in tightly-knit communities the people concerned may never recover. It is therefore crucial for governors to take advice from their fellows, from teachers and the head and from people knowledgeable about schools in general or about the events concerned in particular before expressing opinions publicly which may be based on inaccurate or erroneous information.

6

Difficult situations

In this section we have included some of the things that can happen to you as a governor, and suggest some ways in which you might react. The answers are not by any means clear cut, and it is up to you to use your judgement.

It would be a useful exercise for you first to read the 'problem' and try to use your commonsense on it. Then read our comments and see how they compare with your own judgement. Sometimes our comments are very brief, but where the problem is complex our commentary is accordingly fuller.

These are all, incidentally, based on real life events which have come before governing bodies for discussion or decision.

Accidents to pupils

Problem   There has been an injury to a pupil during the school day. The Head reports to the governors' meeting that the child was taken promptly to hospital, but the parents have decided to sue for negligence.

Comment   Sadly, every year children of school age are injured in accidents, most only very slightly. When this happens in school the staff fill out accident report forms which may well be mentioned at your meetings. Very occasionally you may be told that parents have actually consulted solicitors about legal action: for that reason it is worth your while to know something about the law relating to accidents in school. However, there is no need to feel very worried about this, as you are unlikely to be involved directly, and the matter will be handled by legal experts.

Accidents happen in the street and at home as well as in school and the overwhelming majority are nobody's fault. However, if parents believe that the accident to their child could reasonably have been foreseen or prevented by the school, they are entitled to sue for damages in the courts.

Parents of injured pupils are understandably upset and often angry. Sometimes the injuries can be very severe indeed. However, it is up to them to prove their case, and in law the extent of the injury has nothing to do with whether the teacher or the school is responsible. Obviously, if liability is proved, the compensation awarded will be much greater for severe injury.

Teachers are expected to take as much care of the pupils as reasonable parents would, and this is the test that the courts apply. However, they recognise that the circumstances in the hurlyburly of school are different from life at 27 Lilac Avenue. At home there are usually only one or two children to be looked after by one or two adults, at school children move in groups of twenty and thirty or more, usually under the supervision of only one teacher. Because of the larger numbers, the likelihood of a genuine accident occurring is greater. Larking about and horse-play are an accepted part of a child's growing up. It is up to the courts to say in each case whether they think that the larking about was excessive and should have been stopped. If, for example, in icy weather children make a slide across the playground and one of them falls and is injured, the law would

161

probably take the view that such normally harmless activities have been enjoyed by youngsters since time began: indeed the same pupils who make one slide at lunchtime in the playground probably make another at home the same evening, and parents might even join in, so an accident of that sort does not justify compensation merely because it happened during school hours.

Of course the parents may well argue that they have always kept their child away from such slides, have been known to punish him (in his own interests) when he has dashed along one. To them, the school has not behaved in the way that they as reasonable parents would.

The law's reply is that the school's job would be quite impossible if each and every child had to be treated in exactly the manner required by its parents. For one thing, would that apply equally to very bad parents, and who would decide whether they *were* good or bad? Furthermore, the teacher is an additional parent to a whole group of children, and has to consider what is good for his 'family' as a whole, and not only for one of its members. It is up to the courts of law then to say what a reasonable action would be in each case that comes along. A father cannot dictate to a teacher how his child should be treated, any more than he can dictate to his wife, or godparents.

It would in theory be possible to prevent all accidents in schools. One way would be to remove anything that could cause injury. Top of the list would be opening doors, followed by glass windows. After that we would remove all chairs to prevent pupils falling over backwards, and all desks to prevent fingers being trapped. Scissors, compasses, fountain pens, oil-cans, chisels, swimming baths and football pitches, language laboratories and most certainly science labs would all have to go. And we could pass a law making it necessary to search all pupils twice daily for concealed weapons like nail files, penknives and the vicious conker. Accidents would stop, but so would schools and education.

Despite all this, parents are sometimes advised that their school has not lived up to the standards of care required, and that the pupil has a chance of being awarded compensation in court. It is not malice or a wish to get back at someone that makes parents go through the lengthy, time-consuming and above all expensive legal processes. Rather it is the sheer necessity of now having to provide, perhaps, a life-time's care for a handicapped child. What, for example, of the brilliant pianist whose hand may be damaged permanently one day in the chemistry laboratory because his teacher made a mistake?

Parents usually take teachers' employers to court, because the law holds the employer responsible for accidents caused by his employees. As we have seen, it is the LEA which is the employer in county schools. In the case of voluntary aided schools the situation is more complicated. Although the governors are actually the employers, the law makes the LEA responsible for maintaining the school, so that the LEA gets caught here too!

Clearly, even though the LEA may be forced to pay damages, perhaps running into many thousand of pounds, the teacher certainly does not escape scot-free. His professional reputation suffers very badly and the wear and tear on everyone's nerves waiting for a court judgment – which can take literally years to be given – is enormous (and, of course, is just the same if the teacher is finally held not to have been responsible). The LEA might also decide, in the meantime, that the teacher is too expensive to keep on their staff . . .

If the teacher's negligence were gross in the extreme, the courts could make the teacher himself pay part or all of the damages, but we know of no case where this has happened. Presumably if a teacher were, on his own, to take 100 five-year-olds on a day trip to London and leave them at King's Cross with a cheery wave and a reminder to meet him there next Tuesday, such a case would merit severe treatment of the teacher, and not the LEA.

Before leaving this subject, it is necessary again to draw attention to the Health and Safety at Work Act, 1974. It is not entirely clear just how this Act affects schools, but it seems likely that the responsibility of governors and staff has been, if anything, increased. Governors should make it their business to find out about this important legislation without delay. Your

LEA will have advised the school about its policy, and you should make sure that you know what it is and the part you play. It is no use waiting until there has been an accident to find out that you are in trouble.

The absent teacher

Problem   A teacher at your school has been absent for a week, and you are asked to consider whether the absence should be with or without salary (see Appendix B, Article 9(f)).

It appears that he and his wife attended the funeral of his father-in-law some hundred miles away, a journey which could be accomplished in a few hours in each direction. However, after the funeral his mother-in-law was in a severely depressed state, and the teacher's wife decided that she ought to stay with her mother. The wife said that she needed her husband's support, so they both stayed for the week.

The clerk informs you that it is the policy of the authority to be sympathetic to cases of illness of 'near relatives'. There is no difficulty over two days' absence for the funeral, but you are asked to decide about the remainder of the week. The head tells you that that the teacher is not hard-working, does just enough to get by in school, and is never on the premises after four o'clock.

Comment   There is no simple answer to this: it would be a good idea to ask the clerk what other governors have decided in similar cases, although there is no obligation on you to follow his advice. What does seem clear, though, is that the head should not try to use your discretion in welfare cases to try to discipline mediocre teachers. There are other, direct ways of doing that. In any case, the head is in charge of 'internal management and organisation'.

The late arrival

Problem   A young teacher has been away from your school for a year on a course, for which permission was properly granted.

164

"VERY WELL, MR. JONES, I'LL PUT YOUR REQUEST TO ATTEND A FAMILY BEREAVEMENT WITHOUT LOSS OF SALARY TO THE NEXT GOVERNORS' MEETING"

At the beginning of the school year in September the teacher arrives back several days late. When questioned by the head, the teacher explains that he rang the school three times during August to find out when the term started and was unable to get through. The head confirms that on the dates the teacher rang the school, there was no-one present to answer the phone. Should the teacher be paid for his days of absence?

Comment   Of course not. The teacher had a whole year to establish when he should be back at work, and hardly expected to find anybody there during August. Dates of terms in any case are published at least a full year in advance.

'Shall we let him in?'

Problem   Your primary school is very popular and has no room left for additional pupils in the view of the head and your fellow governors. Accordingly you have decided that no child shall be admitted below the age of five. A family moves into a house very close to your school; the child is under five, but has been at another school since he was four. Should he be admitted to your school?

Comment   Obviously, in letting the child in to your school there is the risk that other parents living nearby with children under five will feel aggrieved. First see if there is another school available and willing to take the child. It is just possible that the authority might be willing to help with transport costs if these are involved. If these possibilities do not work out, you ought probably to admit the child and pray that twenty more cases do not come up at your next meeting. The child's interests should always come first, and it would be harmful to interrupt a child's education at the crucial time when it is first separated formally from its home background.

'Out-manoeuvred by father'

Problem   At the same meeting, another case is brought to your attention. A father has registered his daughter at the school because he is buying a house close by. The head felt obliged to accept the child, although the school is very full. During the fourth week of term the head discovers from correspondence with the father that the family is not after all living where the head was led to believe, but rather in the catchment area of another school. On phoning the father the head discovers that he had done no more than make enquiries about the house, and had no intention of moving there after his child had been accepted at the school of his choice.

Comment   Put this down to experience and don't be caught again. Some children have craftier parents than others. In future the head will be looking for firmer evidence of the parents' intentions.

It is worth noting that at the moment there is no simple and

"I THINK YOU'LL AGREE THAT WE _ARE_ IN THE SCHOOL'S CATCHMENT AREA HEADMASTER"

final legal way of declaring a school to be full. After all, any large school can squeeze in one or two more. The figures used by the architects in designing the school are no use in this matter, and yet common sense tells us that even a very popular school becomes unpopular if governors let it become over-crowded and consequently less efficient.

The existence of the so-called zones or catchment areas for schools is usually taken for granted by both LEA's and parents. Indeed, if LEA did not have a fairly good idea of the area a school was built to serve, it could never tell the architect what to design.

The difficult question for governors and headteachers is always: can these boundaries be used to enforce attendance at this school or that, against parents' wishes?

167

The short answer is: no. British law goes as far as is practicable to guaranteeing that a parent shall have the school he wishes for his child, and it is being proposed at the moment that a parent may choose a school in the territory of any LEA, not only in the area in which he lives. But this must not involve unreasonable public expenditure (i.e. the child must not be sent ten miles to school and the parent claim free travel!); the school must be suitable for the child in question (a pupil allocated to a secondary modern school, for example, could not choose a grammar school – this problem has disappeared with the introduction of all-purpose comprehensive schools) and the school must have a place to offer.

In practice then the existence of a line on a map can not on its own be used to turn down a request for so-called 'extra-zonal' admission. It must be backed up by something much more substantial. Nor, incidentally, can places in a school be kept open for future admissions, say from a growing housing estate. It is tempting to try this, particularly when one knows that the demand will grow. In fact, no one can know how many pupils will also leave during the same period.

The Labour government tried unsuccessfully before losing office in 1979 to give LEAs the power to set limits on the number of pupils entering their schools and forbid heads and governors to exceed these limits. Subsequently the Conservative government tackled the problem by requiring LEAs to seek DES approval before they reduced the number of pupils in a school by 20 per cent or more. Some solution of this sort is essential to prevent a mad scramble for places in the most popular schools when pupil numbers in an area fall dramatically. We already know that the school population will rise again from 1985, and if too many schools have been closed, expansion in the 1990s will be much more expensive.

'I'm not having anyone tell me what my Elvis should wear!'

Problem In an attempt to smarten up your school you have agreed to support the head in introducing school uniform. You are generally successful in this and the idea is popular with parents. However, Mrs Hittemback insists on sending her Elvis to school every day in the most outrageous clothes and the boy, encouraged by his mother, is truculent about the matter and encourages his friends to refuse to wear their uniform. The head delivers Elvis an ultimatum: next time he arrives at school without uniform, he will be sent home again. The head warns you about this in advance and asks for your support.

Comment Be very careful about this one. The head is technically well within his rights, and technically also does not need to consult you beforehand either (see Appendix B, Article 6(b)). The head is responsible for making and enforcing school rules, and obviously the school would collapse if different rules applied to each child. The courts would probably support the head.

However, what good would come of a confrontation with the Hittembacks? Elvis would miss school for some time, and probably get into mischief when the novelty wore off. Mrs Hittemback would tell her story to a local reporter who would see considerable column mileage in the 'poor devoted mother ground down by heartless bureaucrats' (yourselves) story.

The social climate in many areas would be unlikely to support you in such disciplinary measures over a matter like school uniform. Even if you did the instinctive thing and supported your head you might find County Hall breathing down your neck, if for example, the local authority supported Mrs Hittemback and did not approve of school uniform anyway. In short: try to avoid confrontation.

However, since the school has a responsibility for the safety of its pupils, you would be justified in supporting a ban on articles of dress which are likely to be dangerous in the school situation if not at home. Sky-larking boys grabbing at girls' necklaces or long earrings can do a lot of forseeable damage. Similarly high heels are dangerous in stampedes downstairs at lunchtime, and long hair even more so in workshops. This is not a matter of uniform, but of safety.

'I don't care if he does smoke. Mind your own business!'

Problem Your school sets particular store by the good behaviour of its pupils, and has a no smoking rule. One day a teacher leaving school sees a 16-year-old on his way home being offensive to people who live nearby and smoking. The next day the boy is punished by the head, and his father complains to you that he doesn't mind his son smoking and regularly gives him cigarettes. Furthermore the people the boy had been insulting were well-known cranks and were always treating pupils unfairly. The father says that he intends to keep his son away from school until the head apologises and wants the governors to bring pressure to bear.

Comment Stay well away from this one too if you can. It is a fact of British law that when a parent sends his child to a school he is deemed to have accepted the rules of the school. In some ways it is hard on parents when they have a legitimate objection to a rule (for example, they may disapprove of corporal punishment) and it is not possible to go to another school. But the correct thing to do is for them to see the head and try to get the rule changed, and certainly not to encourage their son to defy the rules so blatantly.

Also, British teachers are considered to be more like parents than public officials. It follows then that social training is part of a teacher's job, just as it is a parent's duty. The head was thus justified in taking action.

Whether the punishment for being rude was justified or not is more difficult. It is not necessary for the head to hold a court of enquiry and go to great lengths to establish guilt or inno-cence, only to have reasonable grounds for thinking that a pupil had done something to deserve punishment. Presumably the report from the teacher was just that.

Finally, if the father carries out his threat to keep his son away from school, he will put himself legally in the wrong. There is a legal duty on parents to 'cause (their child) . . . to be educated either by regular attendance at school or otherwise'. Ultimately he could be prosecuted and fined in the courts.

'Teacher's lost my tranny'

Problem During a governors' meeting, one of your col-leagues brings up a delicate matter under 'Any other business'. He has received a complaint from Mr Jones that his son's transistor radio, a Christmas present, was confiscated by his form teacher. When the boy went to collect it after school, the teacher could not find it and said it must have been stolen. Mr Jones had written to the headmaster, who had replied that the radio had been confiscated because it had become a constant nuisance and it was no part of the teacher's job to be responsible for loss arising out of such incidents. The head would certainly not consider any compensation for Mr Jones.

Comment Your colleague has not gone about this important issue in the best way. He is certainly entitled to bring any matter up under 'Any other business', which means just what it says, but he has really tried to turn your meeting into a sudden trial of the head's behaviour, which is almost guaranteed to arouse hostility. He would have been more successful if he had first got in touch with the chairman of governors (or referred Mr Jones directly to him) and let the chairman decide whether or not to put the matter formally on your agenda. The chairman would probably have preferred to ring the head himself and see what was afoot, and could probably have put your colleague's mind at rest before the meeting, where all matters are minuted, even ones which seem important at first sight and turn out to be rubbish!

Despite that, the head seems to have slightly misunderstood the legal position. It is certainly true that a teacher is not responsible for everything a pupil takes to school: he may not even be aware that Mary's fountain pen is solid gold and came from Harrods. But this teacher did what a parent would have done in the same case and took the transistor into his charge. In this case, the law says that he should look after it as well as he would his own property. The law does not say that the teacher must automatically make good the loss: it says that it is up to the parent in this case to show that the teacher was careless with the transistor. This would normally be difficult to prove.

Where parents have gone to the courts of law against schools and LEAs in matters like this, they have rarely been successful. The best approach for Mr Jones would be to write to the local authority giving the full facts: County *might* consider some compensation without admitting that anyone was responsible for the loss, a so-called 'ex-gratia' payment. However, it is most likely that he would get nothing. Had his son lost compulsory games kit, or a coat from the cloakroom, he might have been on better ground, but a transistor radio has no part in normal school life, and was not required in any way. Indeed, the cause of the trouble in the first place was that it was intentionally disruptive!

Going comprehensive

Problem   At one of your meetings you are informed from the chair that the local authority proposes to re-organise your school along comprehensive lines. You agree with this principle; however, you are very unhappy about the proposal for your school. From being a very happy and successful secondary technical school, where pupils could stay to 16 and take 'O' levels and CSE, you are to become a junior high school taking pupils from 11 to 14 only, after which they are to go to another local school of which you have a low opinion. Much anxiety is expressed at the meeting about the proposal.

Comment Many governors have lived through this one in recent years! It is essential to understand that LEAs have to live partly in a world of bricks and mortar. The fundamental problem for them is ensuring that pupils have a school to go to. Schemes of comprehensive reorganisation, therefore, have first to consider the buildings already in existence, what little cash is available to adapt them, and how many pupils each building will hold. In a very real sense you are in the hands of the so-called 'jug and bottle' department, and it is a sad fact of educational life that in very many cases the best educational use of the buildings is the one for which they were first intended. However, the 1980s sees an easing of this problem with a falling school population, and it might even become possible to discard some unsuitable buildings altogether.

If you want to make out a different case to your LEA, then it must not leave out of consideration the other schools with which you are linked. Remember, incidentally, that your ideas will probably affect the primary schools your pupils come from, as well as the schools to which they go when they leave you. It will do your cause little good if you only succeed in annoying the governors of other schools with your ideas.

LEAs cannot do what they want with your school willy-nilly. They usually go to great lengths to get your approval and support, although it has been known for LEAs to sack some governors they appointed when the governors dug in their heels! Just as importantly, they have to get formal approval for their plans from the DES, although under present proposals the DES will become less involved.

This is known as the 'Section 13' procedure, the number of

the appropriate paragraph of the 1944 Education Act. Local Authorities have to give the public detailed information about their intentions for the school. They have to publish it in a local newspaper, and put notices in accessible and conspicuous places, not least of which must of course be the school itself, normally by the gate or front entrance where parents can clearly see it.

After that, it is up to you as governors if you wish to write to the DES and LEA within two months, and argue your case. Any group of ten or more local government electors for your area can do the same, and it makes sense to co-ordinate what you write. After that, the DES gives its decision, and that is final.

Before making objections to a scheme, it is really worth asking yourself if your LEA has much room to manoeuvre. It is very often the case that the buildings and staff available make only one form of reorganisation possible. Where alternative schemes are possible, you will almost certainly be told of them and given the opportunity to have your say. LEAs have nothing to gain by being secretive or unhelpful about their intention. If you want some information, get it from County Hall.

It is by no means the case that the DES will automatically accept the LEA proposals in preference to yours, as any harassed Chief Education Officer will tell you. This is particularly true if you take the time to do your homework as well as he does. Furthermore, the policy at the DES seems to shift from time to time. On one occasion they may lean towards approving 'package deals', that is, schemes which link several schools in an area, so that objections on behalf of one school in the package carry little weight. Another Secretary of State may, after hearing from you, order the LEA not to change your particular school in that way, or to leave you out of the reorganisation altogether.

Vandalism

Problem   In his report to your meeting, the head reports a considerable increase in vandalism in and about the school and asks for any help you can give. He is concerned particularly

174

about relations with the community, since he has received several complaints about malicious acts of damage committed by pupils on the way to and from school. He has punished one pupil for wilfully damaging a piece of scientific equipment lent to him, and would like you to try to get compensation for the loss from the parents. The school building, too, is frequently vandalised in the evenings and at the weekends.

Comment Sadly, this sort of item has figured prominently in recent years on governors' agendas, and unfortunately there is no simple answer. Some governing bodies have found that a special parents meeting called by them at which the co-operation of parents is asked for has produced a notable improvement. Parents are sometimes unaware of the cost to them as tax and rate-payers of damage to school property. Sometimes, too, such a meeting will bring to light information about the culprits upon which the school can act. If your school has a Parent-Teacher Association a joint meeting might help.

As far as punishment is concerned, such acts committed on the journey to and from school are regarded in law as being in the first instance within the head's jurisdiction. Parents sometimes misunderstand this, but it is, nonetheless, the case. If your head feels that he can deal satisfactorily with culprits, then his advice should be followed.

However, the crime might be too serious to deal with in this way, and an approach to the parents might not be fruitful. In such cases the police may be involved, either because you choose to call them in or, more likely, because someone whose property has been damaged does it directly. Certainly if you decide to seek compensation for damage you will have to first secure a conviction in the Juvenile Court. At the moment the limit of the compensation that the court can award is £400 for each offence. Incidentally, any money received in this way belongs to your LEA as the owner of the damaged property, and not to your school. Here again the advice of the clerk will be very helpful to you.

Some schools have recently started to organise voluntary patrols by parents and sometimes staff around school premises at times when they seem particularly prone to vandalism. This is not the place to comment on how successful these might be. However, it is important that the police be consulted and informed before any such operation is mounted. It is also important to clarify with your clerk what the position will be with regard to insurance. While there will probably be little difficulty in ensuring cover for accidents to authorised patrollers, say, for example, by tripping over a milk crate carelessly left in the playground, it is unlikely that you will be covered for the results of an attack if a surprised vandal turns nasty. In such a case you would probably have to turn to the Criminal Injuries Compensation Board.

Dealing with angry parents and incompetent staff

Problem Mrs Smith and her neighbour call to see you one evening. It appears that young Peter Smith has been punished by his History teacher for larking about in class.

Mrs Smith is very angry. She tells you that the teacher is always picking on her Peter for no reason. Furthermore, everybody knows that the teacher is incapable of keeping order in class, and is always giving out punishments, except to the very big boys, who terrify him, and what's more, he does not teach proper History but all this modern rubbish. Mrs Smith goes on to say that she has been to see the head about all this, but the head would not give her much time, and later wrote to her to say that he had investigated her complaints, declared them to be unfounded, and felt the teacher had acted quite properly. He did not agree with Mrs Smith that the teacher should be sacked on the spot, and would take no further action.

Comment The best way to deal with this is to let Mrs Smith have her say (you might not be able to stop her!), but make no promises beyond perhaps saying that you will see if anything can be done. There are several reasons why you should not jump in too hastily, even if you are at first inclined to.

You do not know the full facts. When children get into trouble at school, however slight, they rarely give their parents

176

the full facts. Sometimes, indeed, they genuinely do not hear the teacher when he tells them for the fortieth time to sit down and be quiet. The relationship between teachers, parents and children can easily become emotionally loaded for the worse as well as for the good, and in cases like Mrs Smith's it is as well to let everybody calm down before anything is done.

Mrs Smith is not being very wise when she makes such sweeping statements about the school staff. She is perfectly entitled to tell the head privately just what she thinks of the History teacher and the school in general. But as soon as she tells anyone else, such as the neighbour, she may be called upon to defend herself in court if the head or the History teacher take action for defamation. Mrs Smith would have to show that what she said was true, and it would not be enough to say that she was angry when she spoke, or that she was merely passing on gossip. Defamation is simply the making of statements, either in writing or in speech, which might damage a person's professional standing. According to law, she need make such statements only to one person to make the matter actionable. That person might even be you and would certainly be the neighbour.

Mrs Smith ought to take her complaint, in reasonable language, to the teacher's employer. In a county school, of course, that is the LEA, and she should contact the Chief Education Officer. In an aided school, teachers are employed by the governing body, and Mrs Smith should get in touch with the chairman.

If it turns out, however, that what Mrs Smith says is true, the LEA might consider dismissal of the teacher. Indeed, in this case the head might well come under fire also for defending the teacher as he did, for the head's first loyalty is to the pupils rather than to his colleagues, however much he wishes to stand with them.

Local authorities have the power, as do employing governors, to dismiss for any reasonable cause, and in good faith. Bad time-keeping, absence without reason, refusal to carry out reasonable instructions are some of the grounds on which a teacher like any other employee may be dismissed, with of course the usual right of appeal, perhaps to an industrial tribunal.

There is a real difficulty, however, when one comes to dismissal for general professional incompetence. It is not that teachers have a guaranteed security of tenure: rather there is the difficulty of proving incompetence. A doctor, for example, may regularly administer wrong drugs or treatment, or a factory worker may produce unsatisfactory goods. In teaching, however, good personal relationships are crucial, and these are harder to evaluate. A teacher may find life in one school much more congenial than in another, and, of course, pupils' behaviour varies. A teacher who has been happy and successful in a school for some time may become less so if the school is suddenly reorganised along different lines. Quite apart from this, there is no 'right' way to teach, in the sense that there is a 'right' way to produce cars in a factory.

The most common way for LEAs to deal with this sort of problem is to delay dismissal proceedings until the evidence of incompetence is overwhelming, and helpful advice and warnings have all failed. In the meanwhile, it is possible to consider transferring the teacher to another school. In some cases this solves the problem, if the teacher settles down happily.

On the other hand the teaching profession like any other has its problems and incompetents, and their colleagues in the staffroom would be just as glad as you if they went. If you as a governing body are agreed that a teacher should be dismissed, you can instruct the clerk to set the wheels in motion. Be particularly careful to follow the procedure laid down in great detail. Most appeals against dismissal brought by teachers claim that the procedure was unfair or wrongly carried out and frequently this is upheld. There is little to be gained by letting an industrial tribunal send your problem back to you with a grin on his face, a cheque for compensation in his pocket, and a massive chip on his shoulder.

Corporal punishment

Problem You have been approached by a parent who tells you that one of the teachers at your school has been hitting children very hard. Along with your fellow governors and the headteacher you disapprove of corporal punishment, and believed it to have disappeared from your school. Not wishing to cause unnecessary ill-feeling, you decide to tackle the matter unofficially. You meet the teacher concerned purely by chance away from school and bring the matter up. The teacher surprises you by showing you unsolicited letters from parents, which claim that discipline in the school has gone to the dogs since corporal punishment was abolished, and fully support him in administering such punishment.

Comment First of all, beware of taking on unofficial assignments like this. It would be very foolish of an individual governor to confront a teacher in this way, with no reference to anyone else.

School discipline is certainly an area in which you as a governor should be interested. Through your chairman you could perhaps ask the head to include in his next report to you a paragraph or two on how standards of behaviour in the school have changed, if at all, since corporal punishment was abolished. Remember, though, that even a small school of, say, 200 pupils will have about 400 parents, and there is inevitably going to be a wide range of views from so many people about what 'good' or 'bad' discipline actually means. If you are not satisfied, then you should say exactly what your views are.

Since the head, as we have noted several times, is responsible for internal matters of management, he is entitled to require the teacher not to use corporal punishment. However, no matter what you may think of the ethics of hitting children, the present position is that the teacher has done nothing wrong in the eyes of the law. Legal tradition, the 'common law' of the country, views teachers as we have seen, as extra parents to children in their care. Consequently, just as a parent may chastise his child reasonably, so may the teacher who at the time is responsible for that child. But just as there are limits to what a parent may do to a child, so the teacher is limited. Firstly, the punishment must be reasonable and moderate, and in determining whether this condition has been satisfied the court will consider such matters as the age of the child, whether he has any physical defects, the nature of the offence, the form of the punishment, and the general disciplinary situation in the school. Secondly, the punishment should be administered in good faith: in other words, the teacher should have reasonable grounds for thinking that the child had offended. Thirdly, the form of punishment must be such as is usual in the school, so boiling in oil or thumbscrews are out. Fourthly, the punishment should be such as a reasonable parent might expect in the circumstances of the offence. If any or all of these limitations are not observed, it is possible for a teacher to be convicted in the courts of assault, a criminal offence.

The effect of this is that if the teacher concerned in your school refuses to co-operate, you might, in the last resort, ask the LEA to consider a transfer to another school where no such ban exists. Opinion about corporal punishment within the teaching profession is divided. Many would ban it as a matter of principle, others see it as a vital last-ditch measure for hard-pressed teachers in tough schools. In practice nowadays there is far less than in the past, and it is nearly always administered only by the head or his chosen deputy. A punishment book must be carefully maintained in each school. Critics often point out that the fact that the same names keep reappearing shows that corporal punishment does not work.

A relevant legal case illustrates perhaps how difficult a problem this is. A teacher was assaulted by a violent teenager who was under the influence of drugs, and the teacher was quite badly hurt. He hit the boy and broke his jaw. Judged by the standards and limits mentioned above, the teacher was guilty of assault. However, the judge pointed out, when the teacher was prosecuted, that had the events taken place outside the school the boy would have faced prosecution for a drugs offence, the man would have acted in justifiable self-defence, and might even have been commended for restraining a violent hooligan. He could see no reason why the law should be used to put the teacher in the dock, and would not convict.

Violent pupils – to suspend or not

Problem   A 15-year-old girl at your school has recently assaulted a woman teacher and the staff have decided that none of them will have the girl in any of their classes again. The school is an isolated one and there is no alternative school within a reasonable distance. The chairman and head have interviewed the girl and her parents, and have been promised that she will behave in future and apologise to the teacher concerned, if she can continue her CSE course. Since admissions to the school are in the hands of governors, you are asked to decide.

Comment   Where a child of under sixteen years of age is banned by school authorities (such as the governors) the LEA is put into a very awkward position. The law states quite clearly that the LEA must provide 'efficient, full-time education' for all children of statutory school age in its area.

While you, perhaps, are doing your best to keep your school running smoothly and have decided that the girl is wrecking the place and all your good works and needs to be kept away for everyone's sake, the LEA will be leaning heavily on you to take her back, being afraid in turn that the DES will come down on it like a ton of bricks for not carrying out its duty in law.

The head will be able to tell what the girl's chances are in the CSE examination. If they are good, then she herself will probably see the point of behaving herself from now on, and you would probably feel inclined to readmit her. If the course is too far advanced for her, it might lead to further trouble and you would then have to consider more drastic action such as permanent expulsion. In the short term, however, you ought to accept the assurances given and give her another chance. Be sure though that all the appropriate experts have been set to work, for example, the Schools Psychological and Welfare services where these are appropriate. Home tuition might be another possibility in an extreme case.

The teachers' behaviour, incidentally, is not entirely above reproach. Since they are required to take reasonable care of pupils in their care from the point of view of well-being and safety, they cannot rightly in law turn their backs on her and pretend that she is not there. Should she, for example, suffer an accident which the courts subsequently decide could have been foreseen and prevented by better supervision, then her previous behaviour would not be accepted as an excuse for failing to supervise her properly. Obviously, of course, as a fairly grown-up young lady of fifteen she would not need as much supervision as a child of eight or nine, but the general responsibility in law remains. Should everyone agree that the girl simply cannot be controlled in class, then she should either be suspended until a final decision is taken, or she should be looked after by a colleague, usually the poor old head.

Remember particularly that suspension in state schools is not a punishment. It means simply that the problem is so great that the pupil should be kept away from the school while you and the head decide what is to be done. Indefinite suspension is not permissible, and many LEAs restrict suspension to a maximum of so many days.

Changing school policy

Problem Now that the new head of your primary school has started work, you are disturbed to find that she is not interested in the ITA (Initial Teaching Alphabet) method of teaching children to read. The school has used this method for many years and you and the parents are well satisfied. However, the head tells you in her report that the method will be discontinued from the beginning of the next school year. This bit of information leaks back to the parents and several write to you, mostly attacking the change, but several supporting the new head. When the subject comes up for discussion, the head and the teacher governors argue that it is in the best interests of the school that the system should be changed.

Comment   The first question to ask, perhaps of yourself is: how could a new head be appointed without the governors knowing at the interview exactly what her views were? The basic skills of reading, writing and number work are the bread and butter of primary education, and if applicants are not questioned closely about them, they could be forgiven for thinking that parents and governors had no particular preferences. Now that she has been appointed, she is in charge of teaching methods, and could reasonably say that ITA is a matter of teaching method rather than of curriculum. Perhaps the appointments procedure needs to be revised.

However, there is no need for alarm in this case. There are several widely used methods of teaching reading and skilful teachers use them all equally effectively. Presumably your head will ensure that children are not confused by the change. Probably at first only the new arrivals will use her new scheme, and the older pupils continue with ITA.

Nothing would be gained by insisting that the school continue with ITA if the staff, as it seems, would prefer a change. It would be a good idea to have a meeting with parents at which the new ideas could be explained, and to which parents could be invited whose children had learned to read by the methods supported by the new head. You will probably find that the fears expressed by those parents who opposed the change can be allayed.

Absenteeism

Problem   Young Ira Fiddle at the age of twelve is a very talented musician and the head has given her permission to go to a music teacher every Monday afternoon. Your school has no music teacher who can help her with her violin, and the head thinks that an outside music teacher is the best solution. However this has produced an angry complaint to you from Mrs T.E.E. Bunker. Her son is tipped to be the County Junior golf champion, but the head refused him time off to be coached (he couldn't go after school because it was getting dark too early).

Comment   The head was using his discretion in the best interests of Miss Fiddle, but was, in fact, legally in the wrong. By law children must be educated '. . . by regular attendance at school or otherwise'. The courts have interpreted 'regular' as meaning 'for the whole period that the school is normally open', which means in practice full time from Monday to Friday. The words 'or otherwise' refer to those very exceptional and rare cases where parents educate their children at home, and make no use at all of schools. Once a child is registered at a school he must attend regularly. The head should not have given permission to Miss Fiddle in the first place. In cases like hers, LEAs are sometimes willing to employ peripatetic music teachers who visit several schools in turn to give special help. Golf on the other hand would probably be regarded as outside the normal curriculum, though it might be worth a try.

The devout teacher

Problem   A teacher in your school joins a particular religious sect which requires him to be absent from school on certain feast days. He applies to you for five days of absence without pay for these feasts which are granted. Shortly afterwards he applies for more time off, but you have no more discretionary days left. The application goes to County Hall, but the Chief Education Officer will not grant any more days off. The teacher nevertheless takes unauthorised leave of absence, and tells the head that he intends to take more time off.

Comment   Under one of the provisions of the 1944 Education Act, a teacher may not be disqualified on religious grounds from being appointed or promoted. A teacher cannot be barred from a school solely because he or she is, for example, Jewish or Catholic. The education system goes further and allows, for example, Catholics to take no part in morning assembly: this applies even to headteachers.

It would seem therefore that schools should accept that they should adapt themselves *to some extent* to the religious beliefs of teachers. However, this is a question of degree. A teacher who is continually absent cannot be said to be acting in the best interests of the children he teaches. Governors usually have power to grant a few days off for special cases, but that is usually as far as the LEA is prepared to go.

Finally it should be noted that the Act intended to stop discrimination against teachers for their religious opinions, which have little bearing on their work. Time off, however, may be seen as action not opinion. If in your view the running of the school is seriously disrupted, you would be entitled to take action for unsatisfactory attendance. Dismissal is a real possibility, as it would be in any sphere of working life.

'They want to close our school!'

Problem You read on the agenda for your next meeting that there is a proposal from the LEA to close your school in two years' time because of falling rolls, and because the numbers are already too small to be really viable. Your views are asked for.

Comment By the time you read this, it may well be too late to do anything! The Chief Education Officer might well already have made up his own mind on the evidence *as he has it*, and will almost certainly have consulted the chairman of the Education Committee to see, unofficially, how the Education Committee is likely to react when they are asked later for a final decision. So the moral is: always keep your ear to the ground as a governor, and don't let important issues like this take you by surprise. You may have a friendly councillor in a marginal seat who needs a strong PTA vote next election. Why didn't the head tell you that County Hall officials had been hovering around and asking him all sorts of questions about future numbers of children in the area? And, come to think of it, why hadn't you and your fellow governors been keeping an eye yourselves on pupil numbers? After all, you did know that yours was a small school and that the birthrate was declining, didn't you?

However, all is not lost. Here are some things you could do.

1 Contact the Advisory Centre for Education in Cambridge. They have a useful booklet on what to do.

2 Get all the facts and figures from County Hall or your Area Education Officer and go through the complete case yourself. It's certainly not unknown for County Hall to get things wrong. Don't, however, foolishly assume that County Hall is full of idiots whose aim is simply to do you down. It is not. They have stated a case, and it is up to you to counter it.

3 Any proposals you make should be positive, and not merely defensive.

4 Find out where the LEA proposes to redirect children from your school. If the proposal is to save money on teachers' salaries, check that the LEA is not also proposing to increase the staffs at the schools to which they want to send your children.

5 Check how many pupils in your area will need free school travel if they have to go further to school.

6 Find out what increased costs there will be in the other schools. Extra toilets? Check the Schools Building Regulations, available from your clerk.

7 Get in touch with the other schools. If they have smallish classes of, say, 20–25 they may not like the idea of this favourable position disappearing when your children arrive. Perhaps they will support you.

8 Can you raise money locally to off-set the losses the LEA claims to be making on your school?

9 Find out exactly how many children there actually are in your area, if necessary by knocking on doors. The LEA will probably not have done this.

10 The Section 13 procedure applies to closures as well as to reorganisation. Ensure that, if you have to appeal, the LEA sticks to the letter of the law as far as the procedure is concerned. If they don't, the courts will make them go through the whole consultative procedure again from scratch, which may give you valuable extra time.

11 Particularly, keep in touch with all the other local groups who feel as you do. The best way to fail is to spend your time fighting each other.

12 If yours is a secondary school point out that research by Barker and Gump in the USA found that smaller schools of around 400 pupils were able to offer a good range of subjects and had good personal relationships.
13 Argue that in some areas the two- or three-teacher village school is standard and that some great men and women were educated in very small schools. Money spent on travel and shared facilities is well spent. An inventive LEA can sometimes keep a number of small schools alive if parents so wish by using peripatetic teachers, jointly used centres where specialist facilities, like gymnasia, are available, and by judicious use of buses.
14 Press your LEA to have an adult education policy which allows maximum use of school buildings and facilities during and after school hours. The case for keeping your school going thus becomes stronger. If there is increased leisure in the last part of this century, this will become an important point, especially in rural or inner city areas.

7

Now that you're a good school governor

There is more to being a successful school governor than reading a book about it. On the other hand your willingness to learn about schools, children, curriculum, teachers and the duties of school governors by reading this book is a very healthy sign of interest and goodwill.

The quiz below is mainly lighthearted, but also slightly serious. It is certainly not a properly validated test, merely a set of questions about being a governor. In each section there are five questions. Score one point each time you respond (hand on heart!) 'yes', or give a correct answer which can be verified from local knowledge or reference to this book.

If you score 0 or 1 on any section you may need to take positive steps to improve your knowledge and effectiveness in that area. If you score 4 or 5 you are quite possibly very good at that aspect of your job as a governor. Alternatively you may be a dab hand at magazine quizzes, lucky, or a bit of a fibber.

Children

1. Have you talked to any children in the school (other than your own if you have any attending)?
2. Have you been along to watch any of the children's plays, concerts or sports?
3. Have you looked at any children's work whether up on display or not?
4. Have you ever had a school meal with the children?
5. Do you know how the school handles problem children?

Parents and community

1. Do you ever talk to various parents to see what they like or dislike about the school?
2. Have you ever been along to a meeting of parents?
3. Have you walked around the various parts of the catchment area where parents live?
4. Do you know what kinds of jobs various mothers and fathers have in the area?
5. Do you know what use is made of the school buildings outside school hours?

Teachers and teaching

1. Have you ever talked to any teachers in your school about their views on current issues in education?
2. Do you know which teachers have been on short or long training courses recently and what they did?
3. Have you talked informally to the head, outside the context of the governors' meeting, about life in school?
4. Do you know in general terms how teachers are trained?
5. Do you know what extra activities teachers put on in lunch-hours, after school or at other times?

Curriculum

1. Do you know if the school operates an integrated day? (primary governors) *or*
   Do you know if the school teaches any integrated subjects

like humanities or combined science? (secondary governors)
2. Do you know about any class or individual project work children may be doing?
3. Do you know what the school does for children who are not very good at reading?
4. Do you know what scheme, if any, is used for number work in your school? (primary governors) *or*
   Do you know what choices are available to children at the 'options' stage? (secondary governors)
5. Do you know about anything your school has which is unusual or distinctive in its curriculum, something which perhaps few other schools are doing?

Organisation

1. Do you know the names of your fellow governors?
2. Do you know who your school's HMI is?
3. Do you know what the Education Committee is discussing at present which is relevant to your school?
4. Do you know how decisions are made in the school about changes and policy matters?
5. Do you know how to get an item on the agenda at a governors' meeting?

Future developments

1. Do you know whether the number of children attending your school will increase, decrease or remain the same in the next five years?
2. Have you been along to any meetings of the Education Committee to see what future plans are being discussed?
3. Do you know what the head and teachers are planning to change next year?
4. Do you know which teachers are due to retire in the near future?
5. Do you know how the spread of microprocessors or other technological developments might affect life in your school?

Action
  1. Have you helped raise any money for the school?
  2. If an urgently needed building project were continually put off would you know what action to take?
  3. Are you willing to 'get things moving' if governors' meetings become tedious or pointless?
  4. Have you ever attended a meeting of governors, parents or teachers at which you personally helped set up a 'working party' or 'action group'?
  5. If your school were threatened with closure but you, your colleagues, parents and teachers wished to keep it open, would you know what to do?

Scores (out of 5)

	points		*points*
Children	....	*Organisation*	....
Parents and community	....	*Future developments*	....
Teachers and teaching	....	*Action*	....
Curriculum	....		

Total Score

30-35 points You probably frighten the wits out of the head and your fellow governors with your energy and knowledge, and ought to pause occasionally for breath, food, and to say hello to the budgie and your spouse.

20-30 points Salt of the earth. You are a black belt (10th dan) governor. Two or three like you and the local authority will go bankrupt because your school will get all the resources.

10-20 points You are probably strong on some sections and weak on others. Try to work at those areas where you obtained a low score.

1-10 points If you are a new governor you have probably not yet had the time to learn much about the school. If you have been a governor for a few years, however, you ought to ask yourself if there is anything you can do to be more effective.

0 points Resign. First, however, check your pulse, as you may have died and been allowed to remain a governor post-humously.

Appendix A

NOTTINGHAMSHIRE COUNTY COUNCIL

NOTTINGHAMSHIRE COUNTY COUNCIL

INSTRUMENT OF GOVERNMENT FOR

COUNTY SECONDARY SCHOOLS 1977*

The County Council of Nottinghamshire as Local Education Authority being required pursuant to Section 17 of the Education Act 1944 by Order to make an Instrument of Government in the case of every County Secondary School maintained by them hereby order as follows:

1.   (a) This Instrument may be cited as 'The Nottinghamshire Instrument of Government 1977'.

* Reproduced, as is the material in Appendix B, by courtesy of the Director of Education, Mr J.A. Stone, M.A.

(b) All previous Instruments affecting County Secondary Schools in the area of the Nottinghamshire Local Education Authority are hereby revoked.

2.   (a) In this Instrument unless the subject or context otherwise requires:

'The Authority' means the Nottinghamshire County Council as the Local Education Authority and in so far as the Authority may authorise their functions in regard to education references to the Authority in this Instrument shall be deemed to refer to or to include the Education Committee of the Authority.

'Governors' means the several Bodies of Governors of the County Secondary Schools referred to in the Schedule hereto.

'School' means a County Secondary School maintained by the Authority and referred to in the said Schedule.

'Clerk' means the Clerks appointed to act on behalf of the several Bodies of Governors.

'the Act' means the Education Act 1944, as amended and supplemented by subsequent enactments.

(b) Unless there be something in the subject or context repugnant to such construction, the several words and expressions to which meanings are assigned by the Local Government Act 1972 or by the Act shall have the same respective meanings, but if there shall be any inconsistency the meanings assigned by the Education Act 1944 and subsequent enactments shall prevail.

(c) The Interpretation Act 1889 applies to this Instrument as it applies to the interpretation of an Act of Parliament.

3.   Bodies of Governors shall be constituted as hereinafter provided for the Schools specified in the First Schedule hereto.

4.   Each such Governing Body shall, unless the Authority directs otherwise, consist of the following persons who shall be appointed representative Governors by the Authority and by the appropriate Bodies referred to.

(a) Two persons to be appointed by the Authority, or where the number of Districts served by the school exceeds two such number of persons as may be necessary to ensure one representative for each such District.

(b) Four persons to be appointed by the District Council(s) served by the School in accordance with the numbers specified in the First Schedule to this Instrument.

(c) Three persons being teachers of the school nominated by election from the teaching staff of the school pursuant to arrangements prescribed by the Authority.

(d) Three persons being parents of pupils who are currently in attendance at the school but excluding teaching and non-teaching staff, whether full or part-time, who are employed at the school nominated by the said parents pursuant to arrangements prescribed by the Authority.

5. (a) The first appointments of the Governors shall be made as soon as possible and the names of such Governors shall be notified to the appropriate Area Education Officer on behalf of the Chief Education Officer, or in any other case to the Chief Education Officer.

(b) Subsequent appointments of Governors shall be made as soon as practicable after each four-yearly election of County Councillors.

(c) A Governor being a teacher representative of the teaching staff of the school shall cease to be a Governor when he is no longer employed by the Authority at the school.

(d) A Governor being a parent representative shall cease to be a Governor at the end of the school year in which his child ceases to be a pupil of the school. For the purposes of this Instrument the school year should be regarded as ending on 31st July.

(e) Subject to the other provisions of this Instrument the Governors shall hold office until their successors are respectively appointed and they shall be eligible for re-appointment.

(f) The Governors appointed by the Authority and the

District Council(s) need not be members of the Authority or District Council(s) appointing them.

6. Any Governor who is absent from all meetings of Governors during a period of one year, other than for such reasons as may be acceptable to the Authority, or who is adjudged a bankrupt, or who is declared by the Authority to be incapacitated from acting, or who tenders his resignation in writing to the Clerk to the Governors, shall upon such event cease to be a Governor.

7. Any vacancy shall be reported forthwith to the appointing Body by the Clerk to the Governors.

8. A casual vacancy on a Governing Body shall be filled within three months of the vacancy occurring and the person so appointed shall serve for the remainder of the term for which his predecessor was appointed. A casual vacancy occurring within three months of the expiration of the normal period of office of the holder need not be filled.

9. (a) Any Governor appointed by the Authority or by any other Body shall be removable by the Authority or other Body by which he was appointed.

(b) No person who is related by birth or marriage to any Teacher or other Officer or Servant employed for the purpose of a School shall hold office as a Governor of such School or as a Clerk to the Governors thereof.

10. (a) Except with the approval in writing of the Authority no governor shall take or hold any pecuniary interest in any property held or used for the purposes of the school of which he is a Governor otherwise than as a trustee for the purposes thereof or receive any remuneration for his services as Governor.

(b) If a Governor has any pecuniary interest direct or indirect in any contract or proposed contract or other matter (other than that payable in respect of salary or other emoluments to a member of staff) relating to the school and is present at a meeting of the Governors, at which the contract or other matter is the subject of

195

consideration, he shall at the meeting disclose the fact and shall not take part in the consideration or discussion of or vote on any question with respect to the contract or other matter PROVIDED that this clause shall not apply to an interest in a contract or other matter which the Governor may have as a ratepayer or inhabitant of the area served by the school.

11. The first meeting of the Governors shall be convened by the Clerk as soon as practicable after the date on which this Instrument comes into operation.

12. The provisions of the Second Schedule to this Instrument shall apply to the meetings and proceedings of Governors.

13 This Instrument shall have effect from 8th September, 1977.

SECOND SCHEDULE

1. (a) The Governors shall meet at least once in every school term

(b) The first meeting of a governing body shall be held as soon as practicable.

(c) The quorum of the Governors shall not be less than three or one-third of the whole number of Governors whichever is the greater.

(d) The Governors shall establish such Sub-Committees as they think fit and determine their membership and function provided that no Sub-Committee established shall have a quorum of less than three members of the Governors.

(e) The Area Education Officer shall act as Clerk to the Governors unless the Chief Education Officer shall determine otherwise.

(f) The Chief Education Officer or his authorised representative shall have the right to attend and speak at meetings of Governors or their Sub-Committees.

(g) The minutes of the proceedings of the Governors shall be open to inspection by the Authority.

(h) Representatives of the Press shall not be admitted to meetings of the Governors.

2. (a) The ordinary meetings of the Governors shall be held at such an hour on such days and at such places as the Governors may from time to time determine.

(b) A meeting of the Governing Body may be convened by any two of their number.

(c) Six clear days at least before a meeting the Clerk to the Governors shall send to the usual place of residence of every Governor a summons to attend the meeting specifying the business transacted thereat. Except with the consent of the majority of the Governors present and voting no business shall be considered at a meeting of the Governors other than that specified in the summons.

(d) If at any meeting of the Governors the business specified in the summons is not completed, a special meeting shall be held as soon as possible thereafter to complete the unfinished business. Any meeting may be adjourned by Resolution.

3. (a) The Authority shall appoint one of the Governors as Chairman, who, subject to the other provisions of the Instrument, and unless he otherwise resigns shall hold office until his successor is appointed by the Authority as soon as may be following the first four yearly election of County Councillors held next after his appointment. The Chairman shall be eligible for re-appointment.

(b) The Governors shall at their first meeting following the four yearly election of County Councillors, or as soon as practicable thereafter, elect one of their number, other than a Governor who is a parent governor or a member of the teaching or non-teaching staff of the school, as Vice-Chairman, who, subject to the other provisions of the Instrument, and unless he otherwise resigns, shall hold office until his successor is elected at the first meeting of the Governors, or as soon as is practicable thereafter,

197

following the first four yearly election of County Councillors held next after his election. The Vice-Chairman shall be eligible for re-election.

(c) On a casual vacancy occurring in the office of Chairman the Clerk to the Governors shall notify the Authority who shall appoint a Chairman from members of the Governors to fill the vacancy as soon as practicable.

(d) On a casual vacancy occurring in the office of Vice-Chairman, an election to fill the vacancy shall be the first business to be transacted at the next meeting of the Governors.

(e) In the absence of the Chairman, the Vice-Chairman, if present, shall preside at a meeting of the Governors. If both the Chairman and Vice-Chairman are absent, the Governors present shall choose one of their number, other than a member of the teaching or non-teaching staffs of the school, to preside.

4. (a) Unless invited by a Resolution of the other Governors present at the meeting to remain a Governor who is a teacher of the school shall withdraw from that part of any meeting of the Governors at which there is consideration of the appointment or promotion of a teacher to a post senior to that which is held by him, or consideration of the suspension, dismissal, retirement or personal affairs of a person holding such a post.

    (b) A Governor who is a member of the non-teaching staff of the school shall withdraw from that part of the meeting at which there is any consideration of the appointment or promotion of a teacher or consideration of the suspension, dismissal, retirement or personal affairs of a teacher.

5. Every question to be determined at a meeting of the Governors shall be determined by a majority of the votes of the Governors present and voting on the question, and where there is an equal division of votes, the Chairman of the meeting shall have a second or casting vote.

6. Any resolution of the Governors may be rescinded or varied at a subsequent meeting if notice of the intention to rescind

or vary the same has been given to all the Governors.

7. (a) The Minutes of the meeting of the Governors shall be kept in a book provided for this purpose and shall be signed at the next meeting of the Governors by the person presiding thereat.

(b) The decisions of the Governors shall not be invalidated by any vacancy in their number or by any defect in the election, appointment or qualification of any Governor.

8. The names of the Governors present at a meeting of the Governors shall be recorded by the Clerk.

9. The official correspondence of the Governors shall be conducted by the Clerk to the Governors.

THE COMMON SEAL of the   )
Nottinghamshire County   )
Council was hereunto affixed   )
this   day of   )
                              in the   )

presence of   )

Appendix B

NOTTINGHAMSHIRE COUNTY COUNCIL

ARTICLES OF GOVERNMENT FOR COUNTY
SECONDARY SCHOOLS

MADE UNDER SECTION 17 OF THE

EDUCATION ACT 1944

Whereas the Nottinghamshire County Council as Local Education Authority are required pursuant to Section 17 of the Education Act 1944 by Order to make subject to the approval of the Secretary of State for Education and Science Articles of Government for every County Secondary School maintained by them.

NOW THEREFORE the said County Council acting as the

Local Education Authority hereby Order as follows:-
1. (a) These Articles may be cited as 'The Nottinghamshire Articles of Government 1974'.

(b) All previous Articles affecting County Secondary Schools in the areas of the Nottinghamshire Local Education Authority and the Nottingham County Borough Local Education Authority are hereby revoked.

2. (a) In these Articles unless the subject or context otherwise requires:-

'the Authority' means the Nottinghamshire County Council as the Local Education Authority and in so far as the Authority may authorise their Education Committee to exercise on their behalf any of their functions in regard to education references to the Authority in these Articles shall be deemed to refer to or to include the Education Committee of the Authority.

'Governors' means the several Bodies of Governors of the County Secondary Schools referred to in the Schedule hereto.

'School' means a County Secondary School maintained by the Authority and referred to in the said Schedule.

'Clerk' means the Clerks appointed to act on behalf of the several Bodies of Governors.

'the Act' means the Education Act 1944, as amended and supplemented by subsequent enactments.

(b) Unless there be something in the subject or context repugnant to such construction, the several words and expressions to which meanings are assigned by the Local Government Act 1972 or by the Act shall have the same respective meanings, but if there shall be any inconsistency the meanings assigned by the Education Act 1944 and subsequent enactments shall prevail.

(c) The Interpretation Act 1889 applies to these Articles as it applies to the interpretation of an Act of Parliament.

3. These articles shall have effect subject to:
(a) The provisions of the Act.
(b) The relevant Regulations made by the Minister.

4. These Articles shall apply to the Schools named in the Schedule to these Articles of Government for County Secondary Schools.

5. The School shall be conducted in accordance with the provisions of the Act, with the provisions of any relevant Regulations made by the Secretary of State for Education and Science and with these Articles and for the purpose of ensuring that the School is conducted accordingly the Governors shall make regular visits to the School.

6. (a) The Authority shall determine the general educational character of the School and its place in the local educational system. Subject thereto and to the provisions of these Articles the Governors shall have the direction of the conduct and curriculum of the School provided that they act in conformity with the general policy of the Authority. The words 'conduct' and 'curriculum' shall include arrangements for the secular instruction of pupils elsewhere than on the school premises in accordance with proposals to be approved by the Authority. Fourteen days' prior notice in writing of such arrangements shall be given to the Authority.

(b) Subject to the provisions of these Articles the Head Teacher shall control the internal organisation, management and discipline of the School and shall exercise supervision over the teaching and non-teaching staff (other than the Clerk) appointed solely for the purposes of the School and shall have the power of suspending pupils from attendance for any cause which he considers adequate provided that on the suspension of any pupil he shall forthwith report the case to the Governors who shall consult the Authority.

(c) (i) There shall be full consultation at all times between the Head Teacher and the Chairman of the Governors.
(ii) Suitable arrangements shall be made by the Governors for continuing consultation with the teaching staff and for their views and proposals and those of the non-teaching staff to be submitted to the Governors

through the Headmaster or their representatives. Arrangements shall also be made by the Governors for consultation, when appropriate, with pupils of the school and their parents.

(iii) All proposals and reports prepared by the Head Teacher affecting the conduct and curriculum of the school shall be submitted formally to the Governors. Copies of such proposals and reports need only be forwarded to the Authority upon specific request but the Governors may ask that they shall be so forwarded if it appears to them that they contain a matter of great importance to which the Authority's attention should be drawn.

(iv) The Head Teacher if he is not a Governor shall be entitled to attend every meeting of the Governors except on such occasions and for such items as the Governors may for good cause otherwise determine.

(v) There shall be full consultation and co-operation between the Head Teacher and the Chief Education Officer on matters affecting the welfare of the school.

7. (a) The Governors shall from time to time inspect and keep the Authority informed as to the adequacy, condition and state of repair and decoration of the School premises including the lighting, heating and ventilation thereof, the cleanliness and sufficiency of the sanitary and ablution facilities, and the suitability, condition and sufficiency of the School furniture. The Governors shall also report to the Authority if the School accommodation is or is likely to be more or less than is required for the purposes of the number of pupils attending or likely to attend the School and the necessity or desirability for any improvements to the School premises.

(b) Subject to the other provisions of these Articles the Governors may arrange for minor works of improvement costing not more than a sum to be determined from time to time by the Authority for any single proposal within an Annual allowance to be determined by the Authority provided that the local Clerk of Works shall be notified immediately so that he may arrange where necessary for expert supervision and any expenditure so incurred shall be reported as soon as possible to the Authority.

(c) Subject to compliance with any directions of the Authority the Governors may arrange for the use of the School premises during such hours as they are not required for normal school purposes and receipts for such use shall be paid into the County Fund.

8. Subject to the other provisions of these Articles, School Supplies shall be obtained in Accordance with the directions of the Authority.

9. (a) The Governors shall keep the staffing arrangements of the School under review and shall from time to time advise the Authority in regard to the establishment of Teachers to be employed in the School.

(b) The appointment under the provisions of this Article of all Officers (including Teachers) and Servants required for the purposes of the School shall be in accordance with the directions of the Authority in regard to establishment, remuneration, duties, qualifications, conditions of service and other circumstances in relation to such Officers (including Teachers) and Servants and such appointments shall be made to the service of the Authority.

(c) Subject to the other provisions of these Articles the procedure applicable to the appointment and dismissal of Officers (including Teachers) and Servants employed solely for the purpose of the School shall be as follows namely:-

(i) **Head Teacher**

When the post of Head Teacher of a School becomes vacant the Authority may after consulting with the Governors fill the vacancy by transferring another Head Teacher already in the employment of the Authority. If the Authority do not propose to fill the vacancy in such manner they shall advertise the post and refer a short list to a Joint Committee consisting of the Head Teachers appointment Sub-Committee of the Education Committee and the Authority together with four representatives of the Governors which shall recommend a Candidate for appointment by the Authority.

The Chairman of the said Joint Committee shall be the Chairman of the Education Committee of the Authority or in his absence a Member of the said Education Committee nominated by a majority of the representatives of the Authority present and voting at the Meeting of the said Joint Committee.

The Head Teacher shall be employed under a contract of service in writing determinable (except in the case of dismissal for misconduct or other urgent cause) by either party, upon three months' notice in writing taking effect at the end of the spring or autumn term or upon four months' notice in writing taking effect at the end of a summer term. Unless otherwise determined by the Authority he shall not be dismissed except on the recommendation of the Governors.

A Resolution of the Governors to recommend the dismissal of the Head Teacher shall not take effect until it has been confirmed at a Meeting of the Governors held not less than fourteen days after the date of the Meeting at which the Resolution was passed. The Governors may by a Resolution suspend the Head Teacher from his office for misconduct or any other urgent cause pending the decision of the Authority.

The Head Teacher shall be entitled to appear accompanied by a friend at any Meeting of the Governors or of the appropriate Sub-Committee of the Education Committee of the Authority at which his dismissal is to be considered and shall be given at least seven days' notice of such Meeting.

(ii) Deputy Head Teacher and Senior Master

Unless as a result of re-organisation of secondary education or otherwise, the Authority proposes to fill the post by transfer of a teacher in the service of the Authority the posts of Deputy Head Teacher and Senior Master shall be advertised and the applicants short-listed and interviewed by the Governors who shall recommend the appointment of the successful applicant to the Authority. These appointments shall be determinable upon two months' notice in writing on either side taking effect at the end of the autumn or spring terms, or upon three months' notice taking effect at the end of the summer term.

(iii) Other Teachers

Unless the Authority propose to fill the post from any pool of new entrants to the teaching profession, other appointments shall be made by the Authority in consultation with the Head Teacher and Chairman of the School Governors either by interview after advertisement or by transfer of a teacher in the service of the Authority.

Appointments of other teachers shall in all cases be determinable by either party upon two months' notice in writing taking effect at the end of the spring or autumn term or upon three months' notice in writing taking effect at the end of a summer term.

The procedure for the dismissal or suspension of Deputy Head Teachers, Senior Masters and Other Teachers shall be similar to that hereinbefore specified for Head Teachers except that two Meetings of the Governors shall not be required.

Notwithstanding anything contained in this Article the Authority may after consultation with the Head Teacher and Governors transfer a teacher from a school.

(iv) Non-Teaching Staff

The non-teaching staff shall be appointed by the Authority after consultation with the Head Teacher to the service of the Authority and may be dismissed pursuant to arrangements approved by the Authority which shall provide for the Head Teacher to be consulted as appropriate. Provided that the Governors may in the case of misconduct or other urgent cause suspend a member of the non-teaching staff while their recommendation of dismissal is being considered by the Authority.

(d) The Governors shall conduct their business through a duly authorised Clerk to the Governors who shall be appointed and dismissed in the manner specified by the Authority and whose duties and other conditions of service shall be in accordance with the directions of the Authority provided that the Governors may recommend such dismissal.

(e) The Governors shall forthwith send to the Authority particulars of every appointment made by them and particulars of any recommendations for dismissal under the provisions of this Article.

(f) The Governors shall be empowered to authorise special leave of absence for Head and Assistant Teachers for good and sufficient reasons up to a maximum of five days in any period of twelve months.

10. The Governors shall

(a) Arrange for the admission of pupils to the school in accordance with arrangements made by the Authority which shall take into account

(i) the wishes of parents.

(ii) any school records and other information which may be available.

(iii) the general type of education most suitable for the particular child.

(iv) the views of the Governors and the Head Teacher,

as to the admission of the child at the school.

(b) Assist the Authority in the exercise of its functions under the Education Acts in relation to the enforcement of attendance at School in so far as they are concerned with children who are registered pupils at the school. Provided that in rendering such assistance as the Authority may require the Governors shall act with the advice of the Area Education Officer.

(c) Report to the Authority all cases coming to their notice of pupils who in their opinion should be considered for special educational treatment.

(d) Arrange the times of school sessions within the requirements of the Act.

(e) Take appropriate action in cases of pupils suspended for misconduct, including arranging interviews with parents and, subject to any directions from the Authority, transfer the pupils to other schools where necessary, after consulting the Head Teacher of the School to which it is proposed to transfer the pupil and with the agreement of the Governors of that School.

11. The Governors shall fix the dates of School Holidays and of occasional holidays within the limits determined by the Authority.

12. The Governors shall assist the Authority in the exercise of their functions under the Education Acts in relation to the administration of the School Meals Service, the authorisation of exceptional expenditure under the Scholarships and Other Benefits Scheme and in relation to Educational Journeys and Foreign Travel, provided that in rendering such assistance as the Authority may require the Governors shall act in accordance with arrangements approved by the Authority.

13. The Governors shall comply with any arrangements which may be made from time to time by the Authority in regard to the supply of library books to the school.

14. The Governors shall furnish to the Authority such returns and reports and maintain such records as the Authority

may require and such records and other documents shall be open to inspection by any Officer duly authorised in that behalf by the Authority.

15. The Clerk shall if asked to do so, forward to the Authority the detailed Agenda for each Meeting of the Governors at the same time as such Agenda is circulated to the Governors and he shall upon request also forward to the Authority within seven days after each Meeting such number of copies of the Minutes of the Proceedings of the Governors as may be required by the Authority.

16. The Governors may make the representations and recommendations to the Authority in regard to any matter which affects the education and welfare of the pupils attending the School.

17. The Governors shall ensure that all records which are required to be kept at the School pursuant to the Regulations of the Secretary of State or by direction of the Authority are maintained and preserved in accordance with such Regulations and directions and in particular they shall ensure that a School Log Book is maintained by the Head Teacher in accordance therewith. The Log Book and other records required to be kept at the School shall be inspected by the Governors at least once during each School term and an appropriate entry in relation to such inspection shall be made in the Log Book and other records hereinbefore referred to.

18. (a) No expenditure shall be incurred or approved by the Governors under any of the powers conferred by these Articles unless such expenditure is covered by an Estimate which has been approved by the Authority and is incurred or approved in accordance with the Standing Orders of the Authority in force for the time being.

(b) (i) All monies received by the Governors on behalf of the Authority shall be paid into the County Fund in such manners as the Authority may prescribe.

(ii) Subject to such directions as may be given by the Authority the Governors shall undertake such duties in regard to the disbursement of monies on their behalf as the Authority may reasonably require.

(c) Records of School private funds shall be maintained in the manner prescribed by the Authority.

19. The Governors shall refer to the Authority all matters requiring legal advice or proceedings or the preparation of contracts, agreements or other documents of a legal character and shall furnish the Authority with such information as may be required for the purpose of dealing with such matters.

20. A copy of these Articles shall be given to each Governor upon appointment and further copies shall be available for inspection in each School.

21. These Articles shall have effect as from the 1st day of April, 1974.

THE COMMON SEAL of the)
Nottinghamshire County)
Council was hereunto affixed)
this   day of)
                        in the)
presence of   )

Appendix C

FURTHER READING

The books listed below constitute a small starting point, and you should have no difficulty finding other books which deal in detail with particular aspects of school life.

Some specialist libraries will have tens of thousands of books on education, and perhaps between ten and fifty texts on each quite small specific topic. Faced with such a wide choice you are best advised, if you find you are interested in a particular aspect of education, to consult a good librarian, bookseller, or the head or teachers at your school, who will often be pleased to give you advice. Moreover, in most cases they will be delighted that you are showing such interest in education.

Books

D. Ayerst, *Understanding Schools* (Pelican, 1967)

A good general introduction to some of the issues that come

before Governors. There are chapters on 'Why learn Latin (or, come to that, Chemistry)?', 'Which is the right primary school?', and 'The uniformity of examinations'.

G.R. Barrell, *Teachers and the Law,* Fifth Edition (Methuen, 1978)

A standard reference work packed with authoritative and useful information about legal matters. A complete and detailed guide to the law as it affects all aspects of the teacher's job.

J. Blackie, *Inside the Primary School* (HMSO, 1967)

Although beginning to look a little out of date, this still gives a sound picture of what happens in many primary schools. Written by a former HMI it reveals familiarity with many schools and deep concern for the education of young children.

T. Burgess, *Home and School* (Pelican, 1976)

A book aimed at parents which covers children's development, primary and secondary school curriculum and many other matters of interest to anyone with a child at school; but it is also of use to people interested generally in home and school.

T. Burgess and A. Sofer, *The School Governors' and Managers' Handbook and Training Guide* (Kogan Page, 1978)

A little 'war economy' in appearance, but nevertheless full of helpful advice to governors about meetings, duties, powers and so on. Also contains a sensible set of suggestions about training governors to do their job effectively.

A. Clegg and B. Megson, *Children in Distress* (Penguin, 1970)

The writers use their wide knowledge of schools to describe the one in eight children who need help which they often do not receive. The book deals with 'twilight children', work-shy parents, and other sources of distress to children, describing in detail what schools can do to help.

J. Gretton and M. Jackson, *William Tyndale* (Allen and Unwin, 1976)

A kind of serious 'who-dunnit?' about the real-life distress of the William Tyndale Junior School, written by two journalists who 'covered' the case for the press. Very good as an outsider's view, and sends up warning signals for Governors about how and when to spot things going wrong.

J. Holt, *How Children Fail* (Pelican, 1976)

One of several books (others include 'How Children Learn') by the author, a teacher who observed his own classes and sensitively recorded what children do at school to guess the teacher's intentions or to evade them.

M. Kogan, *County Hall* (Penguin, 1973)

Very readable discussion between the author and three experienced Chief Education Officers about how the education system works.

National Association of Governors and Managers, *The Government of Special Schools*, (1979)

A leaflet giving valuable information about being a governor of a special school.

R. Pedley, *The Comprehensive School* (Pelican, 1969)

A trail-blazing book, passionately advocating comprehensive schools, at a time when they were a much more controversial issue than at present. Very readable, although some of the arguments now seem perhaps a little old-fashioned.

R. Rogers, *Schools Under Threat* (Advisory Centre for Education, 1979)

A vital book if your school is threatened with closure and you wish to organize an appeal. Full of good strategic ploys and hints.

J. Stone and P. Taylor, *The Parent's Schoolbook* (Pelican, 1976)

An extremely useful paperback which deals with several

213

topics in alphabetical order under headings such as 'choice of school', 'governors', 'non-teaching staff', 'suspension', 'truancy', etc. A little tendentious in that it gives the impression here and there that heads and teachers are a bit naughty, but full of accurate, well-written and up-to-date information.

G. Taylor and J.B. Saunders, *The New Law of Education* (Butterworths, 8th edn, 1976)

The standard 'Bible' in the Law of Education and used by Chief Education Officers, the DES and all administrators. Very expensive, but your local library will get or have a copy. A reference book, not to be read from cover to cover!

Newspapers and periodicals

Most national newspapers, many local newspapers and a number of magazines employ an Education Correspondent who will give information in his column about current issues. Particularly authoritative are *The Times Educational Supplement* and the *Education Guardian*. The journal *Education* is widely read by educational administrators and teachers and it too contains up to date and authoritative accounts of recent developments, including useful digests which summarise important issues. The journal *Where?* produced by The Advisory Centre for Education is also informative and worth reading.

Events can change so rapidly in education that a watchful eye must be kept on developments. All accounts of educational issues and of practice in schools, including this book, can soon become out of date.

BOOKS MENTIONED IN THE TEXT

Aspects of Secondary Education in England: A Survey by HMI (DES)

(HMSO, 1979)

Banbury Study (of mixed ability teaching): D. Newbold, *Ability Grouping — the Banbury Enquiry* (NFER, 1977)

R.G. Barker and P.V. Gump (on school size), *Big School, Small School* (Stanford University Press, 1964)

N. Bennett, *Teaching Styles and Pupil Progress* (Open Books, 1976)

Bullock Report: A Language for Life (HMSO, 1975)

Crowther Report: 15 to 18 (HMSO, 1975)

DES, *A View of the Curriculum* (HMSO, 1980)

Mixed Ability Work in Comprehensive Schools: a discussion paper by a working party of HMI (HMSO, 1978)

Newsom Report: Half our Future (HMSO, 1963)

Parliamentary Select Committee report: *The Attainments of the School Leaver* (HMSO, 1977)

Plowden Report: Children and their Primary Schools (HMSO, 1967)

Primary Education in England (DES) (HMSO, 1978)

Robbins Report: Higher Education (HMSO, 1963)

Taylor Report (on school governors): *A New Partnership for our Schools* (HMSO, 1977)

W. Taylor, *The Secondary Modern School* (Faber, 1963)

H.A. Thelen (on 'teachability') *Classroom Grouping for Teachability* (Wiley, 1967)

Warnock Report: Special Educational Needs (HMSO, 1978)

K.B. Start and B.K. Wells, *The Trend of Reading Standards* (NFER, 1972)

215

Index

216

NOTES

NOTES

NOTES

NOTES

NOTES

NOTES

NOTES

NOTES

NOTES

NOTES